CORVETTE
Catalogs

CORVETTE
Catalogs

A Visual History from 1953 to the Present Day

Terry Jackson

DEDICATION

This book is dedicated to my fellow journalists at The Sacramento Bee and in particular to my colleagues on the City Desk who humour my lust for fast cars.

MALLARD PRESS

An imprint of BDD Promotional
Book Company Inc.
666 Fifth Avenue
New York, NY 10103

Mallard Press and its accompanying design and logo are trademarks of BDD Promotional Book Company, Inc.

First published in the United States of America in 1991 by the Mallard Press

ISBN 0–7924–5518–5

This book was designed and produced by
Quintet Publishing Limited
6 Blundell Street
London N7 9BH

Creative Director: Terry Jeavons
Designer: Peter Radcliffe
Artwork: Danny McBride
Project Editor: Lindsay Porter
Editor: Phil Dracket
Photographer: Ian Howes

Typeset in Great Britain by
Central Southern Typesetters, Eastbourne
Manufactured in Singapore by
Tien Wah Press (Pte) Ltd.

CONTENTS

INTRODUCTION

FROM DREAM CAR TO WORLD CLASS SPORTS CAR

Imagine for a moment that the year is 1953. It's a cold, wet January in New York but the people on the street are in good spirits. World War II is fading from mind; a war hero, Dwight David Eisenhower, is about to assume the reins of the presidency; and the Korean conflict seems very far away. America's economy is booming and the average citizen is enjoying a prosperity that is unmatched in the world's history. The stores along Fifth Avenue are packed and people are commuting into the city from homes in new suburbs.

Detroit, the automotive Mecca of the world, is in its heyday. Sales are skyrocketing, two-car families are starting to become commonplace and no one has ever seen a Japanese car on an American highway.

As a celebration of this Yankee hubris, on a wintry 17 January, General Motors – the industrial giant of the world – has transformed the grand ballroom of New York's famed Waldorf Astoria hotel into a transportation Taj Mahal.

Called Motorama, the GM annual display at the Waldorf is a showcase for the best Detroit can offer. The public, the press and, not incidentally, the New York money men are invited to see what the present and the future holds for American drivers.

The show is heavily orientated towards fantasy with a number of concept and design cars on display. Most will never turn a wheel in anger. In fact, most can't turn a wheel, being little more than shells on static platforms.

At the centre of this display is a car unlike any ever offered from Detroit. As a response to a small but growing

BELOW *The 1955 Brochure marks the birth of what was to become America's first and only true sports car.*

Real driving comfort . . . the Corvette way!

SECURITY AND LUXURY for driver and passenger are the keynotes of the snug Corvette cockpit. Individual bucket seats have form-fitting foam rubber cushions. The floor is covered in soft carpeting, backed by sponge rubber. Large pockets and ash trays in doors also serve as arm rests. Beautifully balanced instrument panel includes key-turn starter, electric clock, tachometer, hooded radio speaker.

POTENT "BLUE-FLAME" 6 engine, with three side-draft carburetors, 8 to 1 compression ratio, and overhead valves, puts a flashing 155 horsepower under the throttle. It has a dual exhaust system, efficient cooling and lubrication, and a shielded electrical system . . . plus Chevrolet's traditional six-cylinder economy of operation and maintenance.

A cyclone of power
with the new 195-h.p. V8 engine

A breath-stopping surge of power that surpasses anything you have ever imagined—that's the story of the Corvette's new 195-h.p. V8 engine. Here is a "dream" power-plant . . . ultra-compact, free-breathing, super-efficient, the most modern valve-in-head V8 engine in the world . . . and it can be serviced by any Chevrolet dealer. Dual exhausts, a four-barrel carburetor, 8 to 1 compression ratio, and a high-lift camshaft squeeze latent energy out of every drop of gasoline . . . and careful counter-balancing of the entire engine *after assembly* keeps it smooth as a jet of steam.

Geared-to-the-road stability

The Corvette is a sports car . . . not a scaled-down convertible. At any speed it offers a sense of security, an inherent balance that is astonishing. Low-slung, with a center of gravity only 18 inches above the pavement, its outrigger rear springs and broad-based front tread let it cling to the road like a cat. The steering gear has 16 to 1 ratio for instant response. Its big 11-inch brakes have bonded linings and a grip that would stop a truck. Everything is designed to give the absolute, precise command that only the driver of a true sports car can know.

demand for sports cars, GM has obliged with a white roadster called the Corvette. As the sleek, small, sexy car sits on a turntable, rotating under the hot glare of spotlights, an attractive woman gives the crowd a sales pitch while other women hand out brochures to passers-by. The speech and the pamphlet both refer to the Corvette as a breakthrough in the world of motoring,and so it is. The body is made of a new substance, GRP (Glass Reinforced Plastic) – much better known now as fibreglass – it has an automatic transmission called Powerglide,and the engine is a three-carburettor six-cylinder, the Blue Flame. More importantly, there is a strong hint that the Corvette could one day soon appear in Chevrolet showrooms across the country, available to anyone with the purchase price.

Thousands of people saw that first Corvette, heard the pretty lady give her sales talk and then went away with a not-too-well-produced pamphlet extolling the virtues of the Motorama roadster. It is doubtful if many who visited the Waldorf in January 1953 recall the exact words of that talk, but some of those first Corvette brochures still exist as historical records of the birth of America's first and, to date, only true sports car.

Nearly 40 years have passed since that first brochure appeared and the Corvette has seen many changes, from dream car to sports car, to drag racer, to luxury car, to its latest incarnation as a world class sports car that can compete with the best.

There are many ways to examine the complex and fascinating history of America's sports car,but there may be none so revealing as a look at how the Corvette has evolved through its sales catalogues and brochures. For example, in those early years the amount of effort that went into the Corvette sales brochure was about equal to the impact the car was having on overall Chevrolet sales. In fact, there

AUTOMOBILES CHEVROLET, 1963

NEW CORVETTE

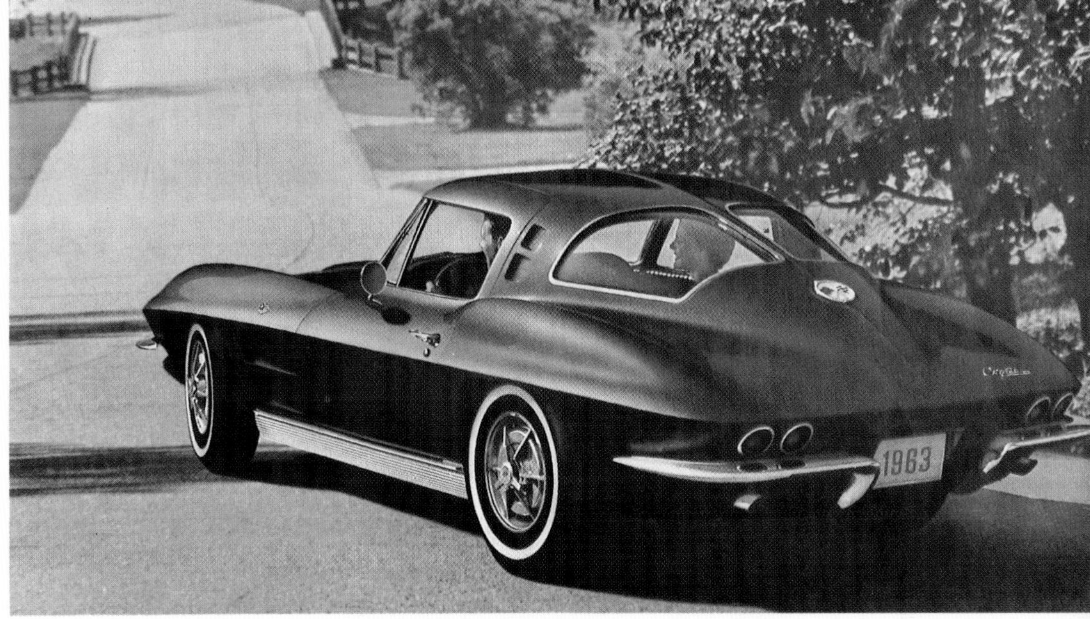

ABOVE *The 1960s was the golden age of the Corvette, symbolized by the styling of the 1963 Sting Ray.*

were probably many times more brochures printed in 1955 than the 700 Corvettes sold that year.

However, as the Corvette improved and Chevrolet came to grips with the role that this fibreglass two-seater was playing, the sales literature became more sophisticated. By 1957, Corvette brochures were full of talk about the merits of fuel injection and sintered, otherwise heat-tempered, metallic brake-linings while the talk surrounding the full-sized Bel Air was about the lack of a pillar on the four-door version and the availability of brocade seat covers.

Into the early 1960s, photographs in Corvette literature showed drivers racing and rallying their cars and the

ABOVE *With the inflated price of oil in the 1970s, Corvette literature emphasized luxury options over high performance.*

emphasis was on high-performance options. When the stunning 1963 Sting Ray was unveiled, the promotional prose acknowledged that the new Corvette was a styling coup. For the first time there was serious talk about aerodynamics, fully two decades before that word would become commonplace in car brochures.

As the 1960s matured, big-block firepower was the order of the day, replacing the Corvette theme of high-revving small-block V8s. The legendary Chevy 427-cubic-inch V8s were the epitome of the Corvette image, so much so that multiple versions were offered to buyers. Option lists became so long and intricate that each year the Corvette catalogue became mandatory educational reading for a nation of consumers hooked on high-performance.

When the pontoon-fendered Corvette appeared in 1968, the sales brochures brought into the car-buyer's lexicon words such as fibre optics, Astro ventilation and fibreglass belted tyres. The march towards more horsepower continued until the early 1970s,when brochures began detailing such heretofore unknown concepts as air pollution controls and catalytic converters.

Corvette was changing with the world as a perusal of the brochures shows. No longer were there photos of drivers at the race track or on rallies. The word luxury was more prevalent than the phrase high-performance. By the mid-1970s, when the American motorist was coping with sky-rocketing gasoline prices and a real fear of shortages, the Corvette was becoming a boulevard cruiser.

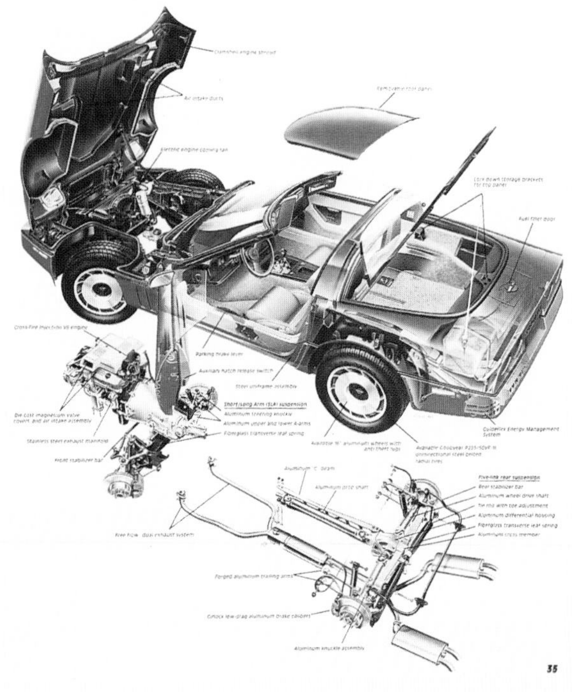

RIGHT *In the 1980s, automotive technology was once again in the forefront.*

Sales literature of the day put more emphasis on options such as air-conditioning, AM–FM stereo radios and leather seats than engine and transmission combinations. It was still a status-symbol car,but that status had more to do with style than substance. Heritage was a watchword of Corvette brochures by the late 1970s and early 1980s. Special editions were cranked out to commemorate the car's history and longevity and brochures were as likely to show past Corvettes as the model in dealer showrooms.

BELOW *With the ZR–1, Corvette takes its place among the world's supercars.*

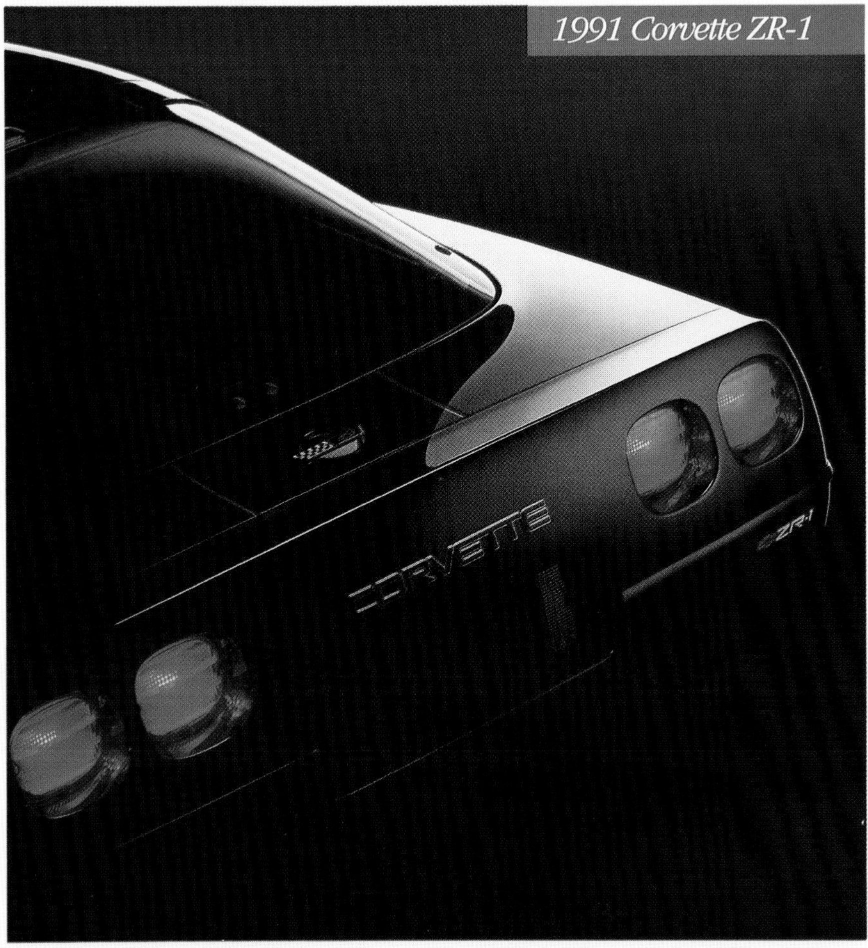

Then, in one swoop, the tenor and outlook changed in 1984. Once again catalogues were full of talk about stunning performance and cutaway technical drawings detailed an all-new platform. The new car fulfilled all the promises of the sales literature and then some. New words were again being introduced to driving enthusiasts by way of the Corvette. There were discussions of Gatorback tyres, tuned port injection and top speeds of 150 mph-plus (241 kph). Each year's model brought improvements in handling and top speed,and the sales brochures were like primers on the latest in automotive technology.

In 1990 the Corvette took a leap ahead into the ranks of the world's supercars, wonderful machinery like the Ferrari Testarossa. The latest Corvette, the ZR-1, was a technological *tour de force*. However, given the demand for the car and its $59,000 price, many Corvette admirers will have to rely on the brochures to bolster their fantasies.

For 1991, there is a facelift for the Corvette and some of the ZR-1's performance has begun to spill over on to the basic model.

Taken as a whole, the Corvette sales literature does a creditable job of providing an insight into the development of America's only true sports car. There is the gee-whiz feeling that accompanied the introduction of the first car, the push for respectability as a sports car in the 1950s, the pride of styling in the 1960s,and the race for more horsepower. And there is the slide into the luxury market as real world problems put the brakes on fuel-thirsty big-block engines; the refinement of the Corvette into a touring car; the sudden re-emergence of performance and handling,and then the Corvette's claim to world-class status.

Though initially produced as throwaway sales tools, the Corvette catalogues have become integral parts of the Corvette legend.

CHAPTER I

1953–1959: THE RISE TO RESPECTABILITY

The first Corvette pamphlet handed out to Motorama visitors in 1953 gave no clue to the car's genesis as the brainchild of Harley Earl, General Motors' vice-president in charge of styling. Earl saw in the Corvette a product that would challenge British cars such as the Jaguar XK120 and the MG TD, which were starting to win a following in America. The Jaguar was the car that Earl had in the middle of his sights, as a careful reading of that brochure shows.

The first Corvette had a 102 in (2591 mm) wheelbase, the same as the Jaguar. The weight was 2705 lb (1217 kg), within 150 lb (68 kg) of the heavier Jaguar. The Corvette had side curtains rather than roll-up windows, the same as the Jaguar. Both cars relied on six-cylinder powerplants under the hood,though the British car's double overhead-camshaft design was far more sophisticated than the Corvette's Blue Flame pushrod engine.

There was no doubt that the Corvette was being positioned as a uniquely American car: 'With an eye to the future, Chevrolet introduces in an experimental model The Corvette, the American sports car of the future.'

Earl was confident that the car would be well received by the upper-crust of American drivers,but prospective buyers

Agile performance

For swift acceleration, hill climbing, and cruising, there's nothing quite like the Chevrolet Corvette—and it handles like a dream. To make it swift, Chevrolet engineers combined great engine power with light car weight. As the result, the engine must pull only 21 pounds per horsepower. Contributing to the Corvette's swiftness, too, is the light wind resistance of its low, streamlined, plastic body. Short length (only 14 feet) and easy steering simplify maneuvering in traffic and parking. A very low center of gravity, outrigger type rear springs, and broad wheel treads stabilize the car and allow fast "cornering." Extra-large brakes insure smooth, positive stops. Balanced suspension provides a level, comfortable ride, and gives you a safer, more certain "feel" of the road. Response of the car to your control is always immediate and positive.

Sensational styling

The low-set Corvette body expresses the swiftness that is so dramatically demonstrated by the car's performance. Taking full advantage of the new body material—glass-fiber reinforced plastic—Chevrolet engineers have created a sports car body in which all contours are smoothly streamlined. There are no disturbing projections. The license plate and headlights are recessed and all hinges are concealed. Adding to the fleet appearance are the chrome-bound, wrap-around windshield, jet-type rear fenders, and sunbursts of chrome in the full-size wheel disks. A new kind of styling, too, is apparent in the chrome radiator grille, bumperettes, and moldings that protect the fenders and rim of the cockpit.

Luxurious comfort

In the spacious Corvette cockpit, you're surrounded by all the luxuries you want in a sports car. Form-fitting seats with foam rubber cushions are smartly upholstered in leather-grained vinyl. The driver's seat is adjustable. Stowage pockets are built in the doors and the carpet is backed by soft sponge rubber. The steering wheel is equipped with horn blowing ring and direction signal lever. The Powerglide selector lever is below your right hand. Controls and instruments, including a tachometer, are arrayed before you. The windshield has dual wipers, defroster slots, and a washer, while inside and outside mirrors provide views to the rear. For extra ventilation, there is a screened cowl ventilator. Ash receptacles, cigarette lighter, electric clock, and courtesy light are standard; the favorite-station, signal-seeking radio and recirculating heater are extra-cost accessories.

RIGHT *1954 brochure promoting the 2 seater Corvette.*

RIGHT *1959: The Corvette was aimed at as wide a range of customers as possible.*

were told precious little more about the new car other than what was printed in that first brochure.

It would be a no-option car that first year. Customers would have to accept Polo White as a body colour and Sportsman Red as an interior colour. All would come with the Powerglide transmission, a feature Earl was certain would make the Corvette appeal to a wide range of customers, including women.

It was a modest beginning and much of the 1950s would be spent trying to improve and develop Earl's experimental vehicle into what he had first envisaged.

The man who deserves the most credit for salvaging the Corvette is Zora Arkus-Duntov, who became chief engineer. When the sales catalogues touted high-performance options, they were for the most part included at the insistence of Arkus-Duntov, and by the close of the 1950s he had made Earl's dream of an American sports car a reality.

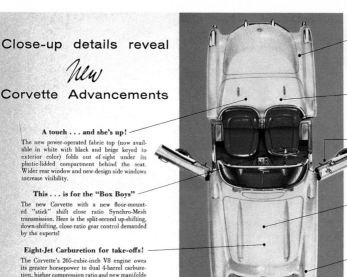

Whether you're casual drive
or connoisseur

New!

-compression "Turbo-Fire V8" engine

carburetors

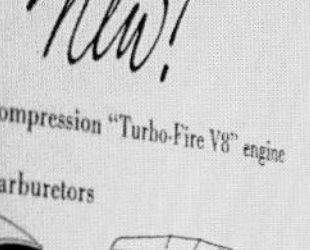

-nforced
-d-top

• New electrically operated fabric top standard

• Weather-tight roll-up windows

-ssion with floor-mounted "stick" shift

-ide with floor-mounted gear selector

-nded headlights

-ear body and fender styling

-panels

steering wheel

-it and body color combinations

optional

Close-up details reveal *New* Corvette Advancements

A touch . . . and she's up!
The new power-operated fabric top (now available in white with black and beige keyed to exterior color) folds out of sight under its plastic-lidded compartment behind the seat. Wider rear window and new-design side windows increase visibility.

This . . . is for the "Box Boys"
The new Corvette with a new floor-mounted "stick" shift close ratio Synchro-Mesh transmission. Here is the split-second up-shifting, down-shifting, close-ratio gear control demanded by the experts!

Eight-Jet Carburetion for take-offs!
The Corvette's 265-cubic-inch V8 engine owes its greater horsepower to dual 4-barrel carburetion, higher compression ratio and new manifolds with "twin pipe" exhausts.

Avant-Garde styling with a touch of tradition
The Corvette is a true sports car—not a scaled-down convertible. Now it's even more adventurous-looking with graceful new fender lines, new side panel and hood treatment and simulated knock-off type wheel covers.

Quick change! A roadster or coupe!
A plastic hardtop featuring a wraparound rear window is available as extra cost equipment. It is easily and securely installed with only five knurled set screws.

Let it rain, let it snow!
Corvette offers the convenience of roll-up regulators that quickly raise and lower the new windows. Power window lifts are available as an extra cost option.

A hood full of "Horses" add a carload of Safety!
The new "Turbo-fire V8" engine is a real life-saver when only sheer *passing power* can leave hazards behind and whisk you to safety. New cylinder heads up Corvette's compression ratio to 9.25 to 1!

"Out-front" styling for looking ahead
The raised-forward portion of the fender houses an improved design headlight that projects forward to extend the fender-line and contribute to Corvette's rakish look.

LEFT *Three years on, and the 1956 brochure still illustrates the original colour options.*

DETROIT PUBLIC LIBRARY
AUTOMOTIVE HISTORY COLLECTION
AUTOMOBILES
1953 CHEVROLET
Entirely NEW
through and through

LEFT *When the 1953 model year began in September of 1952, sedans such as this Bel Air were about the most exciting cars that Chevrolet had to offer. The Corvette was still coming together as a concept vehicle.*

BELOW *The first Corvette sales brochure was a pamphlet handed out to visitors at General Motors' Motorama show at the Waldorf Astoria in New York City, 17 January, 1953. Unlike the other show cars there, the Corvette was destined for production. Price would be $3,498.*

RIGHT *'Sports Car of the Future' was the theme for the Corvette when it was unveiled. Chevrolet publicly called the new two-seater an experimental model but it was clearly ready for production. The brochure pointed out the glass reinforced plastic body, the three-carburettor Blue Flame six-cylinder engine and the then-revolutionary use of the two-speed Powerglide automatic transmission. Production began in June of 1953 and just 300 Corvettes were built. Serial numbers in 1953 ran from E53F001001 to E53F001300.*

WINDSHIELD—Chrome-bound, one-piece, curved Safety Plate Glass; 55-degree slant. HOOD—Glass-fiber hood, with hinges at front. HEADLIGHTS—Recessed in fenders; parking lights beside ends of radiator grille. RADIATOR GRILLE—Chrome airscoop radiator grille. FRONT GUARDS—Chrome grille guard; chrome fender guards. FRONT SUSPENSION—Knee Action, with direct double-acting shock absorbers, and ride stabilizer. STEERING—Full anti-friction steering gear, Center-Point Steering linkage.

The Chevrolet Corvette . . . outstanding performance . . . amazing acceleration . . . very low center of gravity

HEIGHT—33" at door; 47" at windshield. LENGTH—102" wheelbase; 167" over-all. WIDTH—70" over-all. WEIGHT—Approximately 2900 pounds curb weight. TOP—Rakish, manually adjusted, lightweight fabric top; folds into concealed compartment at front of rear deck. BODY—Special open-cockpit, 2-passenger, glass-fiber body. ENGINE—160-h.p. high-compression 6-cylinder valve-in-head special "Blue Flame" Engine, with triple side-draft carburetors and dual exhaust system. TRANSMISSION—Powerglide Automatic Transmission, with floor-mounted selector lever. WHEELS—6.70 x 15, whitewall tires; chrome wheel disks with simulated "knock-off" hubs. Front tread, 57"; rear tread, 59". BRAKES—Hydraulic 4-wheel 11" Jumbo-Drum self-energizing brakes, with bonded linings. Mechanical actuation of rear wheel brakes for parking. CHASSIS FRAME—X-member-braced Box Girder Frame. GASOLINE TANK—18 gallons behind seats; concealed filler on left side.

TAIL LIGHTS—Jet-type tail, stop, and direction signal lights in ends of air-fin fenders. LUGGAGE LOCKER—Capacious, with counterbalanced lid; spare wheel and tire mounted flat below floor. LICENSE PLATE—Recessed in rear deck lid; indirectly lighted. REAR GUARDS—Chrome center guard, between dual exhaust ports; chrome fender guards. REAR AXLE—Low numerical ratio hypoid axle; Hotchkiss drive. REAR SUSPENSION—3-leaf, semi-elliptic springs;

THE SPACIOUS CHEVROLET CORVETTE COCKPIT

COLORS—Scarlet and White. SEATS—Form-fitting individual bucket seats; driver's seat adjustable. ARM RESTS—Built in doors; capacious stowage boxes in doors below saddle covers. STEERING WHEEL—Nearly vertical 17¼" wheel; horn-blowing ring. TRANSMISSION SELECTOR LEVER—Floor-mounted, in sports car tradition. INSTRUMENTS—Airplane type; include center-mounted tachometer showing engine revolutions per minute; hooded speedometer and radio speaker. DOOR CONTROLS—Push button outside; release lever inside. SIDE WINDOWS — Separate windows, snapped in chrome top moldings of doors.

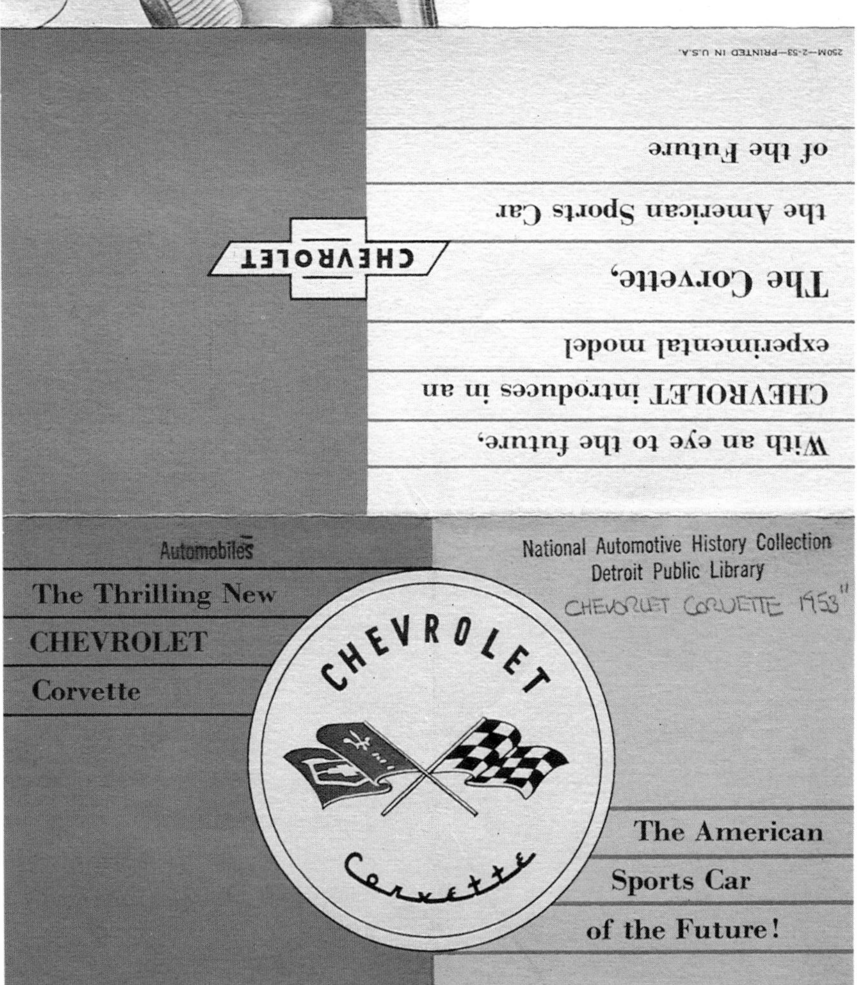

250M-2-53—PRINTED IN U.S.A.
CHEVROLET
With an eye to the future,
CHEVROLET introduces in an
experimental model
The Corvette,
the American Sports Car
of the Future
Automobiles
National Automotive History Collection
Detroit Public Library
CHEVROLET CORVETTE 1953"
The Thrilling New
CHEVROLET
Corvette
CHEVROLET
Corvette
The American
Sports Car
of the Future!

CHEVROLET
AUTOMOBILES
1954
See for yourself how
much more Chevrolet offers-
Bruce Bomberger

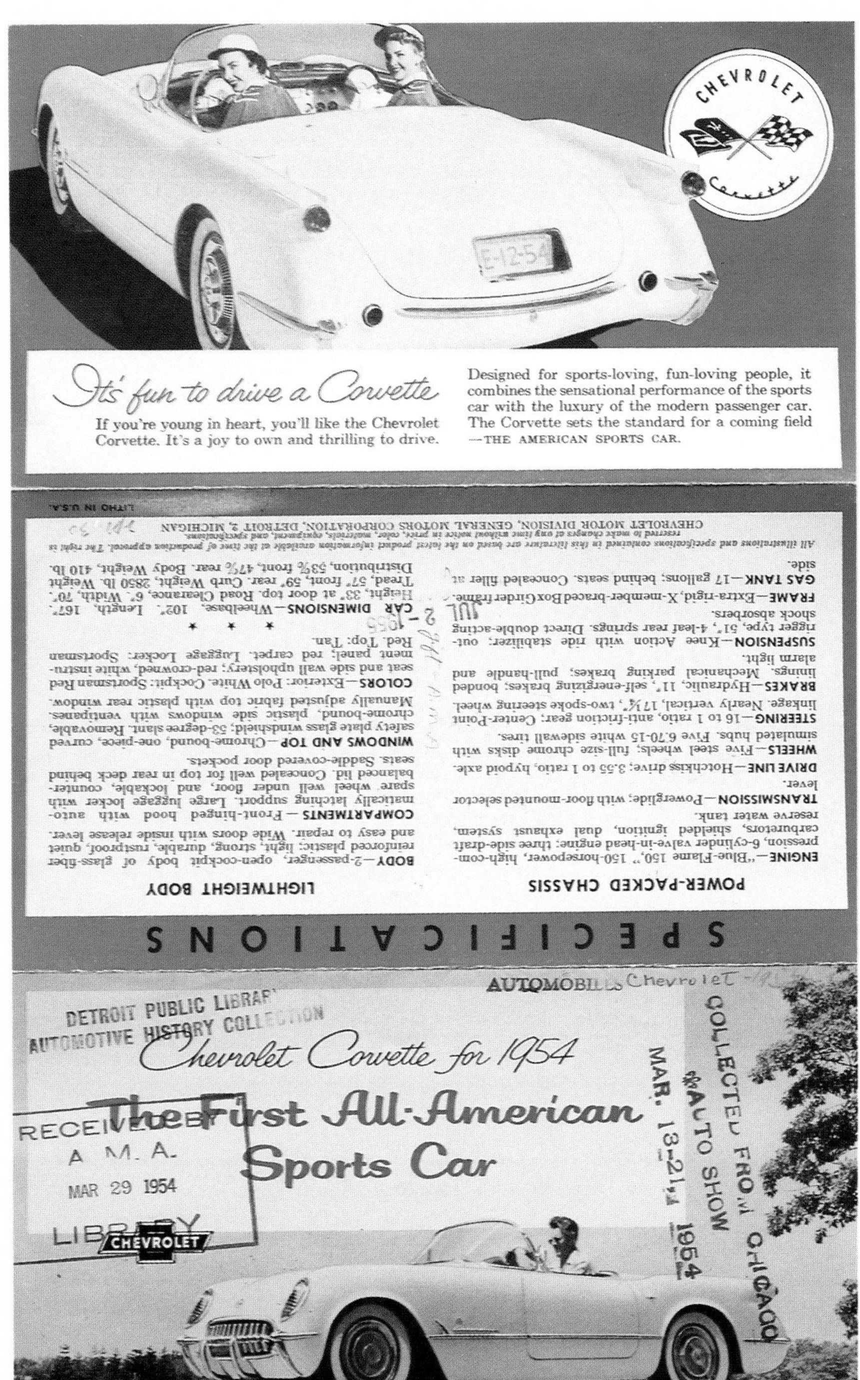

OPPOSITE *Chevrolet dealers still touted big, solid sedans when the 1954 model year began. But alongside these tall, boxy cars, dealers also offered a svelte two-seater, the Corvette. The 300 1953 Corvettes had been offered for sale to high-profile people such as movie stars. It wasn't until 1954 that the Corvette became available to the common man.*

LEFT *For the first time, photos of the Corvette with people behind the wheel appeared in sales brochures. It's interesting to note that women are shown behind the wheel, an indication of the market Chevrolet saw for its automatic-transmission sports car. For 1954, the Corvette was largely unchanged from the 1953 model. One change, however, is that white was not the only colour available. Though not mentioned in early brochures, Corvettes could be ordered in Pennant Blue, with a tan interior, Sportsman Red, and the familiar Polo White, both with red interiors. About 16 per cent of Corvettes in 1954 were blue with red accounting for only four per cent and white making up most of the rest. Black was a special order colour and only a handful were built.*

1954

AUTOMOBILES • *The Chevrolet Corvette*

CONVERTIBLE COUPE

The sports car gains new all-weather utility in this new experimental model. The *removable* top—of the same glass fiber plastic construction as the body itself—may be left behind in the garage on warm and sunny days.

BELOW *1954 marked the first year of Corvette options. In reality, these options were standard on most of the cars and were only listed to make the Corvette seem cheaper. For 1954 the price was dropped from $3,498 to $2,774 – the least expensive Corvette ever. But sales brochures do not reveal that the Powerglide transmission was a $178.35 mandatory option and most cars came fully equipped, boosting the price almost back up to the 1953 level. Serial numbers ran from E54S001001 to E54S1004640.*

Agile performance

For swift acceleration, hill climbing, and cruising, there's nothing quite like the Chevrolet Corvette—and it handles like a dream. To make it swift, Chevrolet engineers combined great engine power with light car weight. As the result, the engine must pull only 21 pounds per horsepower. Contributing to the Corvette's swiftness, too, is the light wind resistance of its low, streamlined, plastic body. Short length (only 14 feet) and easy steering simplify maneuvering in traffic and parking. A very low center of gravity, outrigger type rear springs, and broad wheel treads stabilize the car and allow fast "cornering." Extra-large brakes insure smooth, positive stops. Balanced suspension provides a level, comfortable ride, and gives you a safer, more certain "feel" of the road. Response of the car to your control is always immediate and positive.

Sensational styling

The low-set Corvette body expresses the swiftness that is so dramatically demonstrated by the car's performance. Taking full advantage of the new body material—glass-fiber reinforced plastic—Chevrolet engineers have created a sports car body in which all contours are smoothly streamlined. There are no disturbing projections. The license plate and headlights are recessed and all hinges are concealed. Adding to the fleet appearance are the chrome-bound, wrap-around windshield, jet-type rear fenders, and sunbursts of chrome in the full-size wheel disks. A new kind of styling, too, is apparent in the chrome radiator grille, bumperettes, and moldings that protect the fenders and rim of the cockpit.

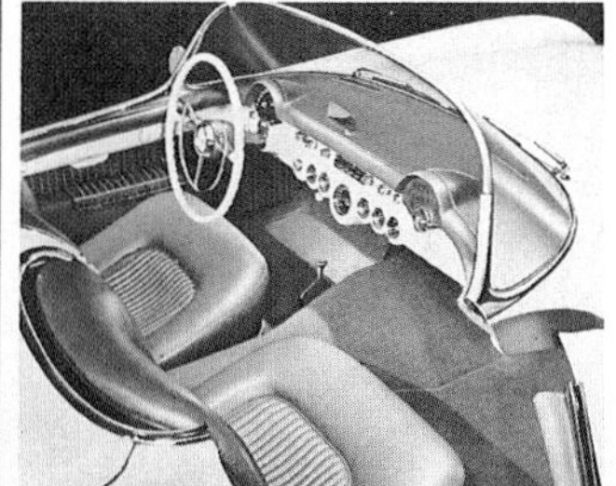

Luxurious comfort

In the spacious Corvette cockpit, you're surrounded by all the luxuries you want in a sports car. Form-fitting seats with foam rubber cushions are smartly upholstered in leather-grained vinyl. The driver's seat is adjustable. Stowage pockets are built in the doors and the carpet is backed by soft sponge rubber. The steering wheel is equipped with horn blowing ring and direction signal lever. The Powerglide selector lever is below your right hand. Controls and instruments, including a tachometer, are arrayed before you. The windshield has dual wipers, defroster slots, and a washer, while inside and outside mirrors provide views to the rear. For extra ventilation, there is a screened cowl ventilator. Ash receptacles, cigarette lighter, electric clock, and courtesy light are standard; the favorite-station, signal-seeking radio and recirculating heater are extra-cost accessories.

ABOVE *Corvettes were not well suited to the rain, a reality that Chevrolet seemed to be acknowledging when it introduced this concept Corvette that sported a removable hard top. This idea would come into production two years later. That was too late for some Corvette buyers, who became disenchanted with the car. Aside from the lack of roll-up windows and a snug top, buyers in 1954 complained about the lack of door handles and locks, as well as shoddy workmanship and a lack of a manual transmission. More than 3,600 Corvettes were built in 1954 but nearly a third of them were unsold when the 1955 model year began.*

New precision of command . . .

effortless ease in traffic with the smoother Powerglide automatic.

The new Corvette blends sports car suspension and vivid acceleration with the quicksilver smoothness of an improved and specially modified Powerglide automatic transmission. Teamed with either the special Corvette version of the Chevrolet "Blue-Flame" 155-h.p. six, or the new "Turbo-Fire V8" (with horsepower boosted to 195 in the Corvette), Powerglide offers a superbly balanced rear axle ratio for all road conditions and split-second shifts between ranges. In the sports car tradition, it has a central floor-mounted range selector of the Safety-Shift pattern that permits manual selection of Low Range at the driver's will.

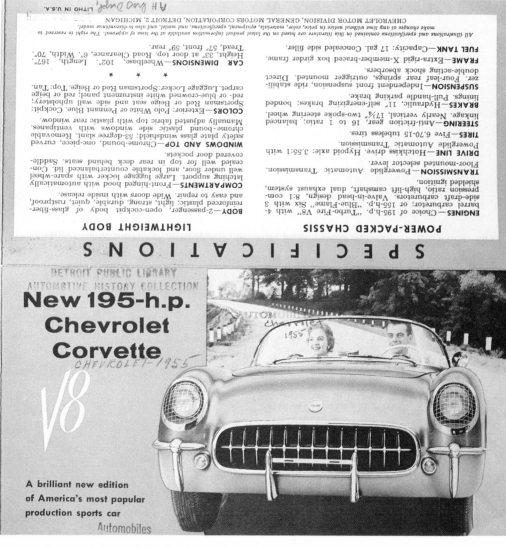

THE SLEEK REAR DECK of the Corvette conceals a generous luggage compartment—far more spacious than most sports cars. The spare tire is in a well under the floor; the radio antenna is built into the deck lid.

New 195-h.p. Chevrolet Corvette

CHEVROLET-1955

V8

A brilliant new edition of America's most popular production sports car

Automobiles

SPECIFICATIONS

POWER-PACKED CHASSIS

ENGINES—Choice of 195-h.p. "Turbo-Fire V8" with 4-barrel carburetor; or 155-h.p. "Blue-Flame" Six with 3 side-draft carburetors. Valve-in-head design, 8:1 compression ratio, high-lift camshaft, dual exhaust system, shielded ignition.

TRANSMISSION—Powerglide Automatic Transmission. Floor-mounted selector lever.

DRIVE LINE—Hotchkiss drive. Hypoid axle: 3.55:1 with Powerglide Automatic Transmission.

TIRES—Five 6.70-15 tubeless tires.

STEERING—Anti-friction gear, 16 to 1 ratio; balanced linkage. Nearly vertical, 17¼" two-spoke steering wheel.

BRAKES—Hydraulic, 11" self-energizing brakes; bonded linings. Pull-handle parking brake.

SUSPENSION—Independent front suspension, ride stabilizer. Four-leaf rear springs, outrigger mounted. Direct double-acting shock absorbers.

FRAME—Extra-rigid X-member-braced box girder frame.

FUEL TANK—Capacity: 17 gal. Concealed side filler.

LIGHTWEIGHT BODY

BODY—2-passenger, open-cockpit body of glass-fiber-reinforced plastic; light, strong, durable, quiet, rustproof, and easy to repair. Wide doors with inside release.

COMPARTMENTS—Front-hinged hood with automatically latching support. Large luggage locker with spare-wheel well under floor, and lockable counterbalanced lid. Concealed well for top in rear deck behind seats. Saddle-covered door pockets.

WINDOWS AND TOP—Chrome-bound, one-piece, curved safety plate glass windshield; 53-degree slant. Removable chrome-bound plastic side windows with ventipanes. Manually adjusted fabric top with plastic rear window.

COLORS—Exterior: Polo White or Pennant Blue. Cockpit: Sportsman Red or Beige seat and side wall upholstery; red- or blue-crowned white instrument panel; red or beige carpet. Luggage Locker: Sportsman Red or Beige. Top: Tan.

* * *

CAR DIMENSIONS—Wheelbase, 102". Length, 167". Height, 33" at door top. Road Clearance, 6". Width, 70". Tread, 57" front, 59" rear.

All illustrations and specifications contained in this literature are based on the latest product information available at the time of approval. The right is reserved to make changes at any time without notice in price, color, materials, equipment, specifications, and model, and also to discontinue model.

CHEVROLET MOTOR DIVISION, GENERAL MOTORS CORPORATION, DETROIT 2, MICHIGAN

LITHO IN U.S.A.

ABOVE *V8 Power arrived in 1955. By the mid-1950s, the powerful V8 was the engine in demand by buyers and Chevrolet finally delivered the Turbo-Fire V8 in 1955. Although the engine would be a boon to the entire Chevy line up, it was a natural for the Corvette. At 195 horsepower, the V8 made a screamer out of the car. The promotional prose in the 1955 Corvette brochure was brimming with enthusiasm that pointed out the Corvette was 'a sports car . . . not a scaled down convertible,' presumably a reference to Ford's new two-seat Thunderbird.*

Fresh from the dreams
of America's foremost
automotive designers . . .
THE CHEVROLI
COPYRIGHT 1955—CHEVROLET MOTOR DIVISION, GENERAL MOTORS CORPORATION

ABOVE *The stylists at Chevrolet were hard at work on restyling the Corvette. This version made the show car circuit in 1955 but it's doubtful it was ever seriously considered for production. Some styling themes, notably the rear deck, appear to be related to the styling on the Corvair when it appeared in 1960. Although designers were at work on a new Corvette for 1956, there was some doubt the car would survive. Sales were so slow that just 700 Corvettes were built in 1955, compared to the 16,000 Thunderbirds sold by Ford. Those strong Ford sales, however, stiffened Chevrolet's resolve to make the Corvette a success.*

Biscayne
Here is an exploration in elegance—a superlatively luxurious experimental car for four passengers that illustrates an entirely new way of thinking about automotive design. Slim and functionally compact, the Biscayne's classic purity of line is accented by the audacious overhead sweep of the Stratospheric windshield, no center pillars, the boldly indented side panel, the air-scoop grille that serves as a bumper. And under the low-set hood is a startling preview of tomorrow's performance . . . a 215 horsepower V8 by Chevrolet.

A cyclone of power

with the new 195-h.p. V8 engine

A breath-stopping surge of power that surpasses anything you have ever imagined—that's the story of the Corvette's new 195-h.p. V8 engine. Here is a "dream" power-plant . . . ultra-compact, free-breathing, super-efficient, the most modern valve-in-head V8 engine in the world . . . and it can be serviced by any Chevrolet dealer. Dual exhausts, a four-barrel carburetor, 8 to 1 compression ratio, and a high-lift camshaft squeeze latent energy out of every drop of gasoline . . . and careful counter-balancing of the entire engine *after assembly* keeps it smooth as a jet of steam.

Real driving comfort . . . the Corvette way!

SECURITY AND LUXURY for driver and passenger are the keynotes of the snug Corvette cockpit. Individual bucket seats have form-fitting foam rubber cushions. The floor is covered in soft carpeting, backed by sponge rubber. Large pockets and ash trays in doors also serve as arm rests. Beautifully balanced instrument panel includes key-turn starter, electric clock, tachometer, hooded radio speaker.

POTENT "BLUE-FLAME" 6 engine, with three side-draft carburetors, 8 to 1 compression ratio, and overhead valves, puts a flashing 155 horse-power under the throttle. It has a dual exhaust system, efficient cooling and lubrication, and a shielded electrical system . . . plus Chevrolet's traditional six-cylinder economy of operation and maintenance.

Geared-to-the-road stability

The Corvette is a sports car . . . not a scaled-down convertible. At any speed it offers a sense of security, an inherent balance that is astonishing. Low-slung, with a center of gravity only 18 inches above the pavement, its outrigger rear springs and broad-based front tread let it cling to the road like a cat. The steering gear has 16 to 1 ratio for instant response. Its big 11-inch brakes have bonded linings and a grip that would stop a truck. Everything is designed to give the absolute, precise command that only the driver of a true sports car can know.

ABOVE *The V8 option was a bargain – at about $135 over the standard six. Only six of the 1955 Corvettes came with the six-cylinder engine. Aside from the V8 option, the specification page remained unchanged from 1954. Most detrimental to sales was the continued use of the Powerglide automatic as the only transmission. A three-speed manual transmission was on the way but it didn't make it until very late in the model year. Serial numbers ran from VE55S001001 through VE55S001700.*

BELOW *When the 1956 model year began, there was a new Corvette that could rightly be considered a quantum leap from the car introduced three years earlier. With a better product to sell, Chevrolet began producing brochures that had more of a hard-edged sales tone to them and men, rather than women, were featured as Corvette drivers. The Corvette was no longer a 'ladies car,' as some critics of the day had charged. Full colour photographs began to appear and several different brochures were produced throughout the model year.*

REVEAL

NEW

Corvette

ADVANCEMENTS

folds out of sight under its covered compartment. Wider windows increase visibility.

Quick change! A roadster or coupe!

smartly-conceived plastic hardtop featuring a wrap-around rear window is available at extra cost. It is easily and securely installed with only five knurled set screws.

Let it rain, let it snow

Corvette offers the convenience of new "roll-up" regulators to quickly raise and lower the new side windows. Power window lifts, only one of Corvette's several new power features, are available at extra cost.

This . . . is for the "box boys"

The new close-ratio Synchro-Mesh with a new floor-mounted "Stick" shift, provides the split-second upshifting, down-shifting, gear control demanded by the experts!

New "going" look

Now Corvette is even more adventurous-looking with graceful new fenderlines, new side panel and hood treatment and simulated knock-off type wheel covers.

New "out-front" styling

The raised forward portion of the fender houses an improved design headlight that projects forward to extend the fenderline and contributes to Corvette's rakish look.

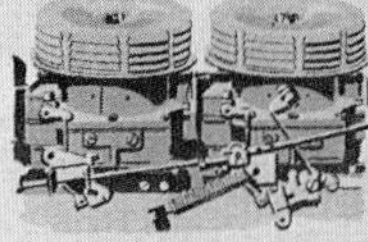

Eight-Jet take-offs!

The Corvette's 265-cubic-inch V8 engine owes its greater horsepower to dual 4-barrel carburetion, higher compression ratio and new manifolds with "twin pipe" exhausts.

A hood full of "horses"

The new "Turbo-Fire Special V8" engine is a real life-saver when only sheer *passing-power* can whisk you to safety. New cylinder heads up compression to 9.25 to 1!

Sensational to *Go* in . . .

Ease into Corvette's luxurious cockpit. Flick its "Turbo-Fire Special V8" engine into life and listen to the cultured baritone of its twin exhausts. Let out the clutch of this tiger-tempered sports car and—GO!

Here in one superbly engineered machine you have whip-lash acceleration, cat-sure cornering and the safest, most positive braking.

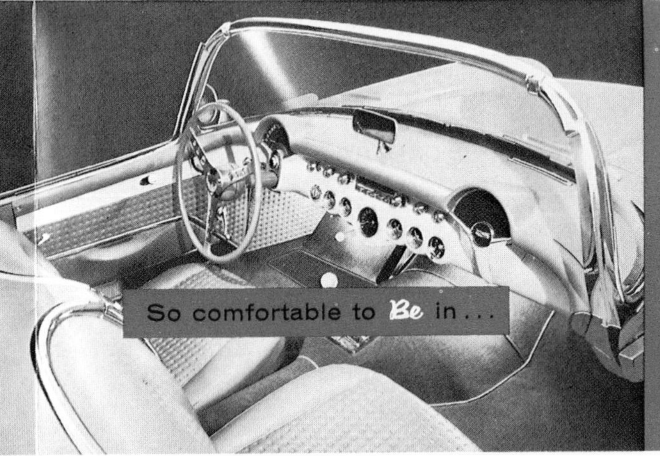

So smart to be *Seen* in . . .

Brilliant styling and color . . . flashing, jewel-like color-contrasts of saddle-stitched bucket seats, body, and top make an irresistible bid for attention and admiration. Surely, Corvette will be the year's most envied car!

Sensational to GO in . . .
So smart to be SEEN in . . .
So comfortable to BE in!

The new Corvette is not a cut-down convertible. It is a true-blooded, tiger-tempered sports car in the noblest tradition.

Whip-lash acceleration, cat-sure cornering and handling are matched with positive safety braking and the vivid luxury of its saddle-stitched bucket seats. Brilliant styling and *color* . . . flashing, jewel-like color contrasts of cockpit and body, cowl and top make an irresistible bid for attention and approval. Surely, Corvette will be the most envied car in any setting!

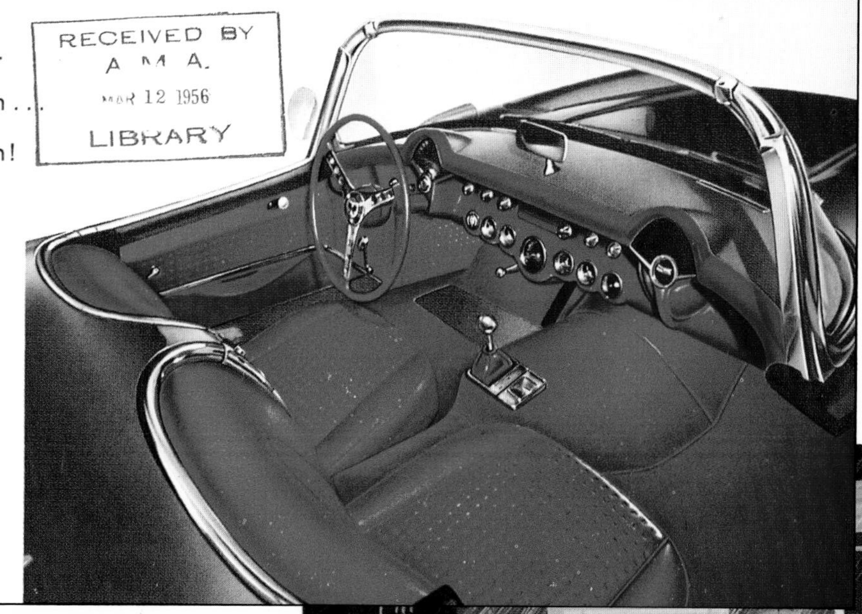

ABOVE *The dashboard of the Corvette remained unchanged on the 1956 model but between the seats there was for the first time a shift-lever that operated a manual transmission. It was a three-speed unit mated to either a 3.55 to 1 or a 3.27 to 1 ratio rear axle. Powerglide remained an option.*

RIGHT *Despite the allure of a much improved Corvette, Chevrolet was still primarily in the business of selling sedans. In fact, Chevrolet sold far more taxicabs, shown in this rare brochure, than Corvettes. For 1956, Corvette production hit 3,388.*

1956 Chevrolet Taxicabs

RIGHT *Outside, the 1956 Corvette still stands as one of the most attractive cars ever built. The style of the distinctive nose on the original car was retained, yet improved with new headlamps and a refined, if toothy, grill. The rear end was improved with recessed tail lights and the relocation of the exhaust tips to the chrome fender bumpers. A curious styling addition was the return of the fender-mounted cockpit air scoops that first appeared on the Motorama Corvette. They were non-functional. The most striking features were the scooped-out side coves that ran from the rear of the front wheel well back to the middle of the cockpit doors. When set off in a contrasting colour, the coves added tremendous flair to the Corvette.*

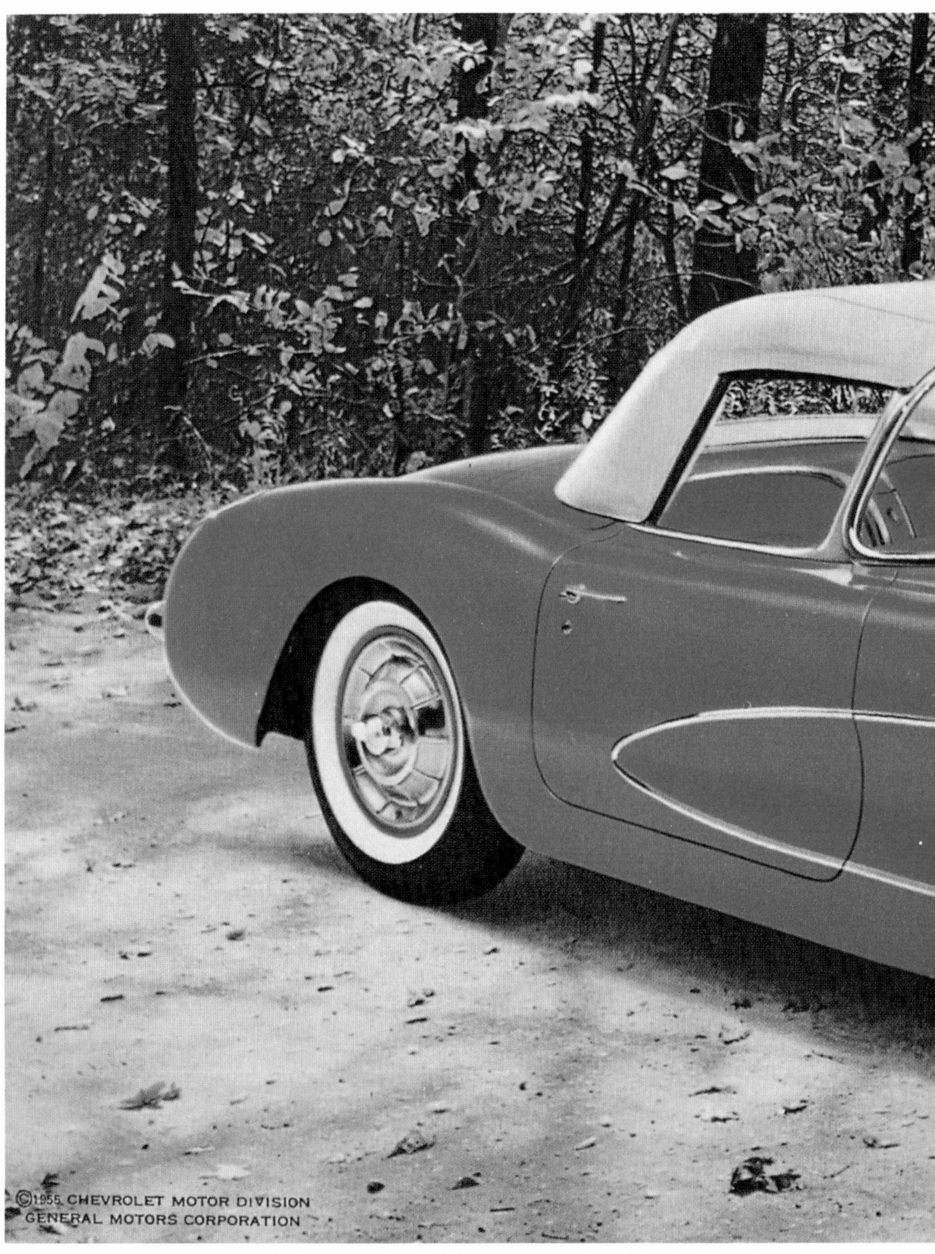

Action is the

Since its initial introduction in limited
Corvette has commanded the attention
experts and enthusiasts everywhere.
well-informed admirers have come
suggestions and comments that have
tant design factors in the New Corvett

"Even *more* action!" clamored the in
fans. "Even *more* convenience!" pe

with the accent

BELOW *The 1956 Corvette also answered the demand for more creature comforts and silenced critics who had complained about leaky side curtains and an ill-fitting top. The new bodywork also incorporated outside door handles and locks, roll-up windows, a convertible top with better visibility and a power lift and an optional removable hardtop. Serial numbers for the 1956 models ran from E56S001001 to E56S004467.*

19 LIVELY NEW CHEVROLETS FOR 1956!
Starring the most glamorous 4-Door Sport Sedans in any price class!
Not one, but two—a Sport Sedan in both the Bel Air and "Two-Ten" series!

ABOVE *The theme of sportiness was beginning to spill over into the rest of the Chevrolet lineup. Rounded curves began to replace the boxy shapes of past years and lower and wider was a common theme.*

CHEVROLET – 1956

THE NEW CORVETTE

BY CHEVROLET

SPECIFICATIONS

ENGINE

"Turbo-Fire Special V8." Valve-in-head design, 265-cubic-inch displacement, 3.75" bore x 3.0" stroke, 9.25:1 compression ratio. 225 horsepower at 5200 rpm. Torque 270 foot-pounds at 3600 rpm. Special high-lift camshaft, high-speed valve mechanism. Polished aluminum rocker covers. Dual four-barrel carburetion, buff aluminum racing-type air cleaners, special intake manifold. Full pressure lubrication system with full-flow oil filter.* High-power exhaust headers and full dual exhaust system. Shielded ignition, 12-volt electrical system. Engine precision balanced after assembly.

TRANSMISSION

Choice of special high-performance 3-speed close-ratio Synchro-Mesh (2.2:1 low and reverse, 1.31:1 second, 1:1 high) with high-capacity 10-inch coil-spring clutch, or optional Powerglide special automatic transmission.* Floor mounted gear or range selector.

REAR AXLE

High torque capacity axle; 3.55:1 ratio standard, 3.27:1 ratio optional with either Synchro-Mesh or Powerglide.

CHASSIS

Extra-rigid X-member-braced box girder frame. Independent coil front suspension with ride stabilizer. Self-lubricating four-leaf rear springs, outrigger mounted. Direct double-acting shock absorbers. Full anti-friction 16:1 ratio steering gear, balanced linkage. Competition-type steering wheel with three shock absorbing spring-steel spokes. Hydraulic 11-inch self-energizing brakes with new bonded linings, pull-handle parking brake. Suspended brake pedal. Choice of black or white sidewall* standard 6.70-15-4 ply tubeless tires or optional 6.70-15-4 ply high-speed nylon racing type.* Decorative wheel covers with simulated knock-off knobs. 17-gallon fuel tank with concealed side filler.

BODY FEATURES

Glass-fiber-reinforced plastic with sculptured side panels; light, strong, durable, quiet, rustproof, easy to repair. Distinctive embossed hood, front hinged, with automatic support, inside release. Simulated twin fender air scoops. Two-passenger compartment, large luggage locker with spare-wheel well under floor, concealed top well behind seats. Unique Corvette crossed-flag emblems on hood and trunk lid. Twin exhaust ports integral with rear bumpers. Chrome-bound, one-piece, curved safety plate glass windshield. Power-operated fabric top with wide plastic rear window. Richly trimmed quick-change hardtop* with rear-quarter windows and full-vision rear window.

INTERIOR FEATURES

Form-fitting vinyl-covered seats, individually adjustable, with safety belt.* Wide doors with built-in arm rest, push-button door handle; key lock, inside door release, swing-out door hinges. Choice of crank-operated or power* window lifts. Ash tray and glove compartment between seats; padded roll on instrument panel and doors, rubber-backed carpeting, metal door kick panels, sills, and step plates. Signal-seeking radio,* heater,* directional signals, electric clock, cigarette lighter, tachometer, outside and inside rear-view mirror, windshield washer.*

COLORS

Onyx Black with Red interior and Black or White top, Venetian Red with Red interior and Beige or White top, Cascade Green with Beige interior and Beige or White top, Aztec copper with Beige interior and Beige or White top, Arctic Blue with Beige or Red interior and Beige or White top, Polo White with Red interior and White or Black top.

DIMENSIONS

Wheelbase, 102". Length, 168.01". Overall height: top down, 49.20"; Convertible top, 51.09"; hardtop, 50.98". Height at door 32.55". Road clearance 6". Width, 70.46". Tread, 57" front, 59" rear.

*Optional at extra cost.

at the time of publication
ipment and specifications.

2, MICHIGAN

LITHO IN U.S.A.

Since its initial introduction in limited volume, the Corvette has commanded the attention of sports car enthusiasts. Now its major new design factors will be welcomed as answers to the needs expressed by this well-informed group. Drivers who scorn the "scaled down convertible" and will accept nothing less than an authentic, competition-type sports car will quickly sense that *action* is the keynote of the new Corvette V8. But convenience is accented too, and you will find many luxury features seldom available in a car of this caliber.

Live, Lithe, Luxurious Action

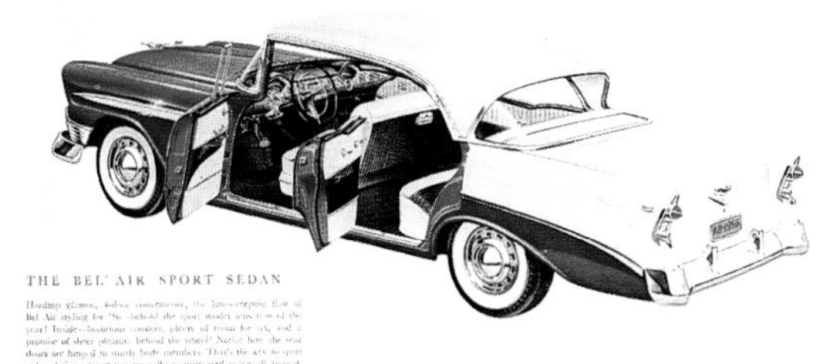

ABOVE *The 1956 model year saw the introduction of a pillarless four-door sedan, called a Sports Sedan.*

BELOW *On those occasions when a Corvette driver exceeded the speed limit, it was highly likely that a Chevrolet-built police car was in hot pursuit.*

RIGHT *Coupes and sedans were the mainstay of Chevrolet's business in 1956 but as the family cars became sportier, the image of the Corvette became important for its 'halo' effect on other sales.*

Introducing the All-New Bel Air 4-Door Sport Sedan
BEL AIR SPORT SEDAN
Hardtop glamor, 4-door convenience and long, low Bel Air lines—it's the sport model sensation of the year in *any* price class! Contemporary interior styling features rich charcoal gray trimmed with ivory vinyl.
Your Choice of Two Lively New Sport Coupes!
BEL AIR SPORT COUPE
For '56—bold new Motoramic styling from handsomely recessed headlamps to rakish rear fender cutouts . . . new colors and combinations to choose from . . . the brilliant performance of V8 or 6 . . . plus traditional Chevrolet quality in every detail!
"TWO-TEN" SPORT COUPE
Chevrolet's *fourth* hardtop for 1956—this spirited sport model, a star of the "Two-Ten" Series! You'll like its roominess and fine-car feeling, its silk-smooth, road-hugging ride! Best of all, you'll like its low price.
COPYRIGHT 1955—CHEVROLET MOTOR DIVISION, GENERAL MOTORS CORPORATION

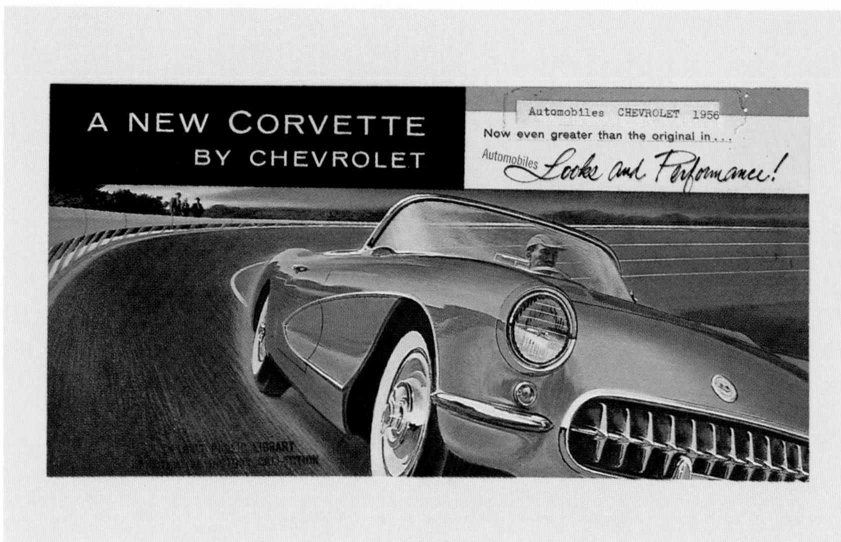

A NEW CORVETTE
BY CHEVROLET
Automobiles CHEVROLET 1956
Now even greater than the original in . . .
Automobiles Looks and Performance!

LEFT *The performance promise made by the 1955 V8 Corvette was delivered in the 1956 model. The Blue Flame Six was gone for good and in its place was an upgraded 265-cubic-inch V8 introduced in 1956. In its standard trim the engine was now rated at 210 horsepower. But the hot setup was a 225-horsepower version topped by two four-barrel carburettors. A few special camshaft versions of the two-four-barrel engine were built with horsepower boosted to 240. The 240-horsepower engine was a special-order item not mentioned in the sales brochure.*

BELOW LEFT *Despite all the upgrades elsewhere, the interior of the Corvette remained mostly unchanged into the 1956 model year. The instrument panel was poorly designed by sports car standards.*

BELOW *The new car was to a large degree the result of work by Zora Arkus-Duntov, a Belgian-born engineer who had a love affair going with sports cars. He joined the Corvette team in 1954 and was committed to high performance.*

Close-up details reveal New Corvette Advancements

A touch . . . and she's up!

The new power-operated fabric top (now available in white with black and beige keyed to exterior color) folds out of sight under its plastic-lidded compartment behind the seat. Wider rear window and new-design side windows increase visibility.

This . . . is for the "Box Boys"

The new Corvette with a new floor-mounted "stick" shift close-ratio Synchro-Mesh transmission. Here is the split-second up-shifting, down-shifting, close-ratio gear control demanded by the experts!

Eight-Jet Carburetion for take-offs!

The Corvette's 265-cubic-inch V8 engine owes its greater horsepower to dual 4-barrel carburetion, higher compression ratio and new manifolds with "twin pipe" exhausts.

Avant-Garde styling with a touch of tradition

The Corvette is a true sports car—not a scaled-down convertible. Now it's even more adventurous-looking with graceful new fender lines, new side panel and hood treatment and simulated knock-off type wheel covers.

Quick change! A roadster or coupe!

A plastic hardtop featuring a wraparound rear window is available as extra cost equipment. It is easily and securely installed with only five knurled set screws.

Let it rain, let it snow!

Corvette offers the convenience of roll-up regulators that quickly raise and lower the new windows. Power window lifts are available as an extra cost option.

A hood f... add a ca...

The new "Turbo-fi... saver when only sh... hazards behind and... cylinder heads up (... to 9.25 to 1!

"Out-front" sty...

The raised-forward ... an improved desig... forward to extend th... to Corvette's rakish...

Action is the keynote . . .

Since its initial introduction in limited volume, the Corvette has commanded the attention of sportscar experts and enthusiasts everywhere. From these well-informed admirers have come many of the suggestions and comments that have been important design factors in the New Corvette V8.

"Even *more* action!" clamored the insatiable rally fans. "Even *more* convenience!" petitioned the spectator-owners whose love for luxury matches their discernment of lines and styling.

Now we confidently present the newest Corvette for your own critical appraisal. Its design incorporates new ideas from professional drivers—ideas that have been evaluated and refined to bring about the most spectacular evolution in the world of sports cars. That's the New Corvette V8!

with the accent on Convenience

New!

- 225-h.p. High-compression "Turbo-Fire V8" engine
- Dual 4-barrel carburetors
- Glass-fiber reinforced quick-change hard-top optional
- New electrically operated fabric top standard
- Weather-tight roll-up windows
- 3-speed transmission with floor-mounted "stick" shift or special Powerglide with floor-mounted gear selector
- Redesigned extended headlights
- Classic design rear body and fender styling
- Sculptured side panels
- Competition-type steering wheel
- Contrasting cockpit and body color combinations
- Racing-type tires optional

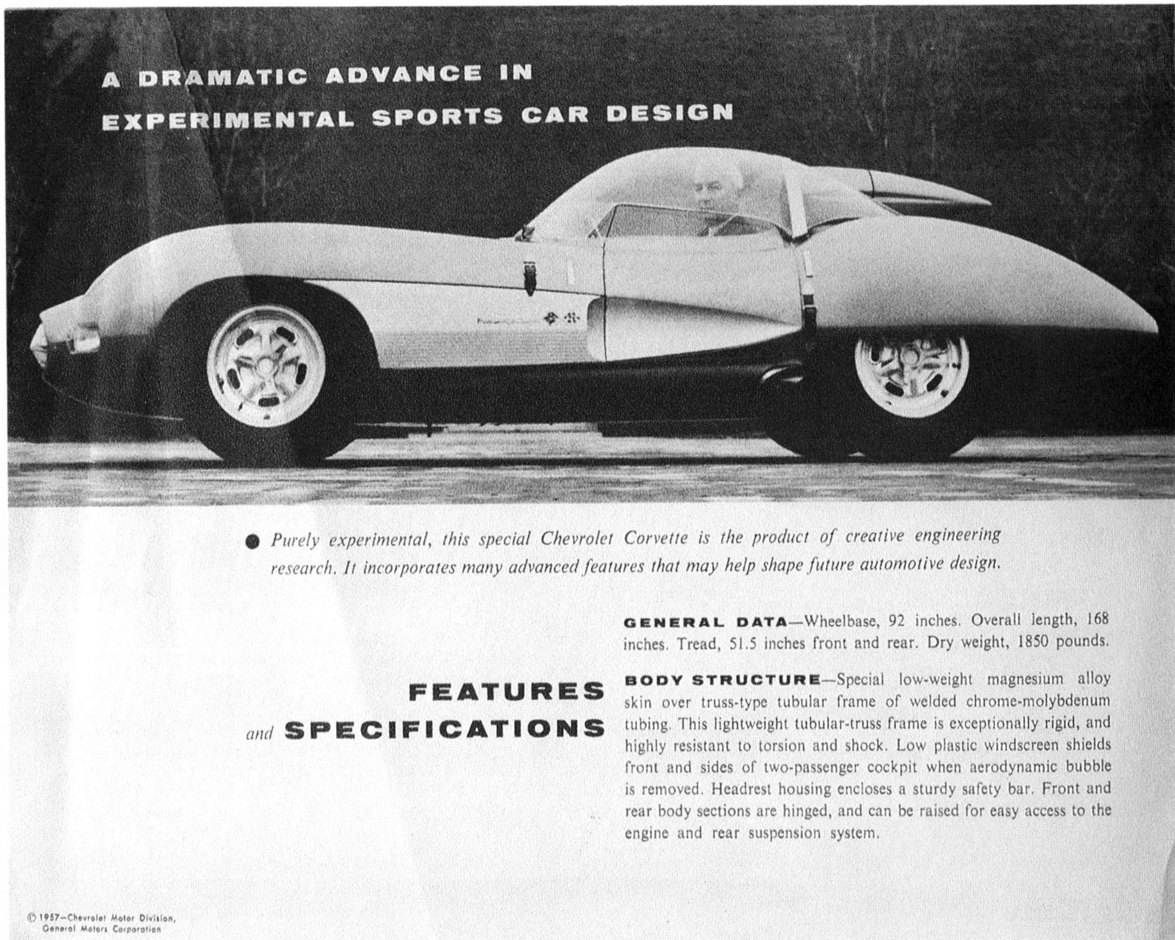

A DRAMATIC ADVANCE IN
EXPERIMENTAL SPORTS CAR DESIGN
● Purely experimental, this special Chevrolet Corvette is the product of creative engineering research. It incorporates many advanced features that may help shape future automotive design.
FEATURES and SPECIFICATIONS
GENERAL DATA—Wheelbase, 92 inches. Overall length, 168 inches. Tread, 51.5 inches front and rear. Dry weight, 1850 pounds.
BODY STRUCTURE—Special low-weight magnesium alloy skin over truss-type tubular frame of welded chrome-molybdenum tubing. This lightweight tubular-truss frame is exceptionally rigid, and highly resistant to torsion and shock. Low plastic windscreen shields front and sides of two-passenger cockpit when aerodynamic bubble is removed. Headrest housing encloses a sturdy safety bar. Front and rear body sections are hinged, and can be raised for easy access to the engine and rear suspension system.
© 1957—Chevrolet Motor Division, General Motors Corporation

ABOVE *The performance theme was stressed even more strongly in the 1957 Corvette, which on the outside remained unchanged from 1956. Racing had become a major sales tool for Chevrolet though there was a corporate racing ban in effect. Arkus-Duntov arranged for a specially-built Corvette, called the SS – shown here with him behind the wheel and with a plexiglass top – to compete at Sebring. Though the car did not finish, it was an example of the commitment Arkus-Duntov and others at Chevrolet had to high-performance cars. Some of that racing experience spilled over into the showroom for 1957. By specifing RPO (Regular Production Option) 684, a buyer would get a racing suspension that included heavier springs, sway bar, Positraction rear axle, finned brake drums with special linings and quicker steering. The option was a hefty $725 and it was specified mainly for cars destined for racing. There was also a special version of the new 283-horsepower fuel-injection engine that was also intended for racing. Designated RPO 579E, it had a cold-air induction system and a special tachometer was mounted on the steering column. To prove it was not intended for the faint-hearted, Chevrolet would not sell it in a Corvette that also had a cockpit heater.*

CHEVROLET'S NEW CORVETTE

LEFT *When the 1957 Corvette debuted, the car's future was assured. It was now fast, stylish and fun to drive. Gone were the problems of no manual transmission and only a six-cylinder engine.*

EVERY IN

A CHAMPIC

LEFT *The 1957 catalogue could boast of a variety of special features and options. A buyer could choose a four-speed or the trusty two-speed Powerglide. There was the option of a detachable hardtop, and the windows could be had with either manual cranks or power lifts. Combined with the 1957's undeniably good looks, it was a winning package.*

EVERY INCH A PRIZED POSSESSION!

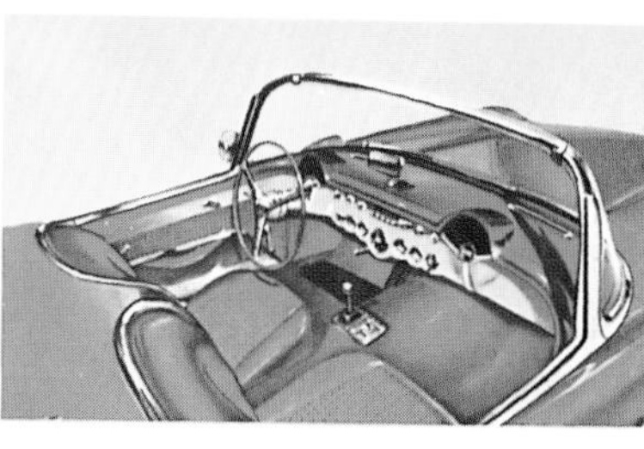

SETTING THE PACE FOR SPORTS CAR INTERIORS

GRACEFUL AND GALLANT IN EVERY LINE

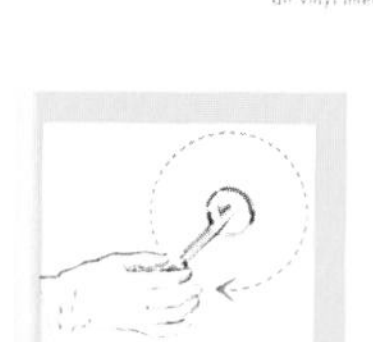

WEATHER-TIGHT ROLL-UP WINDOWS

SIMULATED KNOCK-OFF HUBS

STICK SHIFT

POWERGLIDE

CHOICE OF FABRIC OR HARD TOPS

SERVICE — AS CLOSE AS YOUR NEAREST CHEVROLET DEALER

RIGHT *More power was the battle cry when the 1957 Corvette arrived. Sales brochures touted the arrival of more horsepower in the form of more cubic inches – the 265-cubic-inch V8 had grown to 283 cubic inches – and fuel injection. Called Ramjet Fuel Injection, the Corvette system was mechanically actuated and produced, in its top form, 283 horsepower – one horsepower per cubic inch. In reality, the gross horsepower rating was higher than 283 – probably closer to 290 – but the chance for some catchy advertising copy was too good to pass up.*

SENSATIONAL **NEW FUEL INJECTION**

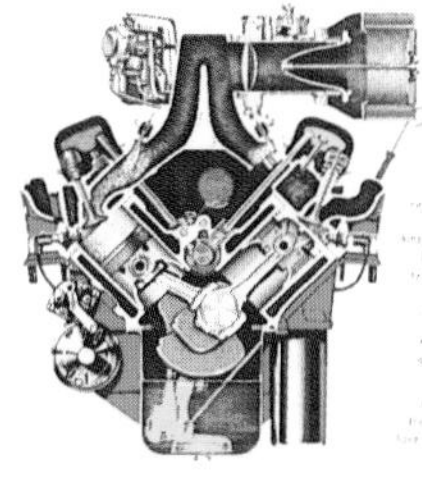

FOR THE FIRST TIME IN AUTOMOBILE HISTORY—

ONE H.P. FOR EVERY CUBIC INCH!

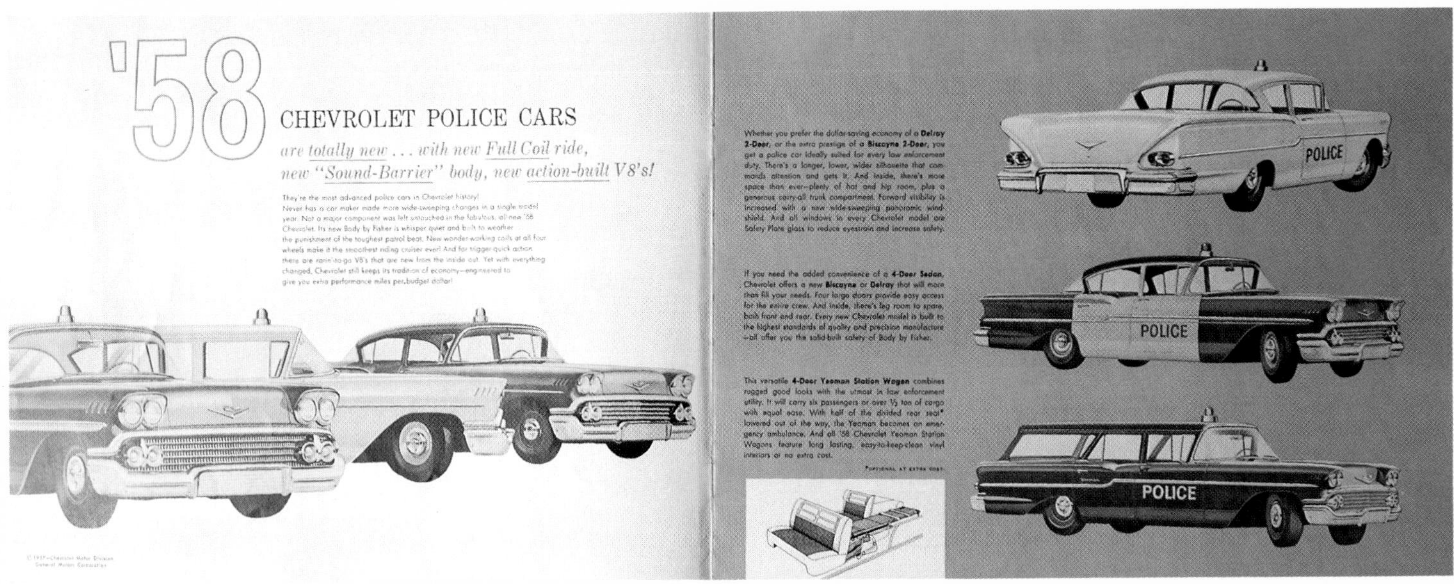

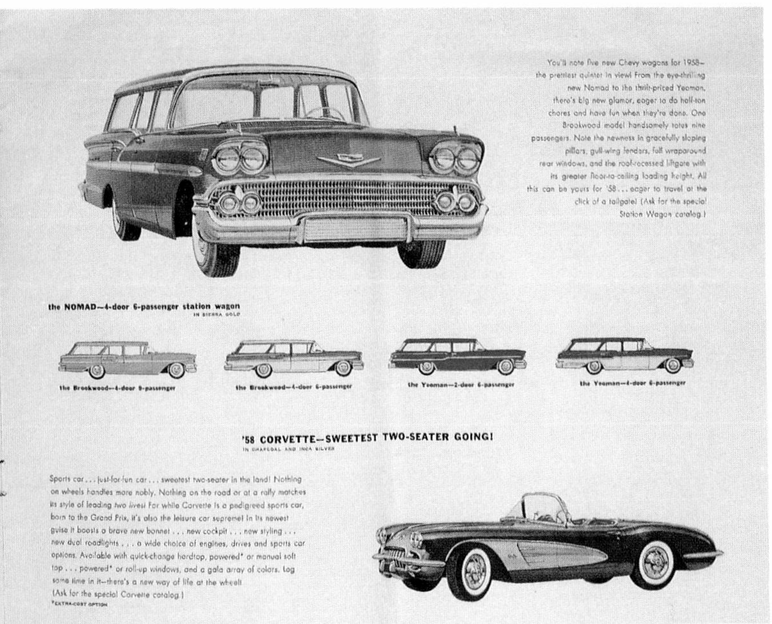

LEFT *The Corvette was still small potatoes to Chevrolet, as shown in this full-model sales brochure. More space is given to station wagons than the Corvette. Nonetheless, sales for 1958 continued to climb, topping 9,100. Serial numbers that year ran from J58S100001 to 109168.*

ABOVE *Chevrolet police cars, such as the one pictured in this brochure, would have to go a long way to catch a 1958 Corvette. Brochures also hailed new horsepower for the top-rated fuel-injected engine. It was rated at 290 horsepower, up from the advertised rating of 283 for the 1957 engine. In reality, there was likely no change in the engine from 1957 to 1958, since the 283 horsepower rating was artificially low.*

RIGHT *By the start of the 1959 model year, the Corvette was recognized as America's sports car. The two-seat Thunderbird became a four-seat luxury car in 1958, leaving the sports car field to the Corvette.*

1959
Chevrolet
CORVETTE
DETROIT PUBLIC LIBRARY
AUTOMOTIVE HISTORY COLLECTION
AMERICA'S
SPORTS CAR

LEFT *Almost as if in apology for the chrome excesses of 1958, Chevrolet cleaned up the car in 1959. The chrome on the trunklid was banished, as were the fake louvres on the hood. On the pure sales pitch side, the Corvette remained relatively unchanged. Engine choices remained the same as they were in 1958,though brochures were also full of talk of a new 'parallelogram' rear suspension. In reality, chief engineer Arkus-Duntov had added simple radius rods to the suspension to try to control wheel hop, given the massive amount of power the car's dated chassis was being asked to deliver.*

BELOW *Racing is very much a part of the Corvette image and nearly all of those raced came directly off the showroom floor. Among options available are 'road tamed' versions of the metallic-lined drum brakes that previously were race-only options. They are coded RPO 686. Checking the box next to RPO 684 brought on a host of handling and braking upgrades as well. These two options were favoured by those who had racing in mind for their Corvettes.*

RIGHT *Styling on the 1959 Corvette seems classic even today. In contrast, the big tail fins that accompanied almost every other American car in 1959 seem comical by today's standards.*

LEFT *By 1959, the Corvette was many things to many people. It was a boulevard cruiser to most buyers but it was also a rally and race car to some. Chevrolet capitalized on this versatility in its brochures.*

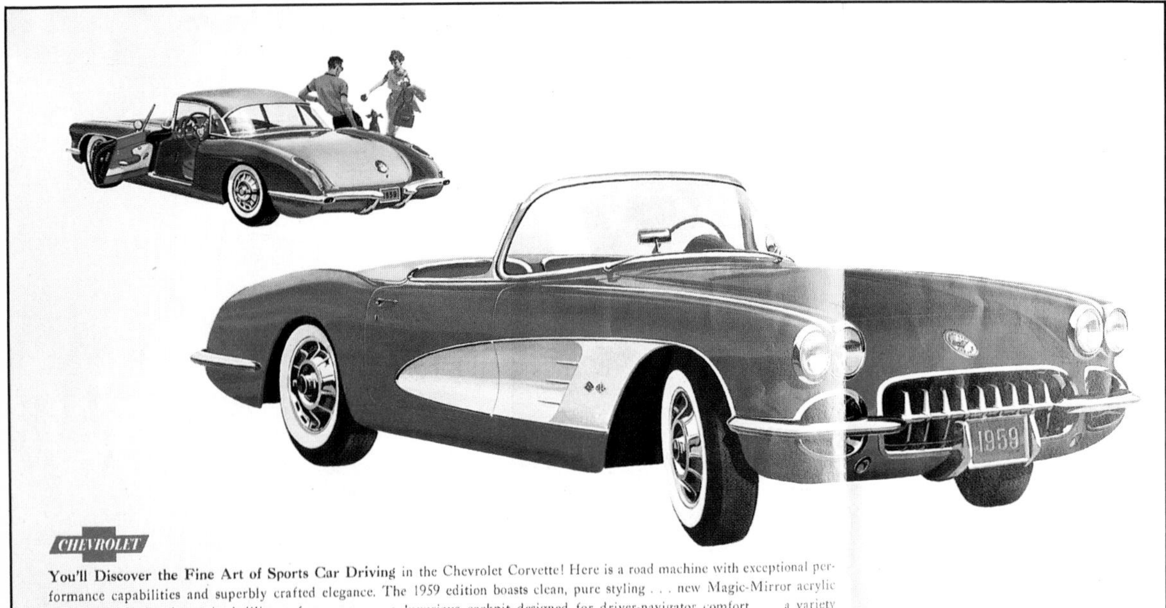

CHEVROLET
You'll Discover the Fine Art of Sports Car Driving in the Chevrolet Corvette! Here is a road machine with exceptional performance capabilities and superbly crafted elegance. The 1959 edition boasts clean, pure styling . . . new Magic-Mirror acrylic lacquer finish that keeps its brilliance for years . . . a luxurious cockpit designed for driver-navigator comfort . . . a variety of power teams engineered for driving fun. In every way, the Corvette is an authentic sports car . . . America's sports car.

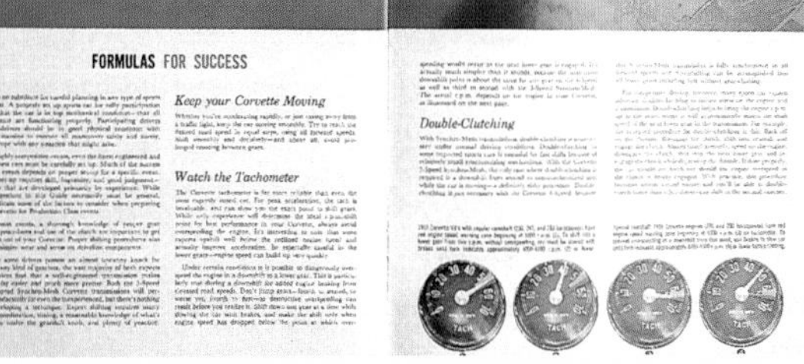

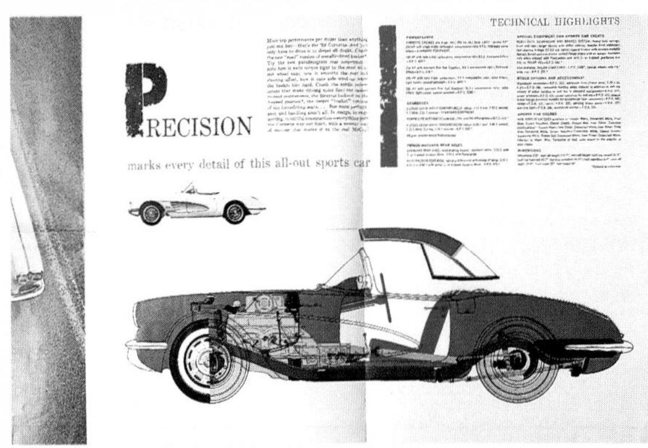

PRECISION
marks every detail of this all-out sports car
TECHNICAL HIGHLIGHTS

ABOVE *In its most potent form, the Corvette had few peers when it came to raw power. Zero to 60 mph (97 kph) times were well under six seconds and top speed was more than 135 mph (219 kph). Yet with its live rear axle and its inherent understeer it was a forgiving car to drive fast.*

RIGHT *GM recognizes that many Corvette owners are inexperienced when it comes to driving a high-performance automobile. As almost an educational service, Chevrolet produces a booklet that explains the fine points of shifting, double-clutching and handling in a Corvette.*

BELOW RIGHT *Chevrolet sells the technology of the Corvette through the use of vague but attractive cutaway drawings. The most innovative mechanical feature in 1959 was the addition of a reverse lock-out mechanism to the four-speed manual transmission. It prevented the driver from inadvertently selecting reverse gear.*

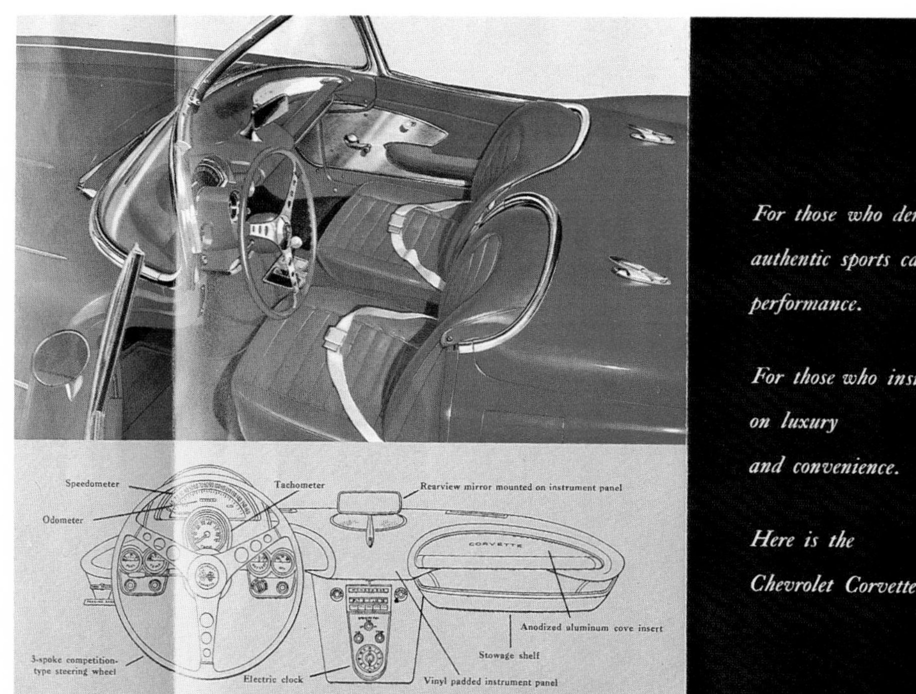

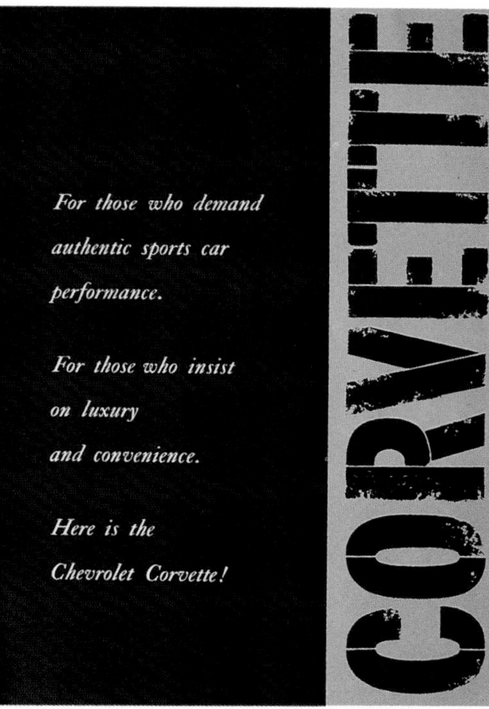

For those who demand authentic sports car performance.
For those who insist on luxury and convenience.
Here is the Chevrolet Corvette!
CORVETTE

LEFT *New seats with more deeply-bucketed bottoms appeared in 1959. They are a welcome addition to the revamped dashboard that appeared the year before. The gauges were now grouped directly in front of the driver instead of being spread across the dashboard.*

RIGHT *Corvette closes out the decade with a car that is a quantum leap ahead of the 1953 Motorama car. Sales for 1959 inch up to 9,670, with serial numbers running from J59S100001 to J59S109670. Basic price was $3,875.*

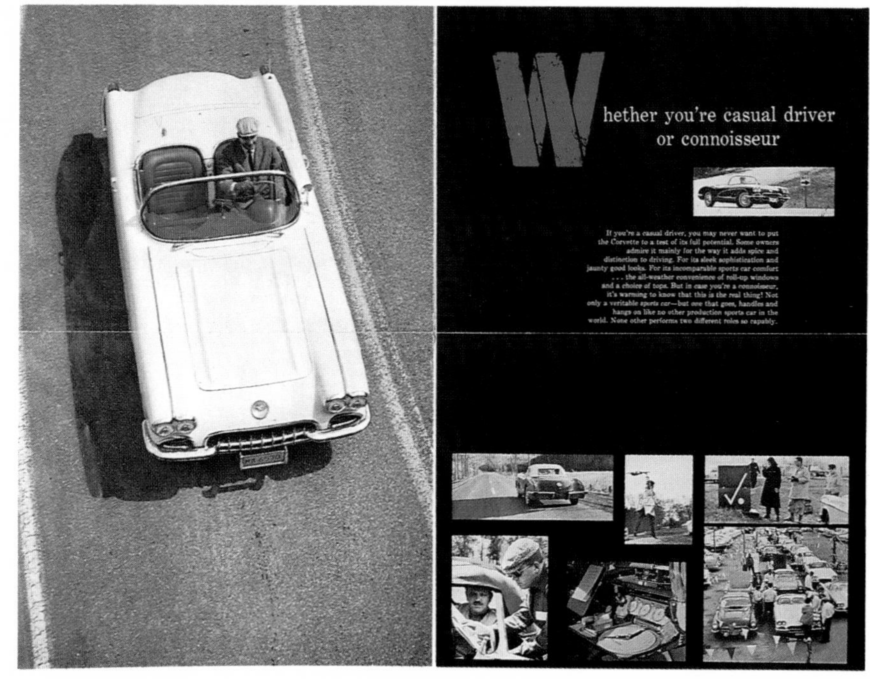

CHAPTER TWO
THE 1960s: CORVETTE REACHES NEW HEIGHTS

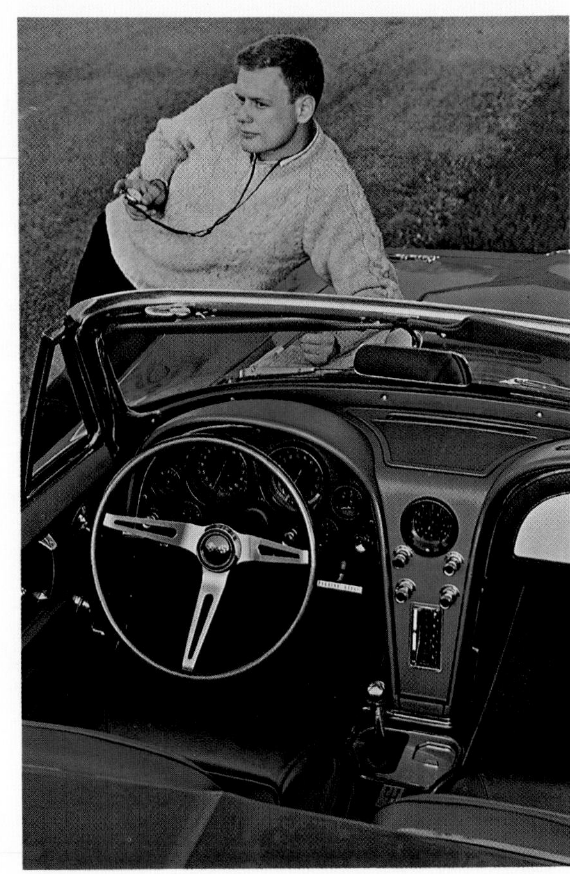

RIGHT *Corvette marketing took advantage of the boom in youth culture.*

The 1960s were a remarkable time. Spacecraft would fly to the moon, colour television would come to almost every household in the United States, an entire culture based on youth would spring up and America's love affair with the automobile would reach its zenith.

In this exhilarating time, America's only sports car, the Corvette, will reach new levels of power and sophistication.

From a styling viewpoint, the car will become the vision of William L. Mitchell, a protégé of Harley Earl, creator of the first Corvette. Mitchell will first make his mark with the stunning 1963 Sting Ray design, a body shape that stands today as one of the most forward-thinking designs ever. He will follow up that coup with the 1968 Mako Shark design, which fails to draw much praise from the automotive press but becomes the most enduring and popular Corvette shape ever.

On the inside, the Corvette will change from a car with a chassis design rooted in the 1930s to a sophisticated sports car with four-wheel independent suspension and four-wheel disc brakes. The engineering achievements will be the work of Zora Arkus-Duntov, who is the link between models of the 1950s and 1960s. The Corvette chief engineer will also be the leading architect of awesome horsepower gains under the hood. Although a proponent of small-block V8s that gather their horsepower from high revolutions, Arkus-Duntov will bow to market pressure and bring to the Corvette some of the most powerful big-block V8s ever offered in a production automobile.

Throughout all of this, the Corvette will become a more user-friendly car, through the addition of creature comfort options such as power steering, power brakes, tilt/telescope steering wheels, leather interiors, air-conditioning and more compliant suspensions.

When the decade ends, the Corvette from all aspects will be at a pinnacle of performance that won't be matched or surpassed until the 1980s. Free of such concerns as complex air pollution engine controls and the need for fuel economy in the face of high gasoline prices, the 1960s are a time that can rightly be called Corvette's golden era.

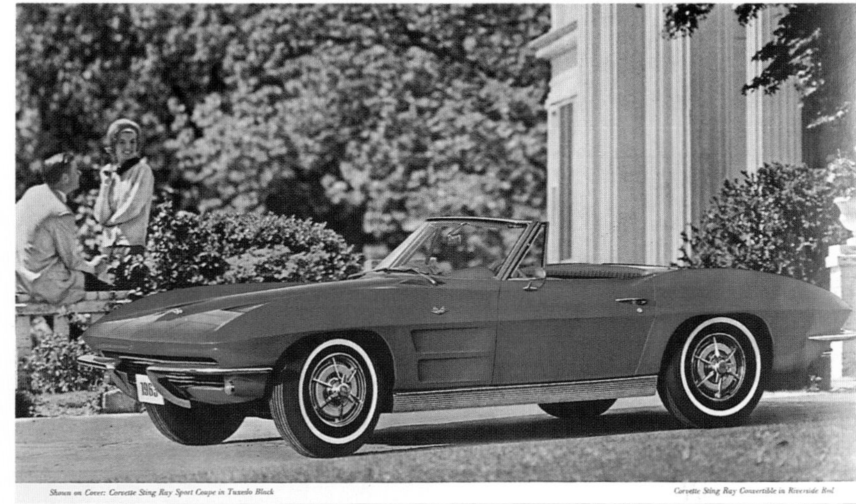

Shown on Cover: Corvette Sting Ray Sport Coupe in Tuxedo Black

Corvette Sting Ray Convertible in Riverside Red

NEW GRACE
AND ELEGANCE
SILHOUETTE
AMERICA'S SPORTS CAR

Corvette steps out smartly with an exhilarating new look for '63. A freshly elegant look that promises to lift the spirits of any buff who takes the wheel. It's the Corvette Sting Ray! Two sparkling new models, both pointing the way to a classic new concept in American sports car design.

Catch an eyeful of the Corvette newcomer, the exciting Sport Coupe. Graceful body panels and compound-curved side windows emphasize the miles-ahead aerodynamic design. Power-operated, retractable headlamps rotate out of sight to blend into the unobstructed hood line. Doors extend upward into the roof, adding armchair ease and comfort to sliding in and out. This is the Corvette Sting Ray Sport Coupe. Clean, taut, fresh in every detail.

You'll find the Convertible is jauntier than ever in '63. Uncluttered lines accented front and rear by trim wrap-around bumpers. The subtle contour of the smoothly molded rear deck. A gleaming aluminum grille, retractable headlamps and a sweeping hood-length windsplit. Top up or down, graceful streamlining is the goal. And the Corvette Sting Ray Convertible achieves it.

300-hp, 350-hp, 390-hp, 400-hp, 435-hp. Say when.

To propel your Stingray you can choose this 427 CID powerplant with a special high domed hood—or any one of its spirited brothers. The choice you make depends primarily on what kind of spirited performance suits you best. Check the specifications and pick the transmission and rear axle ratio that fit your idea of sports car capability and you'll have a tailor-made package.

How about triple 2-barrel carburetion? You get it with the 435-hp and the 400-hp 427 CID engines. Want Turbo Hydra-matic? It's available with all three Turbo-Jet 427 V8's in addition to the standard 300-hp V8. Prefer 4-Speed? With all engines except the 300-hp and the 435-hp, you have a choice of gear ratios. Depending on engine, axle ratios range from 3.08 to 4.11. If your choice is the Turbo Hydra-matic, you still get up to 3 choices.

New Corvette power team features for '69 include new, larger 350 CID 300-hp engine as standard, or a 350-hp version is available. More new features include sturdier engine construction on the 350 CID, thicker bulkheads and main bearing caps, firmer crankshaft clamping with longer washer head bolts, extra-firm 4-bolt main bearing cap attachment and improved cooling system.

We even have a special engine (L-88) that we don't recommend for street use.

Transmissions: Standard 3-Speed fully synchronized; 4-Speed fully synchronized (wide-range or close-ratio); Turbo Hydra-matic shifts automatically unless you want to shift it—through three forward ranges.

Four-wheel disc brakes are still standard on Corvette—and in stopping ability, fade resistance and modulation they're very much appreciated by just about anybody interested in sports cars. Other Corvette features include a new anti-interference ignition system, a high-output Delcotron generator, new high-capacity energizer-type side terminal battery, rust-proof fiber glass body—and a thoroughness and attention to detail that Corvette owners fully understand.

Standard equipment safety and security features on the 1969 Corvette include: energy-

435-hp Turbo-Jet 427 V8.

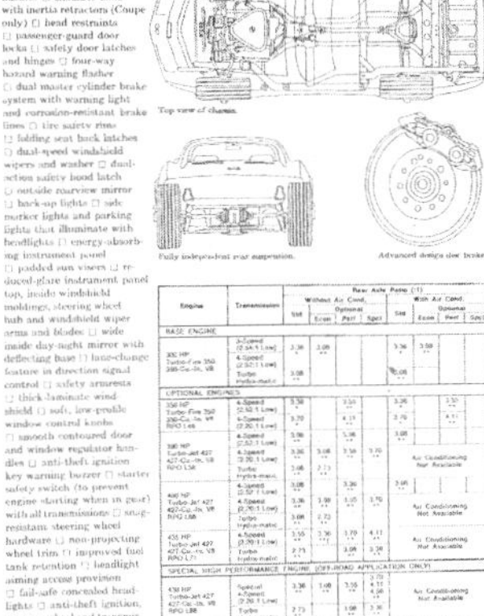

absorbing steering column □ seat belts with pushbutton buckles □ shoulder belts with inertia retractors (Coupe only) □ head restraints □ passenger-guard door locks □ safety door latches and hinges □ four-way hazard warning flasher □ dual master cylinder brake system with warning light and corrosion-resistant brake lines □ tire safety rims □ folding seat back latches □ dual-speed windshield wipers and washer □ dual-action safety hood latch □ outside rearview mirror □ back-up lights □ side marker lights and parking lights that illuminate with headlights □ energy-absorbing instrument panel □ padded sun visors □ reduced-glare instrument panel top, inside windshield moldings, steering wheel hub and windshield wiper arms and blades □ wide inside day-night mirror with deflecting base □ lane-change feature in direction signal control □ safety armrests □ thick-laminate windshield □ soft, low-profile window control knobs □ smooth contoured door and window regulator handles □ anti-theft ignition key warning buzzer □ starter safety switch (to prevent engine starting when in gear) with all transmissions □ snag-resistant steering wheel hardware □ non-projecting wheel trim □ improved fuel tank retention □ headlight aiming access provision □ fail-safe concealed headlights □ anti-theft ignition, steering wheel and transmission selector lock.

LEFT *1969: The 1960s saw massive increases in horsepower.*

ABOVE *1963 brochure with the innovative Sting Ray design.*

CORVETTE
custom features
for driving enjoyment
AUTO COMPASS
PUSH BUTTON
WINDSHIELD WASHER
DELUXE HEATER
AND DEFROSTER
DELUXE WONDER BAR RADIO
America's number one
SPORTS CAR
1960
30

LEFT *Compared to what would come later in the decade, this listing of Corvette options is paltry. A heater, a radio and windshield washer would become standard equipment, but not in 1960.*

RIGHT *The theme of the Corvette still revolved around performance with lots of talk in the catalogue about handling and power. The top-of-the-line engine listed for 1960 was a 315-horsepower version of the venerable 283-cubic-inch V8 topped with aluminium cylinder heads. Unfortunately, the option was never produced because the aluminium cylinder heads were too fragile for mass production.*

You want to fit and feel right in a sports car cockpit. You want space inside, comfortable seats, pleasing appointments. The Corvette achieves all this in a way that sets it apart from others. Wide doors open into a cockpit of uncompromising standards. Contoured, individually adjusted *bucket seats* are padded with foam rubber, covered with luxurious yet practical vinyl. *Cockpit colors* are keyed to new exterior Magic-Mirror finishes. Inside, new larger-twist *carpet* stretches from door-to-door. *Instrument cluster* includes a big *tachometer* for ready reading. Between the bucket seats is a *key locking compartment* for maps, operations manual and other odds and ends.

◄ Corvette's distinctive *wrap around windshield*, of Safety Plate Glass, gives driver and navigator excellent forward visibility.

The Corvette offers you a choice of two standard tops. There's a manually operated rubberized fabric *soft top* (upper right), or an easily removed fiber glass *hardtop* (lower right). Both are carefully fitted for weather tight protection. If you like, take both tops—the second comes at nominal extra cost. Or, there's a power-operated soft top* for the ultimate in quick top operation. ►

*Optional at extra cost.

ENGINEERED IN THE FINEST SPORTS CAR TRADITION

Vital statistics determine a sports car's agility and feeling for fun. Power-to-weight, gearbox choices, rear axle ratios, brakes, steering, suspension system — all must fit together for a sports car to live up to its proud name.

The Corvette offers virtually unlimited components for the sports car you want. All have come about because the Corvette bears the unmistakable stamp of Chevrolet's vast engineering facilities and ever-constant objective to build the world's finest production sports car.

The unique fiber glass reinforced plastic BODY on the Corvette is an excellent example of this. By its very nature, fiber glass reinforced plastic is ideal for a sports car body. Lightweight, which contributes to the car's greater performance. Tremendously strong. Safe. It also offers the benefits of rustproof and corrosion-resistant qualities.

Underneath the sleek Corvette body lies a rugged box-girder FRAME. This sports car-type frame forms the foundation for the special way the Corvette stays put on the curves and holds onto the straights. Up front the taut SUSPENSION is engineered with independent coil springs and improved stabilizer bar. Parallelogram rear suspension is by radius rods and semi-elliptic outrigger-mounted leaf springs and a new stabilizer bar. STEERING is quick and precise. Overall ratio of 21:1 produces responsive HANDLING. Corvette BRAKES are designed for safe, fade-resistant stops. They're big 11-inch hydraulic self-energizing brakes with bonded linings (if you prefer, heavy-duty brakes or sintered-metallic linings* are also available). Constant streams of air flow over the brakes through slotted wheel discs.*

The heart of a sports car is its engine. Engineers around the world acclaim Corvette ENGINES as the finest production power plants on the road. All are valve-in-head V8's with 283 cubic inches (3.88" bore x 3.0" stroke) of pure power potential. In their '60 editions, these engines attain new peaks of performance and efficiency.

The Corvette V8 comes in five versions. If you're a driver who wants a Corvette just for the fun of it, then you may want the standard V8, developing 230 h.p. with single 4-barrel carburetion. Or there's the 245-h.p. edition (shown at right) with twin 4-barrel carburetion. If you're a performance enthusiast, you may want the 270-h.p.* engine with twin 4-barrel carburetion, special camshaft and high-speed valve system. Chevrolet's unmatched achievements in production fuel injection engines are offered in 275-h.p.* and 315-h.p.* versions, the latter delivering well over one h.p. per cubic inch of displacement, alone among all production engines. New, lightweight aluminum cylinder heads, saving 53 pounds, are an important refinement in these Ramjet Fuel Injection power plants. Performance is improved with a higher 11:1 compression ratio.*

In GEARBOX choices, the Corvette offers three floor-mounted transmissions to suit your favorite kind of shifting. Corvette transmissions have earned unprecedented respect for dependability, durability and capability. For those who prefer the convenience of an automatic, the rugged and proven POWERGLIDE is available. For people who prefer to shift by hand, there's the 4-SPEED Close-Ratio Synchro-Mesh* with reverse lockout mechanism and the standard 3-SPEED Close-Ratio Synchro-Mesh.*

A variety of power-tailored gear ratios and rear axle ratios can be chosen. Of special significance to sports car enthusiasts who strive for weight-saving are the new aluminum clutch housings used with the 4-speed and 3-speed transmissions.

This, then, is what the Corvette has to offer. The equipment you choose is strictly up to you. But whatever you pick, you can be confident your Corvette will out-handle, out-corner, outperform anything in its class. This is the promise of driving fun found in the Corvette. Years of refinement, patience and careful attention to minute details have gone into creating this car. This is what the Corvette represents today. A true sports car. America's sports car.

RIGHT *For 1960, the idea of a Corvette with a luxury aspect emerged in the brochures. This was the first glimpse of a side to Corvette that would develop and mature over the next three decades. 'Elegant on the boulevard . . . a luxurious year-round car . . . a comfortable touring car' were all phrases that Chevrolet used to sell the Corvette in 1960. Aside from more sumptuous seats and thicker carpeting, little was new. The boulevard ride was enhanced with a new anti-sway bar up front and the addition of one out back. Gone was the race-orientated RPO 684 heavy-duty suspension.*

CORVETTE! AMERICA'S SPORTS CAR / DESIGNED FOR PERSONAL SPORTS CAR COMFORT

How do you define a sports car?

Is it a machine for the rigors of rallies and the like? Or is it for traffic and countryside?

The Corvette fits them all.

Spend a weekend with it on a rally. The Corvette belongs with the best of them. Experts call its power plant the finest production engine ever built. Corvette gearboxes are admired both here and abroad. Advanced parallelogram rear suspension keeps the Corvette sure and steady over straightaways and through hairpin turns. Air-cooled brakes prove their worth in stop after stop.

Or drive the Corvette to the office. Take it out for a Sunday afternoon or over to the neighbors. It brings spice and spirit to everyday driving. Just consider: Lustrous Magic-Mirror finish outside. Elegant appointments inside. Gleaming aluminum trim. Supple vinyl covered instrument panel. Electric clock. Foam rubber bucket seats. Deep-pile carpet underfoot. Choice of hardtop or soft top.

This is what an American sports car must be. Versatile. Capable. Luxurious. The Corvette by Chevrolet is ideal for people who want a special fun-for-two kind of driving.

The Corvette's roll-up windows are easy to operate—a convenience not found on some other sports cars. Power-operated* windows are also available for those who desire an extra measure of comfort.

©1959—Chevrolet Motor Division, General Motors Corporation

RIGHT *The big news for Chevrolet in 1960 was the introduction of the Corvair, a rear-engine, rear-wheel-drive economy car that was, for an American manufacturer, a bold offering.*

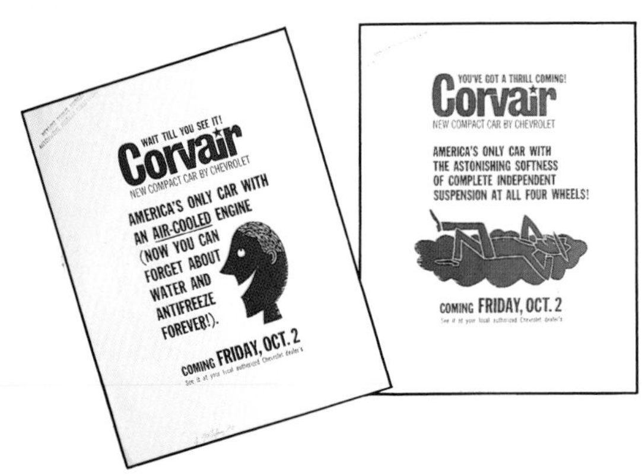

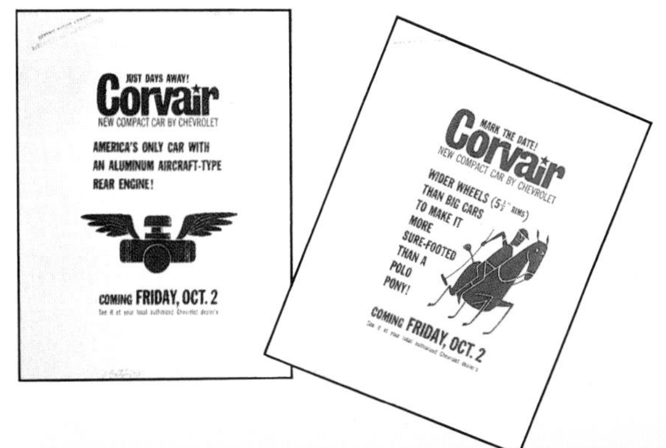

LEFT *As innovative as the Corvair was, it was never the success Chevrolet had hoped for. In its first year, it was outsold by Ford's entirely conventional front-engine Falcon compact.*

LEFT *Open-road touring was the Corvette's strong point, thanks to the high torque and horsepower available from its V8, even in the 230-horsepower base form. To make sure those long hauls could be made with fewer gas stops, shrewd Corvette buyers ordered the optional 24-gallon (91-litre) gas tank.*

Here is the Corvette '60, newly refined version of the car that captures hearts and laurels for sheer good looks and pure performance. An authoritative sports car, nimble and precise—elegant on the boulevard, eager on the road. A luxurious year-round car with roll-up windows and choice of soft or hard top. A comfortable touring car, with deeply contoured bucket seats, deep-pile carpeting and cockpit appointments to suit the most demanding purists. An exhilarating car, with new capability and precision in braking, combined with proved handling, new ride and all-out roadability. Choose from a wide range of new Magic-Mirror colors. Engines range up to 315 h.p., including exclusive Ramjet Fuel Injection*. Transmission choices are standard 3-Speed close-ratio Synchro-Mesh, 4-Speed close-ratio Synchro-Mesh*, or automatic Powerglide*. Try the Corvette—you'll see how it opens up a new life of driving fun.

(Ask for the special Corvette catalog.)

*Optional at extra cost.

LEFT *Although the introduction of the luxury theme tended to soften the Corvette's performance image, there were some new wrinkles for 1960 that helped in the 'go-fast' department. A new aluminium clutch housing helped save 18 lb (8 kg), and the most potent engines came with a lightweight aluminium radiator. Even though most of the changes for 1960 were minor, Corvette sales continue to climb, breaking the 10,000 barrier for the first time. Serial numbers that year ran from 00867S100001 through 00867S110261. The basic price was $3,872.*

LEFT *The sales catalogues for 1961 displayed the new rear bodywork on the Corvette. The fresh rear styling was just a hint of the all-new Corvette that would appear in 1963. The work of William 'Bill' Mitchell, the man now in charge of the Corvette design, the new rear tail was an instant hit. It went surprisingly well with the front end look which had been largely unchanged since 1956.*

BELOW *Although most of the attention is centred on the look out back, the nose of the Corvette also gets a facelift in 1961. Gone are the heavy chrome bezels around the headlights. The trademark chrome teeth are replaced with a bar-and-mesh arrangement. Cockpit room has been increased by cutting down on the width of the transmission tunnel and there are new interior door panels and handles. A host of items, such as sun visors, windshield washers and courtesy lights are now standard. Also standard for the first time are lap seat belts.*

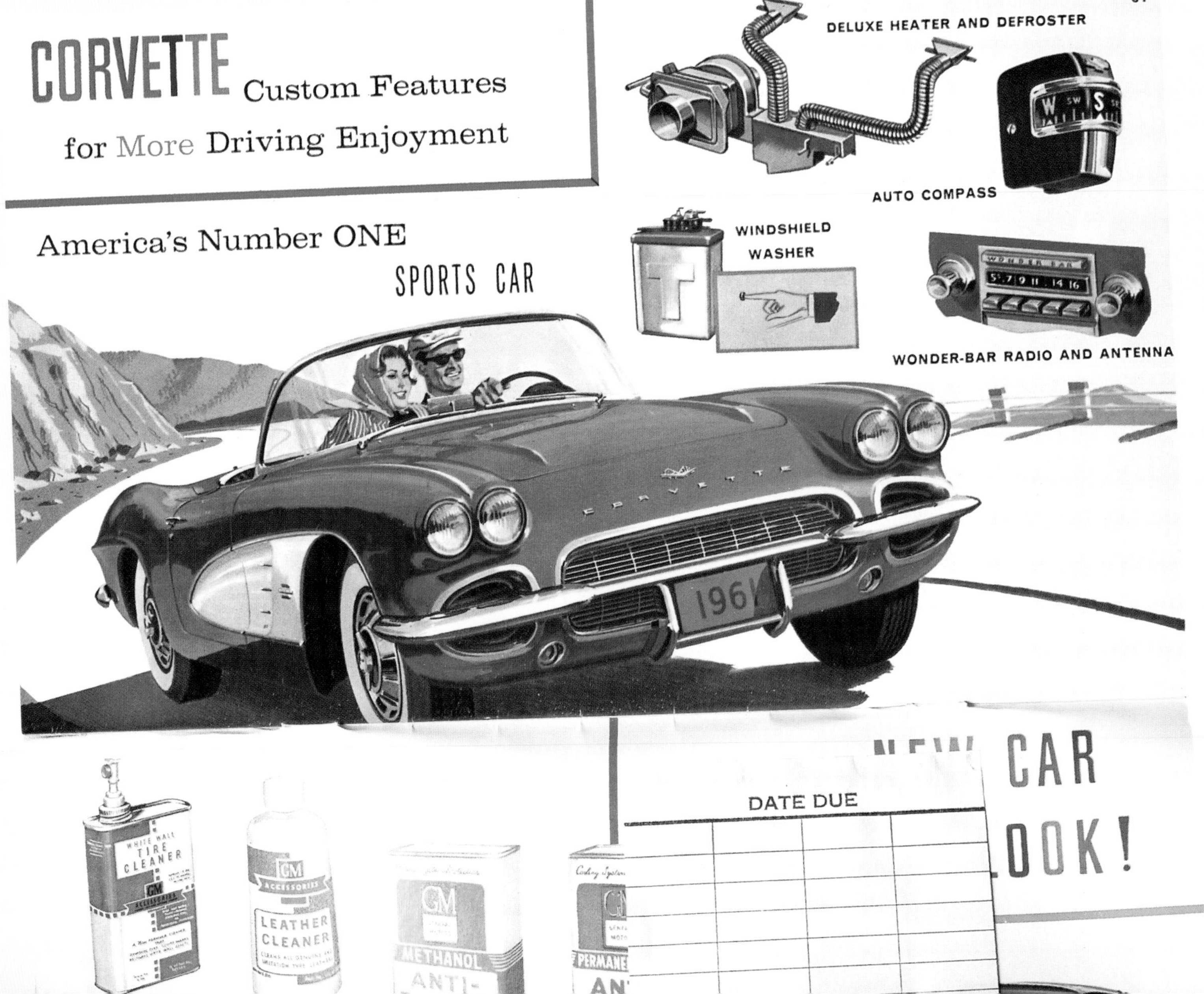

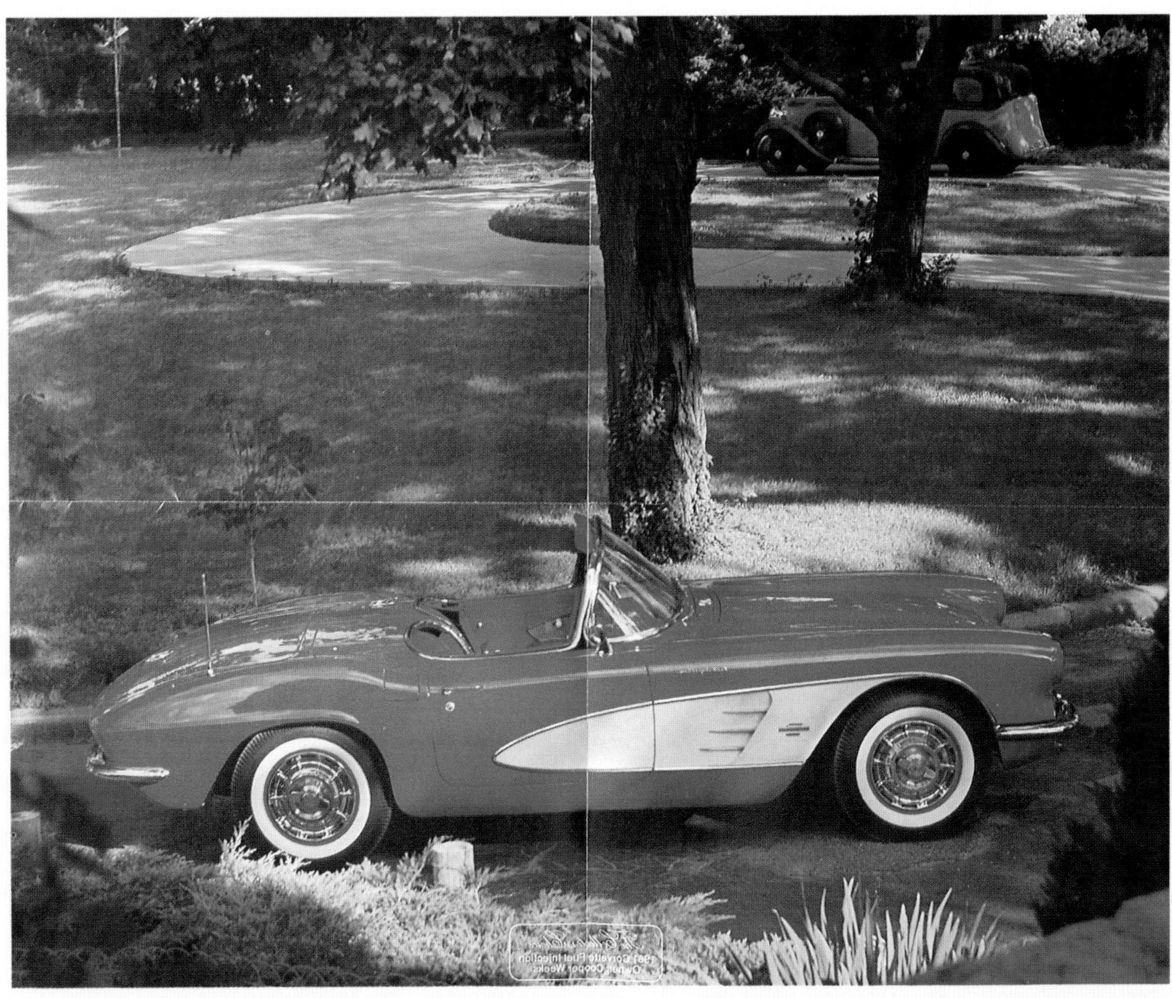

LEFT *The 1961 Corvette is also notable because it is the last model where there was the option of a two-tone paint scheme that accented the stylish side coves. On the mechanical side, the car remained essentially unchanged. The 283-cubic-inch V8 came in five stages of tune, from 230 to 315 horsepower, with the top engine achieving that output thanks to new, cast-iron cylinder heads based on the aborted aluminium design of the previous year. The basic price inched up to $3,934 and sales neared the 11,000 mark. In 1961, serial numbers ran from 10867S100001 to 10867S110939.*

Corvette is equipped with elegance . . . fashioned with true sports car flair!

There's a "just right" feeling when you step through the Corvette's wide door openings and seat yourself in the luxuriously appointed cockpit. First, adjust the foam cushioned bucket seat to your own personal requirements. Give yourself all the foot and leg room you need. Windows, up or down? You can roll 'em on Corvette. Get snug and secure with Corvette's seat belt. It's standard equipment. Now, grasp the floor-mounted stick shift. Work through the gears. Even in a show-room dry run you'll feel the fun of shifting for yourself. If you're more inclined to things automatic, there's sure and smooth Powerglide. By the way, the transmission tunnel is 19 per cent narrower this year. More space in the cockpit. Check the glovebox. It's conveniently located between the seats. And you can lock it. Push-button door handles, side view mirror, metal sill and step plates and inside door locks are Corvette conveniences that can't be found on most other sports cars. Add, too, these four new standard items: dual sun visors, windshield washers, parking brake alarm, courtesy lights.*

**Optional at extra cost*

PERFORMANCE IS THE MEASURE OF A FINE SPORTS CAR . . . AND NO CAR MEASURES UP LIKE CORVETTE . . . Corvette arrives in '61 as the product of careful craftsmanship and creative engineering—the world's finest sports car in its performance class. Experts say so. But for the real say so, you'll have to take to the Corvette. Press lightly on the accelerator. Phenomenal response! Corvette's wonderful power-to-weight ratio gives it that go. The light fiber glass reinforced plastic BODY is over three times as thick as steel, has twice the tensile strength, half the weight. No rust, either. Any one of the five Corvette ENGINES will scamper with amazing responsiveness, operate with scrupulous efficiency. Move from gear to gear. You're sure to feel a real professional grasp with the beautifully synchronized Corvette gearshift. Corvette engineers have designed the TRANSMISSIONS to take optimum advantage of Corvette's high performance engines. This year the standard 3-Speed Synchro-Mesh with standard axle ratio will offer quicker acceleration under most driving conditions while giving greater cruising economy. For all-out performance, the optional 4-Speed transmission* has a lightweight aluminum case, reduces overall weight by 15 pounds, adds new power. Now, see how the Corvette RIDES and HANDLES. Take your first corner. No lean and no sway. As you come out of that turn you'll feel Corvette holding tight and taut on the road. The combination of independent coil springs up front and parallelogram rear suspension produces stability and steadiness. Brake the Corvette. Notice how those big, self-energizing Corvette BRAKES need only a gentle touch, resist fade. There are all sorts of additions to the basic 1961 Corvette driving package. You can find them on the back of this folder. Discuss them with your Corvette salesman after your first test ride. Take it now!

CORVETTE KEY:
1. Self-energizing 11-inch brakes with air-cooling slots in wheel covers. 2. Independent coil spring front suspension, nitrogen bag shock absorbers. Stabilizer bar. 3. Precision anti-friction steering. 4. Fiber glass body. 5. Unit-balanced propeller shaft, universal joints. 6. Rugged box-girder frame

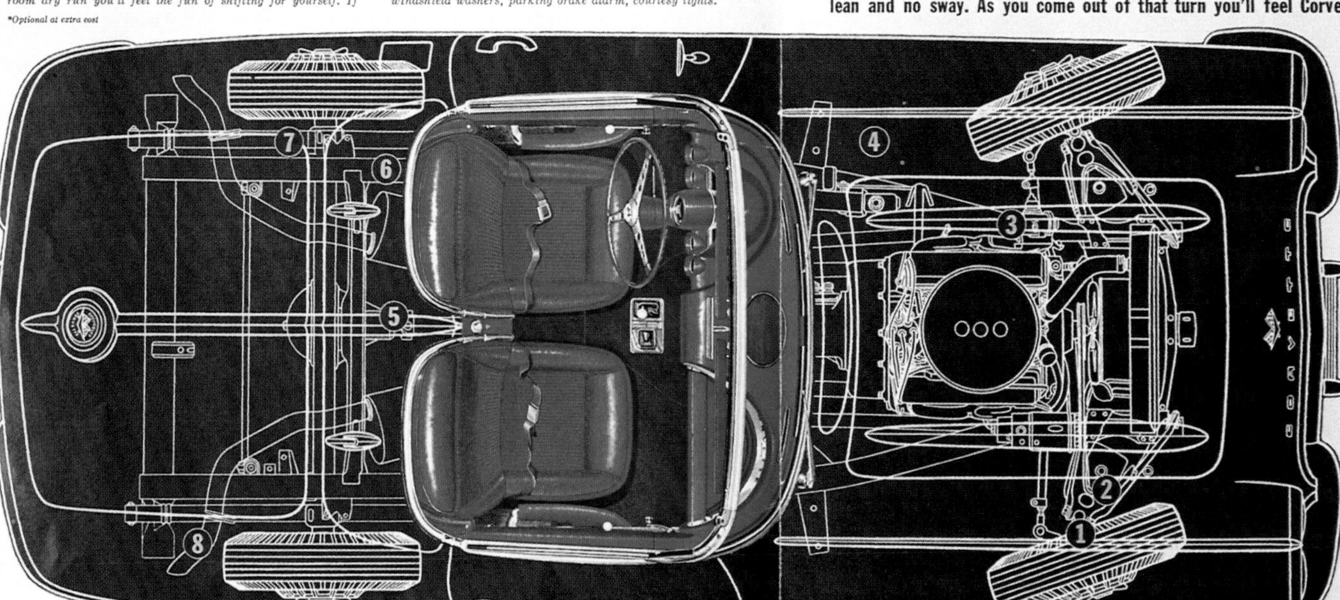

1
2
3
4
5
6
7
8

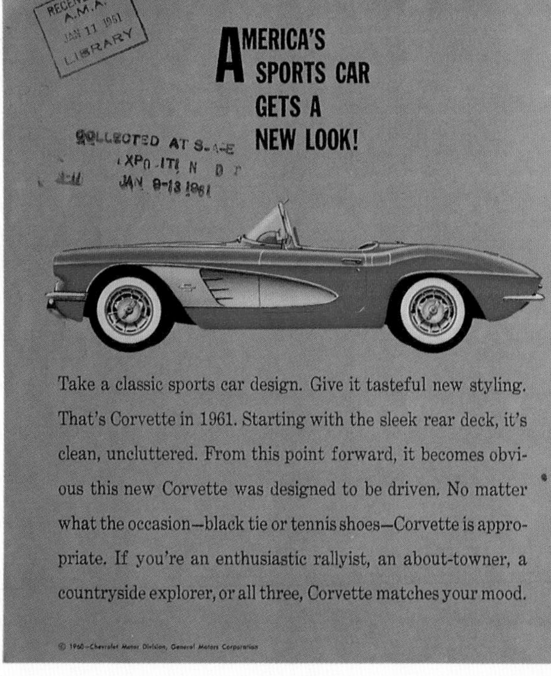

RECEIVED BY
A.M.A.
JAN 11 1961
LIBRARY
AMERICA'S
SPORTS CAR
GETS A
NEW LOOK!
Take a classic sports car design. Give it tasteful new styling. That's Corvette in 1961. Starting with the sleek rear deck, it's clean, uncluttered. From this point forward, it becomes obvious this new Corvette was designed to be driven. No matter what the occasion—black tie or tennis shoes—Corvette is appropriate. If you're an enthusiastic rallyist, an about-towner, a countryside explorer, or all three, Corvette matches your mood.
© 1960—Chevrolet Motor Division, General Motors Corporation

1961

ABOVE *While the first Corvette stressed the Powerglide transmission, the majority sold by 1961 came with the four-speed manual transmission. The Powerglide couldn't handle the power of the three most potent 283-cubic-inch engines.*

RIGHT *Although there was no place outside of Nevada where it could be legally tested, the top speed of a 315-horsepower Corvette was nearly 140 mph (225 kph).*

BELOW RIGHT *Starting in 1962, the option list began growing and becoming more sophisticated on the Corvette. Between the four engine-horsepower choices – 250, 300, 340 and 360 – and the three transmissions – three-speed manual, four-speed manual and Powerglide – there are 10 powertrain options on the Corvette now. Also, air-conditioning and power brakes appear on the list as well.*

RIGHT *Corvette catalogues had a new drawing card in 1962 with the introduction of the 327-cubic-inch engine. Bore and stroke of the trusty 283 V8 were increased to achieve the larger displacement. It would prove to be one of the most popular engines Chevrolet would produce. Outside, the Corvette remained essentially unchanged from 1961. A cleaned-up fake grill in the side cove and the deletion of the two-tone paint option were the most noticeable design changes.*

powered
FOR THE OPEN ROAD
obedient
ON CITY STREETS

Performance is a Corvette hallmark. Take the new Corvette V8s. Each is a 327-cubic-incher with low weight and compactness. The standard 250-hp engine features 4-barrel carburetion, 10.5:1 compression, hydraulic valve lifters and full dual exhaust system with efficient Ram's horn manifolds and reverse-flow mufflers. For higher performance, the 300-hp V8* includes the same equipment with a larger 4-barrel aluminum bodied carburetor and modified intake manifold. For ultra-high performance, try the new—340-hp Corvette V8*—with a large 4-barrel aluminum-bodied carburetor, aluminum intake manifold, 11.25:1 compression ratio, special camshaft and mechanical valve lifters. Peak performance is yours with the instant response of the new Ramjet Fuel Injection V8's* 360 urgent horsepower! This premium performance engine features lightweight valves, special camshaft, mechanical valve lifters and 11.25:1 compression ratio.

Put this abundant power to work. Corvette's fine 3-Speed Synchro-Mesh transmission is standard with all engines. Optional 4-Speed Synchro-Mesh* is tailored to engine choice and rear axle ratio. There's an improved Powerglide automatic*, too, with a new aluminum weight-saving case and major internal changes. Positraction axles* are matched to all engines and transmissions. With the high-performance engines, a wide choice of ratios is available. See the chart above.

personalize
CORVETTE TO YOUR
BRAND OF COMFORT

For driving fun and skill, you have to FIT and FEEL RIGHT inside the cockpit. Corvette's luxurious new interior pampers you with deep-twist carpeting, all-vinyl seats, padded instrument panel, assist bar, deep stowage bin, heater and colors keyed to exterior Magic-Mirror paint choices. First, match up your choice of ENGINE and TRANSMISSION. There are 10 eager engine and transmission combinations. Then choose the kind of TOP—hard or soft—you want. Either top gives you all-weather protection and excellent visibility. If you're an around-towner, you'll like the convenience of the POWER-OPERATED TOP* and POWER WINDOWS.* RADIO* and NARROW BAND WHITE SIDEWALL TIRES* are usual choices for most every driver, and they add a touch of elegance to the appearance. There's not much more you can buy—there's not much more you could want! Unless you're a performance enthusiast. Then, in addition to a high performance Corvette V8, you'll want to specify RPO 686—the special sintered-metallic HEAVY-DUTY BRAKES*—or RPO 687—the complete HEAVY-DUTY BRAKE, STEERING AND SHOCK ABSORBER OPTION*, available with special power teams. 5½" WIDE-BASED WHEELS (RPO 276) and STRAIGHT-THROUGH MUFFLERS (RPO 441, where ordinances permit) are special options.

*Optional at extra cost.

specifications FOR THE '62 CORVETTE

AUTOMOBILES
Chevrolet, 1962

corvette
FOR 1962

CORVAIR STATION WAGON LOADS AND HANDLES LIKE NO OTHER WAGON! After all, loadability is what most station wagon buyers look for first. Which brings up the unique advantages of the '62 Corvair Station Wagons—Monza and 700 models. Key-locking front luggage compartment provides 10 cu. ft. of concealed cargo space. Rear load space adds up to 58 cu. ft. and a load floor nearly 6½ ft. long. And a single, easy motion opens or closes the one-piece counterbalanced liftgate. What's more, these Station Wagons have four doors so you can load from the side. Plus Corvair's Forced-Air Heater that assures full all-around heating. Best of all, there are the rear-engine design benefits in handling, traction and ride that mark every '62 Corvair's sports car feel on the road.

GREENBRIER SPORTS WAGON MOST ADAPTABLE WAGON UNDER THE SUN! For family use, business and all-around pleasure, Greenbrier Sports Wagon has up to 175.5 cu. ft. of *big* cargo appeal. That's close to twice what regular, full-sized station wagons provide. Greenbrier's foam-cushioned seating gives 6-passenger comfort, versatility that lets you fasten the second seat in forward or rear-facing positions. A third seat* allows nine to sit comfortably. Double doors at both the rear and curbside mean two-way loading convenience. Both '62 models—Greenbrier and its companion the Greenbrier De Luxe—are quality finished inside and out.

CORVAIR 700 STATION WAGON in Twilight Blue. Front and back loading, 6-passenger, rear-engine design, a family favorite.

CORVAIR GREENBRIER DE LUXE SPORTS WAGON in Yuma Yellow and Cameo White. Bright exterior trim, special interior appointments.

OPTIONAL AND CUSTOM FEATURES* FOR '62 CORVAIR: Aircraft-type gasoline heater for near-instant warmth . . . air conditioning with new, extra-quiet compressor . . . fold-down rear seat (standard on Monzas) . . . push-button transistor-powered radio . . . Soft-Ray tinted glass. *Ask your Chevrolet Dealer for full information on '62 Corvair equipment—see the complete '62 Corvair Catalog for further details on standard equipment and options!*

'62 CORVAIR

CORVETTE NEW POWER, NEW PROFILE FOR AMERICA'S SPORTS CAR! Most spirited performance in Corvette's history stems from a new, larger displacement line of compact 327-cu.-in. V8's. All four deliver sparkling horsepower, ranging from responsive 250 in the standard Corvette V8 up to an exhilarating 360 in the Ramjet Fuel Injection engine.* Standard 3-Speed Synchro-Mesh or versatile 4-Speed Synchro-Mesh* transmission teams with any engine, while a new automatic Powerglide* is available for two power choices. Style-wise, Chevrolet's new Corvette reveals a neatly altered side view plus tasteful refinements in its identifying ornamentation as well as the front grille. Interiors present their customary richness in bucket seats, deep-twist carpets and luxury appointments, along with newly styled door panels. In addition, Corvette Heater-Defroster (outside air-type) comes as standard equipment. *For full information on '62 Corvette equipment and options, ask to see the complete Corvette Catalog at your Chevrolet dealer's.*

CORVETTE BY CHEVROLET in Roman Red. Most refined model yet of America's only true sports car.

All illustrations and specifications contained in this literature are based on the latest product information available at the time of publication approval. The right is reserved to make changes at any time without notice in prices, colors, materials, equipment, specifications and models, and also to discontinue models. Chevrolet Motor Division • General Motors Corp., Detroit 2, Mich.

**Optional at extra cost.*

'62 CORVETTE

LEFT *The Corvair van and station wagon look very dated next to the Corvette in the Chevy catalogue. With its blacked-out grill and the scarcity of chrome, the 1962 car still looks fresh and exciting by today's standards. More than 14,000 buyers liked the looks as well in 1962. Serial numbers ran from 20867S100001 to 20867S114531.*

BELOW *By the end of 1962, the era of the solid rear-axle Corvette was over. The 1962 car had taken the basic design and engineering about as far as it could go. The era of choice and options was just beginning to dawn on the Corvette and buyers were free to 'design' their own. With the arrival of the Sting Ray, those choices would expand even more.*

NEW CORVETTE

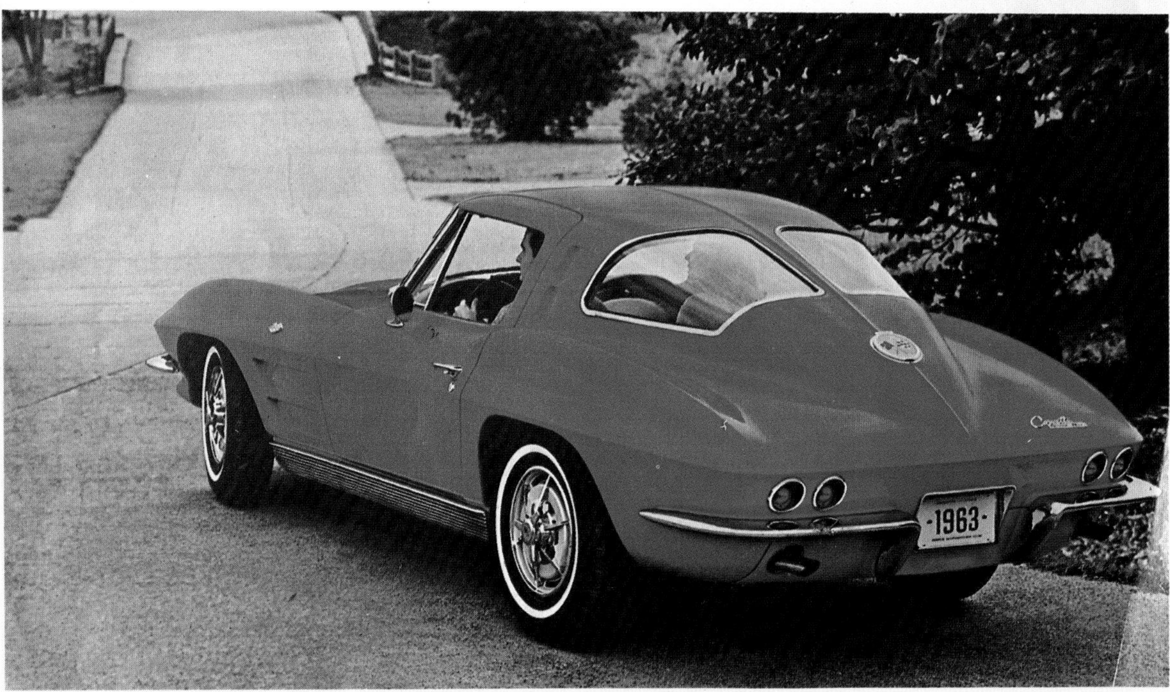

ABOVE *After 10 years as a convertible, the all-new 1963 Corvette saw the introduction of the Sting Ray body style and the first coupe. It was a revolutionary styling statement by William Mitchell, who arguably was the best designer ever to work at General Motors. The most notable feature was the rear window design, which is featured in this brochure. The rear design incorporated a wind split that ran from the windshield back to the rear lip, dividing the rear window via a bar that split the glass in two. Although it remains the most distinctively styled Corvette to date, the split window coupe was not popular with Corvette chief engineer Zora Arkus-Duntov, who argued that it unnecessarily obscured a driver's rearward vision. Arkus-Duntov won the argument and the design appeared only during this year.*

RIGHT *As much as the styling of the 1963 Corvette was the real attention-getter that year, the Sting Ray also had a number of other features that would have made it a best-seller anyway. Handling was improved on two levels. First, by repositioning the passenger compartment, the centre of gravity was lowered to 16.5 inches versus 19 inches for the 1962 car. Secondly, the outdated live rear axle and X-frame setup was ditched in favour of a ladder-type frame and a contemporary independent rear suspension.*

CORVETTE ... Newest in AMERICA'S SPORTS CARS

2 MODELS
SPORT COUPE
CONVERTIBLE

THE CORVETTE STING RAY SPORT COUPE has a wrap-over rear window, doors that wrap into the roof, and a center windsplit on the roof. Seven solid colors (including a premium color) of Magic-Mirror acrylic lacquer are offered on both Corvette models.

THE CORVETTE STING RAY CONVERTIBLE is available with a folding softtop, a removable hardtop or both. The folding top is offered in black, white or beige. Both Corvette models have wheel discs, rocker sill molding and compound-curved door glass as standard equipment.

THE LONG, LOW HOOD flows smoothly down to cover panels that conceal retractable dual headlights. Sporty twin simulated grilles flank the hood windsplit. Crossed flags and a deep "V" form the handsome front emblem.

HEADLIGHTS ARE ROTATED to the exposed position by electric motors. Manual provisions for rotating the headlights are also built into the Corvette. For increased highway safety, the Corvette has amber parking and directional signal lights.

THE REAR SMOOTHNESS of the Corvette is not broken by th… within the pa… below the bo…

18

CORVETTE STING RAY... STAYS AHEAD

THE CORVETTE'S ALL-VINYL INTERIOR comes in dark blue, black, red or saddle. Genuine leather seat trim in saddle color is offered as an option. There are bucket seats, armrests, carpeting, dual red safety reflectors at the inside of each door and crank-operated ventipanes.

A SINGLE HOODED CLUSTER of instruments is on the driver's side. On the passenger side, a similar hooded area houses a large, lighted glove box. Standard equipment includes an electric clock, tachometer, cigarette lighter, dual sunshades and a fashionable steering wheel.

THE '63 CORVETTE BODY combines a structural network of steel and Fiberglas-reinforced plastic body panels for increased rigidity. All doors have advanced double-lip locks.

A WELDED STEEL PERIMETER-TYPE FRAME with five cross members outlines and protects the passenger compartment. The frame is closely integrated to the body.

STRENGTH, AGILITY AND DURABILITY are built into the Corvette chassis. These are some of the outstanding features—spherical front joints, Ball-Race steering, independent rear suspension with three links at each wheel and transverse leaf spring, and self-adjusting brakes with bonded linings. Major chassis parts can go six months or 6,000 miles between lubrications. The front spherical joints, tie-rod ends, and the idler arm and relay rod connection are specially sealed. And the rear axle has permanent-type lubricant.

PLENTY OF POWER UNDER THE HOOD

Three carburetor-type V8's and a Fuel Injection V8 are offered on Corvette. With the Fuel Injection Engine, a warning buzzer sounds if excessive r.p.m.'s are reached. All engines have a Delcotron generator, oil filter and aluminized muffler (right-side muffler also has stainless steel parts). There are 6,000-mile or 60-day oil changes (whichever occurs first) under

19

*Corvette Sting Ray Sport Coupe in Sebring Silver**

Corvette Sting Ray Convertible in Riverside Red with Matching Hard Top

Corvette Sting Ray Convertible in Riverside Red with White Soft Top

Corvette Sting Ray Convertible in Riverside Red

TOPS FOR FASHION IN FOUR NEW LOOKS

Part of the fun of buying a Corvette is deciding which new Sting Ray model strikes your fancy most. If you're normally a coupe fan, naturally the lines of the new Corvette Sport Coupe will hold your attention. On the other hand, you may want a few top-down days. Then you'll prefer the handsome Convertible. The more devoted sunshine lovers will, of course, go for the neat soft-top Convertible. There's also an easily removable hardtop which can be selected in place of the soft top. To make it easier deciding, you can always order the Convertible with both tops, the hardtop at modest extra cost.

Left: Sport Coupe doors extend upward into the roof for comfortable ins and outs. Right: Luggage area behind the seats in the Sport Coupe is spacious and fully carpeted.

NEW CONVENIENCES BLEND SUNDAY-DRIVING EASE WITH SPORTS CAR FUNCTION

Most sports car fans like some dress-up conveniences, too. Things like the new Corvette's functional instrument grouping. Speedometer, tach, new trip odometer, ammeter, oil pressure, fuel and temperature gauges—they're all part of a single smart-looking cluster. There's more to enjoy in a new glove box, passenger assist grip and convenient retractable headlamps. Amber lenses on front parking and turn signal lights offer safer visibility. A center console houses the transistorized signal-seeking radio*, electric clock, ashtray and heater controls. Windows are crank-operated; and for easy opening, so are the new ventipanes. Power steering*, power windows* and power brakes* are also available.

Corvette's efficient blended-air heater is tailored to coordinate with a new cowl inlet ventilation system. Two control knobs let you keep the passenger compartment up to date with the weather, keep the windshield clear of frost.

Corvette adds convenience in the rear of the cockpit, too. Behind those comfortable bucket seats, you'll find a broad expanse of luggage space. Even the spare tire has been moved to a special housing under the body to make more room for suitcases and packages. Two concealed compartments under the luggage area floor provide out-of-sight stowage for tools and valuables.

*Optional at extra cost.

RIGHT *The 1963 Corvette brochures were full of words such as convenience, comfort and choice. It was the year when the option list started to grow so long that few cars were exactly alike. Power steering, power brakes, air-conditioning, leather seats and beautiful knock-off wheels were among the options offered.*

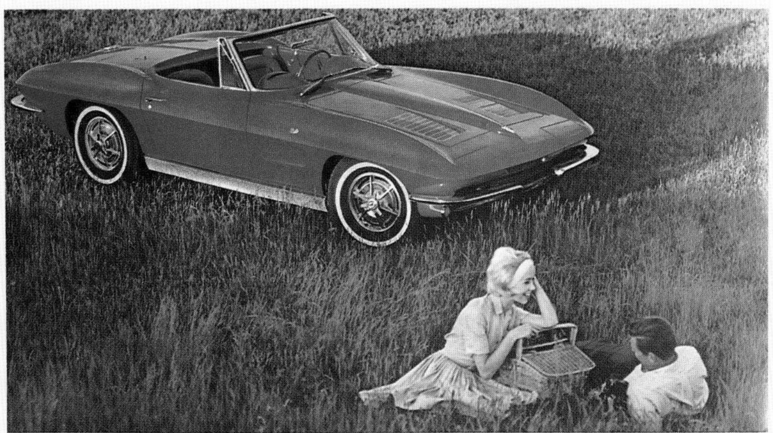

Corvette Sting Ray Convertible in Riverside Red

CORVETTE FEATURES FOR '63

Engines—All engines have independent mechanism for each valve; temperature controlled fan; precision-machined forged steel crankshaft; premium aluminum main bearings; full-pressure lubrication system; full flow oil filter; automatic choke; and a 12-volt electrical system. Oil-wetted polyurethane element in the air cleaner. All-aluminum cross-flow radiator. Positive closed-type crankcase ventilation.

Chassis—Direct double-acting freon-bag shock absorbers. Balanced steering linkage with 19.6:1 overall ratio can be reset to 17:1 (standard with power steering*). Hydraulic 11-inch brakes with fade-resistant bonded linings. Hand-operated parking brake on rear wheels. Black 6.70 x 15" tires standard. Optional* 6.70 x 15" nylon blackwalls or rayon whitewalls.

Exterior Features—Fiber-glass reinforced plastic body with Magic-Mirror acrylic lacquer finish in seven solid colors: Tuxedo Black, Ermine White, Riverside Red, Silver Blue, Daytona Blue, Saddle Tan and Sebring Silver*. Three Convertible tops (white, black and beige) available with any body color. Doors have push-button handles and key locks. Covered well for folding top behind seats.

Additional Optional Equipment*—Sintered-metallic brake linings. Cast aluminum wheels with 6" rims and knock-off hubs. Special performance equipment package (available only on the Sport Coupe with Fuel Injection engine, 4-Speed transmission and Positraction) includes: power-type heavy-duty brakes including finned drums with built-in fans, vented backing plates and front brake air scoops, special sintered-metallic linings and self-adjusting feature when driving forward; dual-circuit brake master cylinder; heavy-duty stabilizer bar; 36-gallon fuel tank; heavy-duty front and rear springs and shock absorbers; aluminum wheels with 6" rims and knock-off hubs.

*Optional at extra cost

Dimensions—Wheelbase, 98". Overall length, 175.3". Overall height: Convertible with soft top up, 49.8"; Convertible with optional hardtop, 49.3"; Sport Coupe, 49.8". Cowl height to ground, 34.9". Door opening height to ground: Convertible, 45.5"; Sport Coupe, 46.7". Road clearance, 5.0". Overall width, 69.6". Tread: front, 56.3"; rear 57.0".

All illustrations and specifications contained in this literature are based on the latest product information available at the time of publication approval. The right is reserved to make changes at any time without notice in prices, colors, materials, equipment, specifications, and models, and also to discontinue models.

Chevrolet Motor Division,
General Motors Corporation, Detroit 2, Mich.

LITHO IN U.S.A.

LEFT *Although the split window coupe was the most memorable feature in 1963, the convertible still commanded considerable interest. Of the more than 21,000 Corvettes built in 1963, half were the traditional convertible. However, as a nod to the realities of everyday driving, more than half the convertible buyers also specified the removable hardtop.*

INSIDE, A LUXURIOUS NEW MEASURE OF CORVETTE COMFORT

A healthy share of the new Corvette's charm is in the feeling you get when you sit behind the wheel. It's almost as if the car was designed to your personal specifications. You're surrounded by a color-keyed interior (black, red, dark blue or saddle) with leather-grained vinyl upholstery on seats and hooded areas of the instrument panel. Upper sidewalls are tastefully trimmed with pleated leather-grain vinyl with carpet below. An optional saddle interior* lets you indulge yourself with genuine leather seats. And underfoot, there's wall-to-wall deep-twist carpeting matched to the interior color scheme. Even the luggage area is carpeted, protecting your baggage against scuffs.

Climb into the Sport Coupe and note how the doors extend upward into the roof to let you slide in easily. Then give those bucket seats a bounce. Sheer foam-cushioned comfort. And whether you're driver or co-pilot, you'll find that Corvette continues to give a full measure of sports car roominess.

This year's Corvette is decked out with plenty of other standard luxury items. A deep-hub steering wheel crowns the new steering column that's adjustable to your driving comfort. Seat belts, inside and outside mirrors and recessed safety reflectors in the door sidewall panels. Long padded armrests, sunshades for driver and passenger. Electric windshield wipers, push-button windshield washer. Directional signals, parking brake alarm, courtesy lights.

**Optional at extra cost.*

LEFT *Interior room grew on the 1963 Corvette improving driver and passenger comfort. As in past years, the instruments were grouped in a pod in front of the driver. In addition to more leg, head and elbow room, the cockpit featured better ventilation.*

RIGHT *Corvette catalogues were full of the usual new model hype about the styling and chassis changes for 1963. But for once, the product matched the hype. The Sting Ray would become an enduring classic.*

RIGHT *The convertible looks equally as sharp as the hardtop. Though the roadster is now worth less than a 1963 split window coupe, the open-air version of the Corvette outsold the hardtop by 325 cars. Serial numbers for the coupe started with the prefix 30837S, while the convertible numbers started with 30867S. The entire serial span ran from 100001 to 121513.*

1963 CORVETTE

Two Corvette body styles are available with the addition of the 2-passenger Corvette Sting Ray Sport Coupe. Aerodynamically clean and in the Gran Turismo style, this new Sport Coupe features wrap-over doors and compound curved side windows and backlight. Dual simulated air exhaust ports decorate the roof side, immediately rearward of the door. The sloping roof line is unbroken through elimination of a rear deck lid, and the fuel filler is concealed beneath the rear deck emblem. In the rear view, the roofline tapers back, to blend out just forward of the body rear panel peak line.

70

Shown on Cover: Corvette Sting Ray Sport Coupe in Tuxedo Black

Corvette Sting Ray Convertible in Riverside Red

NEW GRACE AND ELEGANCE SILHOUETTE AMERICA'S SPORTS CAR

Corvette steps out smartly with an exhilarating new look for '63. A freshly elegant look that promises to lift the spirits of any buff who takes the wheel. It's the Corvette Sting Ray! Two sparkling new models, both pointing the way to a classic new concept in American sports car design.

Catch an eyeful of the Corvette newcomer, the exciting Sport Coupe. Graceful body panels and compound-curved side windows emphasize the miles-ahead aerodynamic design. Power-operated, retractable headlamps rotate out of sight to blend into the unobstructed hood line. Doors extend upward into the roof, adding armchair ease and comfort to sliding in and out. This is the Corvette Sting Ray Sport Coupe. Clean, taut, fresh in every detail.

You'll find the Convertible is jauntier than ever in '63. Uncluttered lines accented front and rear by trim wrap-around bumpers. The subtle contour of the smoothly molded rear deck. A gleaming aluminum grille, retractable head-lamps and a sweeping hood-length windsplit. Top up or down, graceful streamlining is the goal. And the Corvette Sting Ray Convertible achieves it.

Again available with optional removable hardtop, the Corvette Sting Ray Convertible, like the Sport Coupe, retains the Corvette image despite the completely new advanced styling concept. Fast lines of the longer, lower hood are preserved with the addition of retractable headlamps. The aluminum radiator grille extends virtually the full width of the vehicle. As in the rest of the Chevrolet line, parking lamps have amber lenses. New straight windshield pillars complement overall vehicle styling.

LEFT *The basic price of the new Corvette hovered just above $4,000 but most buyers piled on the options and most cars carried sticker prices of $5,000 and above. Basic price on the coupe was $4,252, compared to $4,037 for the convertible.*

Corvette Sting Ray Sport Coupe in Sebring Silver equipped with Sporty Aluminum Wheels* with Knock-off Hubs.*

MORE THAN EVER, A POLISHED PERFORMER ON THE OPEN ROAD

The real driving fun of a Corvette begins with imaginative engineering. Beneath those trim lines, Corvette is sporting engineering features that just plain add ginger to any driving. Take the chassis, for example. Corvette's new frame is stronger and more torsionally rigid than in past models. The new four-wheel independent suspension irons out even the rutted trails, keeps handling steady and sure. Maintenance is easier, too, with a battery-saving Delcotron generator, extended-life exhaust system, and hydraulic self-adjusting brakes. Other '63 innovations include Ball-Race steering, an adjustable steering column and wider wheel rims.

Overall, the new Corvette's weight is distributed in a different way. More than half the weight now rests on the rear wheels—a first among modern American front-engine cars. That means hare-quick maneuverability when turning and cornering, plus improved traction on the rough back roads.

When it comes to efficient power teams, Corvette remains front-and-center. Makes no difference whether you cruise the turnpikes, dodge city traffic or joy ride on country lanes. Pick your power from one of Corvette's big V8's, match it with a versatile Corvette transmission and find out just how a sports car should respond.

**Optional at extra cost.*

LEFT *Viewed from the side, the coupe's voluptuous lines are more pronounced. The fender bulges, though non-functional, add a muscular feel to the design. Aside from chrome rocker panels, there are few tack-on items. Even the characteristic non-functional side vents are kept to a minimum.*

AUTOMOBILES CHEVROLET, 1963

NEW CORVETTE

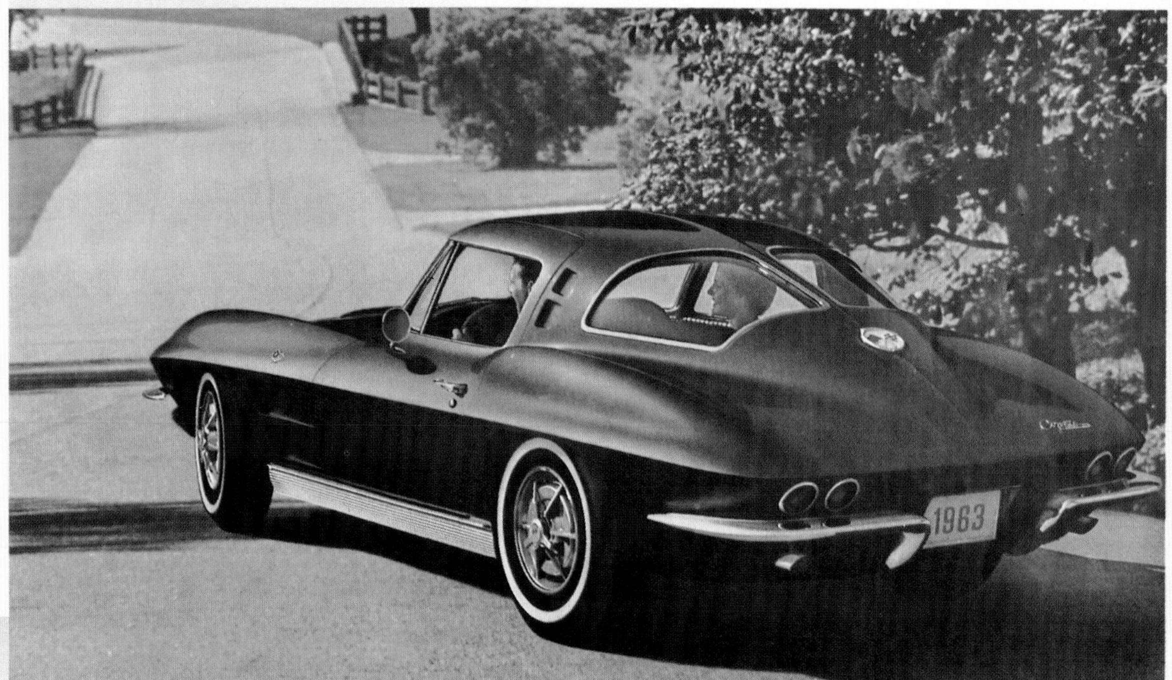

LEFT *Chevrolet had hopes that independent racers would make the 1963 coupe a winner in GT class events. Toward that end, the coupe could be ordered with a list of performance options, including heavy-duty springs, shocks and sway bars, Al-Fin aluminium brake drums with metallic linings, dual master hydraulic cylinders, aluminium knock-off wheels and a 36.5-gallon (166-litre) tank. The entire package of goodies could be ordered under the option code Z06. Unfortunately, the Z06 cars appeared at the same time as the lighter, race-bred Shelby Cobra, and the Sting Rays often were defeated by the Cobras.*

LEFT *The new chassis resulted in a front/rear weight ratio of 49/51 per cent, which gave the Corvette a tendency to oversteer.*

vehicle weight on the rear wheels. As important, variation to the unloaded or curb weight condition is less than 2 percent. This small change from these two extremes provides consistent driving response through the loading range.

With more of the weight in the rear, traction characteristics are improved. This is particularly true during the rearward weight shift at hard acceleration. Weight shift forward during braking gives better proportioning of effort at all four wheels. Lighter front end weight reduces proportionally the steering effort required to turn the car.

Height of the center of gravity is an indication of vehicle stability. In the new Corvette, the C. G. is nearly 17 percent lower than in the previous model. Coupled with the excellent roll axis provided by the new suspension designs, Corvette for 1963 excels in flat cornering.

POWER TEAMS TAILOR-MADE FOR SPORTS CAR FUN

There's a power team to meet your most exacting sports car expectations. Each of the four versions of the big V8 has 327-cubic-inch displacement, 4" bore and 3.25" stroke. The 250-hp standard engine features a single 4-barrel carb, 10.5:1 compression ratio, hydraulic valve lifters and new dual exhaust system. The 300-hp power plant* adds a large aluminum 4-barrel carburetor and larger intake valves. Both the 340- and 360-hp engines* have cylinder heads with large ports, domed aluminum pistons, 11.25:1 compression, high-speed valve systems with specially finished exhaust valves, mechanical valve lifters, ribbed aluminum rocker covers, special camshafts and 5-quart oil capacity (4-quart capacity on 250- and 300-hp engines). The 360-hp Fuel Injection engine* provides a larger volume aluminum manifold with improved ram pipes and warning buzzer for the tach.

The standard transmission is 3-Speed Synchro-Mesh. Ratios: 2.47:1 first; 1.53:1 second; 1:1 third; and 2.80:1 reverse. For a variety of engine and rear axle combinations, 4-Speed Synchro-Mesh* is the answer. Ratios with 250- and 300-hp* V8's: 2.54:1 first; 1.89:1 second; 1.51:1 third; 1:1 fourth; and 2.61:1 reverse. Ratios with 340- and 360-hp V8's*: 2.20:1 first; 1.64:1 second; 1.31:1 third; 1:1 fourth; and 2.26:1 reverse. Both 3- and 4-Speed Synchro-Mesh have a 10" semi-centrifugal diaphragm spring clutch with a lighter aluminum 360-degree clutch housing and floor-mounted shift. 4-Speed transmissions also have a mechanism on the shift lever to prevent unintentional reverse engagement. The automatic Powerglide* transmission, available with two engines, gives really effortless driving. And you'll find Positraction* axle ratios to suit your choice of power teams.

HP	Induction System	Comp. Ratio	Cam, Lifters	Distributor Points, Advance	Transmission	Rear Axle Ratio Std.	Rear Axle Ratio Positraction
250	4-Barrel Carburetor, Dual-Intake Air Cleaner	10.5:1	Std. Cam, Hydraulic Lifters	Single, Vacuum-Centrifugal	3-Speed	3.36:1	3.36:1
					4-Speed* (2.54:1 Low)	3.36:1†	3.08:1 3.36:1
					Powerglide*	3.36:1	3.36:1
300*	Large 4-Barrel Aluminum Body Carburetor, Dual-Intake Air Cleaner	10.5:1	Std. Cam, Hydraulic Lifters	Single, Vacuum-Centrifugal	3-Speed	3.36:1	3.36:1
					4-Speed* (2.54:1 Low)	3.36:1†	3.08:1 3.36:1
					Powerglide*	3.36:1	3.36:1
340*	Large 4-Barrel Aluminum Body Carburetor, High-Flow Air Cleaner	11.25:1	Special Cam, Mechanical Lifters	Single, Vacuum-Centrifugal	3-Speed	3.36:1	3.36:1
					4-Speed* (2.20:1 Low)	3.70:1	3.08:1 3.36:1 3.55:1 3.70:1 4.11:1 4.56:1
360*	Fuel Injection, Special Air Cleaner	11.25:1	Special Cam, Mechanical Lifters	Single, Vacuum-Centrifugal	3-Speed	3.36:1	3.36:1
					4-Speed* (2.20:1 Low)	3.70:1	3.08:1 3.36:1 3.55:1 3.70:1 4.11:1 4.56:1

† 3.08:1 Performance Cruise Ratio optional at extra cost.

Optional at extra cost.

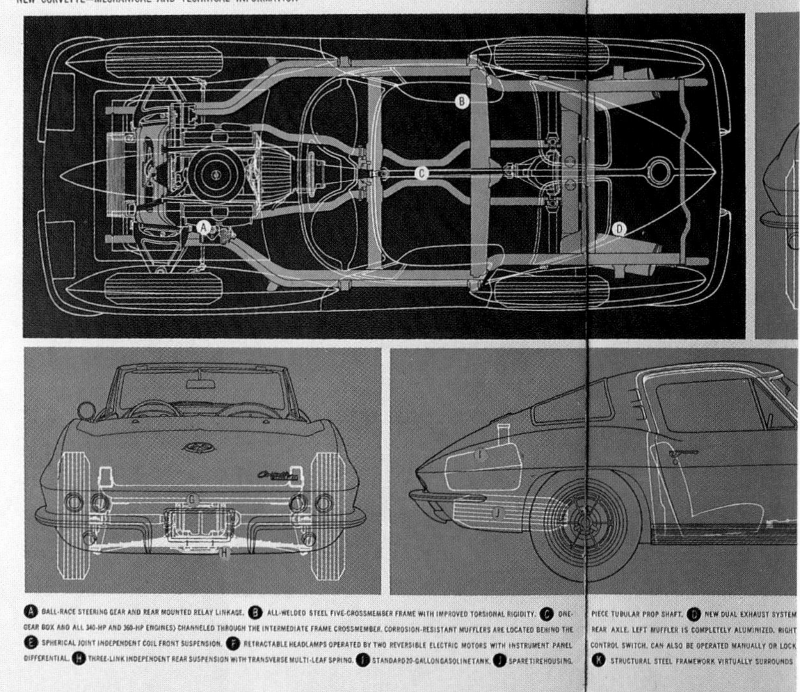

LEFT *Horsepower and Corvette were two words that went together in 1963. The brochures touted the array of engines available. Though all were based on the same cast-iron V8 block, they were all different, from the potent but docile 250-horsepower base engine to the high-compression, fuel-injected 360-horsepower engine which required more attention in tune-ups.*

RIGHT *Despite slight oversteer, the new Corvette chassis was a resounding success. Its independent rear suspension – which used a frame-mounted differential linked to two halfshafts – was lighter and more versatile than the old solid-axle setup.*

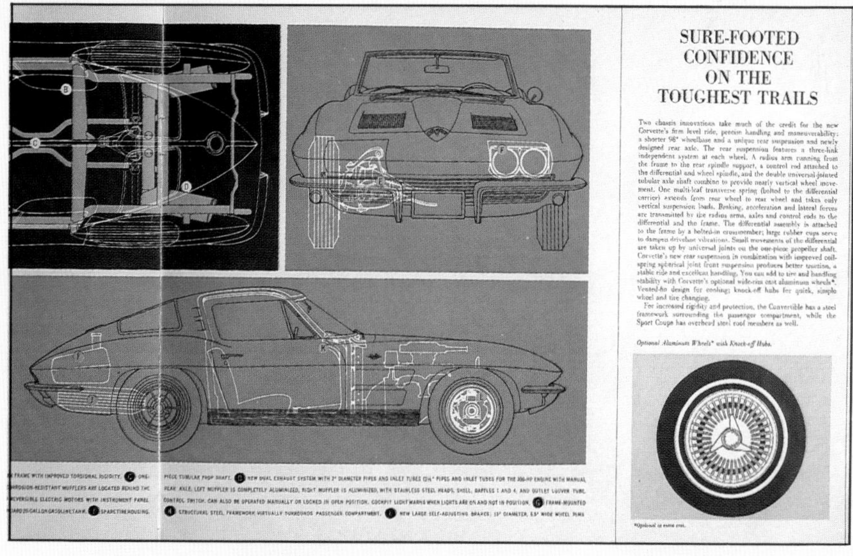

SURE-FOOTED CONFIDENCE ON THE TOUGHEST TRAILS

Two chassis innovations take much of the credit for the new Corvette's firm level ride, precise handling and maneuverability: a shorter 98" wheelbase and a unique rear suspension and newly designed rear axle. The rear suspension features a three-link independent system at each wheel. A radius arm running from the frame to the rear spindle support, a control rod attached to the differential and wheel spindle, and the double universal-jointed tubular axle shaft combine to provide nearly vertical wheel movement. One multi-leaf transverse spring (bolted to the differential carrier) extends from rear wheel to rear wheel and takes only vertical suspension loads. Braking, acceleration and lateral forces are transmitted by the radius arms, axles and control rods to the differential and the frame. The differential assembly is attached to the frame by a bolted-in crossmember; large rubber cups serve to dampen driveline vibrations. Small movements of the differential are taken up by universal joints on the one-piece propeller shaft. Corvette's new rear suspension in combination with improved coil-spring spherical joint front suspension produces better traction, a stable ride and excellent handling. You can add to tire and handling stability with Corvette's optional wide-rim cast aluminum wheels*. Vented-fin design for cooling; knock-off hubs for quick, simple wheel and tire changing.

For increased rigidity and protection, the Convertible has a steel framework surrounding the passenger compartment, while the Sport Coupe has overhead steel roof members as well.

Optional Aluminum Wheels with Knock-off Hubs.*

**Optional at extra cost.*

CORVETTE STING RAY

SPORT COUPE

CONVERTIBLE

CORVETTE:

America's Only True Sports Car

The 1964 Corvette Sting Ray—Sport Coupe and Convertible—features an improved ride and better insulation from road noise. Both models have outstanding features—steel-reinforced Fiberglas body, all-welded steel frame, independent four-wheel suspension, retractable dual headlights. Simulated hood grilles are eliminated for 1964. The new body sill molding features a ribbed area. Corvette convertible can have a folding top, hardtop or, as an option, both. Both Corvettes are available in seven exterior colors in Magic-Mirror acrylic lacquer.

The rear window center pillar on the sport coupe is eliminated for 1964, offering more glass area for improved visibility.

Interiors feature all-vinyl, foam-cushioned bucket seats; door safety reflectors; carpeting; vinyl-coated Fiberglas headlining in both coupe and hardtop; improved ventilation system in the coupe. Interiors are available in black, red, blue, saddle or silver. Leather is available as an option.

The Corvette steering wheel is of simulated wood-grain plastic. The full complement of instruments includes a tachometer. All Corvettes also have cigarette lighter, glove box light, parking brake light, electric clock, floor-mounted transmission shift lever, and a light that warns when headlights are on, but not in fully-aimed position.

Corvettes offer a choice of four 327-cubic-inch V8 engines: 250 H.P., 300 H.P. and 365 H.P. in carburetor-equipped engines and 375 H.P. in the fuel injection V8. There's also a choice of three transmissions: quieter three-speed manual, four-speed manual or Powerglide.

19

LEFT *In 1964, William Mitchell's beloved split rear window is replaced by a single piece of glass. Aside from that, there were few changes in styling. The fake hood louvres of 1963 were removed, though the hood still carried two indentations. The horsepower war continued with the two highest-rated 327 engines receiving increases. The carburetted solid-lifter version was increased to 365 horsepower, and the fuel-injected version soared to 375 horsepower. The latter engine was an expensive option at $538. A fully equipped fuel-injected Corvette would cost more than $6,000 but it would also run the quarter mile in 14.2 seconds. Four gearboxes were offered: a three-speed manual, a four-speed manual, a close-ratio four-speed manual and the Powerglide automatic. Sales would top 22,000. Convertible serial numbers started with 40867S, with coupes getting the prefix 40837S. Production numbers ran from 100001 to 122229.*

ABOVE *The introduction of the 1965 model marked the start of the high-horsepower cubic-inch wars of the late 1960s. Although the catalogues listed the 375-horsepower fuel-injected 327-cubic-inch engine, the star of the show was the 396 cubic-inch big-block option. The new engine, which featured an advanced 'porcupine' pushrod valve design, was called a Turbo-Jet V8. In the Corvette, this engine produced an awesome 425 horsepower, thanks to 11 to 1 compression and solid valve lifters. Although only several hundred Turbo-Jet Corvettes were built, this model marked the end of the high-revving fuel-injected 327 engines.*

RIGHT *Luxury and power were two items that the Corvette catalogues stressed. Though the car was a ground-pounding machine, it could be had in versions that were more subtle and comfortable. Air-conditioning was becoming more popular as an option and the addition of an AM-FM radio option helped sell the image of a Corvette as a boulevard cruiser.*

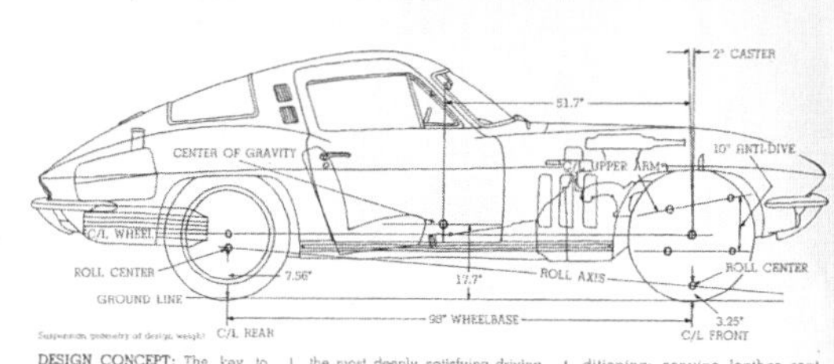

DESIGN CONCEPT: The key to Sting Ray's roadability and handling lies in its 4-wheel independent suspension and its greater rearward weight distribution. Chevrolet engineers chose the fully independent suspension so that optimum use could be made of the great power available. The rearward weight distribution makes it possible to achieve excellent handling and still maintain an acceptably gentle ride. The major vehicle masses — the heavier components of the Sting Ray — are located so that the suspension and steering systems can work with the design, rather than having to compensate for imbalance. The Sting Ray has been basically *right* from its original concept. Constant refinement and continual development have gone forward to make the 1965 Corvette Sting Ray more than ever one of the most deeply satisfying driving experiences available in the world.

EXTRA-COST OPTIONAL EQUIPMENT

The following equipment, shown previously in illustrations or described in the text, is available at extra cost for the Corvette Sting Ray. These options add driving pleasure, or prepare the car for special uses. They allow the Sting Ray owner to equip his car to his own particular tastes.

CHASSIS: Heavy-duty suspension. (Rear spring rate: 305 lb./in. Rear shock absorbers: 1⅜ in. Front spring rate: 550 lb./in. Front shock absorbers: recalibrated. Stabilizer bar: 0.94-inch diameter.) Positraction; power brakes; telescopic steering column; power steering; optional axle ratio; nylon tires; whitewall tires; cast aluminum wheels with wide-base six-inch rims and knock-off hubs.

ENGINE: Off-road service exhaust system; exposed, side-mounted exhaust system; 36-gallon fuel tank (Sport Coupe only). (Note: when 36-gallon fuel tank is fitted, luggage compartment is partially carpeted); transistor ignition and voltage regulator; 300-horsepower engine; 350-horsepower engine; 365-horsepower engine; 375-horsepower Ramjet Fuel Injection engine.

TRANSMISSION: 4-Speed; 4-Speed close ratio; Powerglide.

BODY: Soft-Ray tinted glass; back-up lights and non-glare inside rearview mirror; Four-Season air conditioning; genuine leather seat upholstery; wood-rimmed steering wheel; electric windows; AM/FM pushbutton radio with remote control power antenna; removeable hard top. (Convertible only. You can, however, specify either hard top or soft top at no extra cost—or order both with hard top at extra cost.)

from rubber to roof, a sports car...

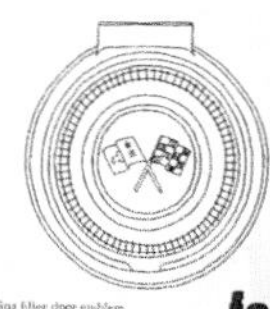

Gas filler door emblem

for performance -and style-minded individuals.

14

RIGHT *Some updates were made to the Corvette interior. One of the most functional was the application of matte black bezel rings to the instruments. In previous years, the rings were chrome and caused glare. New for 1965 was the wood-rim steering wheel which helped enhance the Corvette's image as a GT-class car.*

10

ELECTRICAL SYSTEM: The electrical system of the Sting Ray is based on the powerful 12-volt Delcotron diode-rectified air-cooled generator. A transistor ignition system can be ordered which provides electronic ignition control rather than mechanical. A flashing red warning lamp warns if the electrically operated retracting headlamps have been left on after retraction; a similar warning light is supplied for the hand brake. The wiring system itself is color-coded for ease of maintenance. Ignition system components are shielded in radio-equipped cars to prevent interference. Accessories are fused except for the headlamps and parking lamps; these have circuit breakers rather than fuses.

S-wire spring construction

INTERIOR: A true sports car in every sense, the Sting Ray still offers a completely luxurious driving environment. For 1965, the interior features new trim of durable expanded vinyl with a more subtle texture. Two new interior colors, maroon and green, and striking two-tone combinations of silver/black, white/black, white/red and white/blue complement the other choices of black, red, blue and saddle. Genuine leather upholstery is available for 1965 Corvettes in all of these colors.

The individual bucket-type seats are of "S-wire" spring construction, and have a new bolster-like design for more seating comfort and better lateral support. Both seats are adjustable fore and aft through a range of four inches. New molded panels covering the back of the seats offer protection against scuffing. Carpet for the 1965 Sting Ray is molded to shape for better fit, a more finished appearance and fewer seams. The luggage compartment is completely carpeted; and an under-the-floor storage compartment tucks valuables out of sight. Interior door panels are of a new molded construction; the armrest is integral with the panel and the door pull-handle is separate. Dual sun visors are standard.

Controls for the outside-air-type heater and defroster are located on the central console along with the electric clock and radio controls; vent controls are located under the instrument panel on each side of the steering column.

Matched speedometer and tachometer are the primary instruments in the Sting Ray. Supplementing these are an electric fuel gauge, electric coolant temperature gauge, ammeter, and an oil pressure gauge. A re-settable trip odometer, headlight switch, cigarette lighter, headlamp retractor switch, hood release, and four-position ignition switch complete the instrument panel. On the passenger side, a built-in passenger assist grip is part of the instrument panel hood. The new ignition switch makes it impossible to remove the ignition key from the lock except when the switch is in the "off" or locked position.

DIMENSIONS (in inches)	Sport Coupe	Convertible
Torso	37.0	38.5
Leg	42.7	42.7
Hip	50.9	50.9
Shoulder	48.4	48.4
Entrance room	31.4	30.2

yet this car is plush, convenient...

Instrument panel construction

Sport Coupe door

Options and Custom Features to personalize the Sting Ray precisely to customers' wishes are available at extra cost. Some of them are presented throughout this catalog in illustrations and in text. A listing of them will be found on pages 12 and 14.

loaded with creature comforts...

11

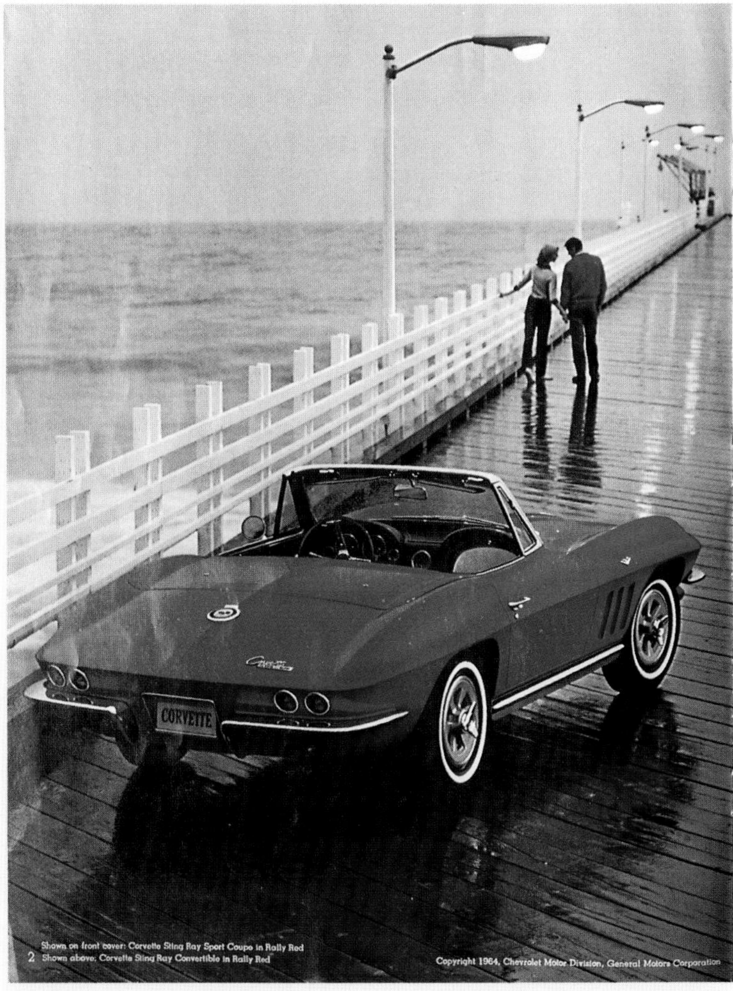

CORVETTE
Shown on front cover: Corvette Sting Ray Sport Coupe in Rally Red
2 Shown above: Corvette Sting Ray Convertible in Rally Red
Copyright 1964, Chevrolet Motor Division, General Motors Corporation

We think it's unwise to just tinker with an American classic like the Corvette Sting Ray. Changes should be meaningful. This fine road machine was and still is America's only true sports car. So for 1965, Sting Ray underwent subtle refinements in styling that only enhance its unique looks. And performance, always a basic measure of Sting Ray's appeal, has been improved still further. A new "street" engine develops 350 horsepower and answers most enthusiasts' needs for traffic and highway driving. The two top V8 power plants offer 365- and 375-horsepower for those who specify all-out go. Best of all, the Sting Ray now has Sport-Master disc brakes on all four wheels that naturally complement the tremendous performance capabilities of the car. The '65 Sting Ray stops smoothly, surely and firmly with braking reserve far beyond normal requirements. More than ever the Corvette Sting Ray is luxurious transportation for two, a different kind of driving experience.

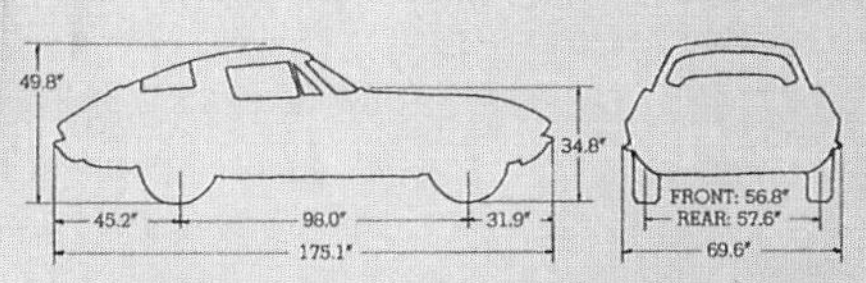

External dimensions, Sport Coupe

this is a different kind of car...

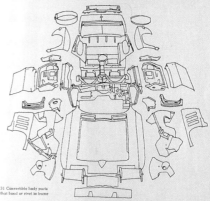

31 Convertible body parts that bond or rivel to frame

A wide range of extra-cost Options and Custom Features is offered for the Sting Ray to fit individual tastes. The illustrations and text of this catalog present some of them; pages 12 and 14 list the options for your convenience.

BODY: Styling changes for the 1965 Sting Ray are simple and effective. A smooth hood without depressions or distractions in the contour. New louvers behind the front wheels that help increase air flow through the engine compartment. A new grille with three black horizontal bars highlighting the center of the grille. New body sill moldings of bright aluminum. These changes only serve to refine what is aerodynamically one of the more efficient cars in the world.

Both Sting Ray models, Sport Coupe and Convertible, use the same one-piece underbody. The Convertible uses 31 fiber glass panels, the Sport Coupe 35. Where rivets can be exposed, the fiber glass parts are riveted to the metal framework; elsewhere, a bonding strip of fiber glass is riveted to the framework and the fiber glass is bonded to this. Sport Coupe bodies are attached to the chassis at six points with rubber "biscuit" mounts, the Convertible at four points.

In comfort and livability, the Sting Ray hasn't changed. Twin retracting headlamps, 3-speed ventilation blower in the Sport Coupe, the wrap-over doors in the Sport Coupe for easy entry and exit, wrap-around bumpers, compound

a true all-American sports car...

3

ABOVE *For 1965, the Corvette would not only go faster, it would stop faster. At long last, four-wheel disc brakes were offered as standard equipment. They would be a stunning improvement over the old drum setup, in modulation, fade and wear. For those who were looking for foolish bargains, the disc brakes could be deleted for a $64 credit. Only a few hundred of the 23,000 Corvettes built that year didn't have disc brakes. Serial numbers in 1964 ran from 100001 to 123562. Prefix for hardtop models was 194375S, 194675S for convertibles.*

RIGHT *The arrival of the 1966 model saw the last vestiges of restraint removed when it came to horsepower. A corporate ban on engines of more than 400 cubic inches in cars smaller than full-sized sedans was erased and the Corvette received the 427-cubic-inch Turbo-Jet V8. A bored out 396 V8, the 427 came in two horsepower ratings – 390 and 425. Although the top rating of 425 horsepower was identical to the 1965 396, there were 50 more foot-pounds of torque.*

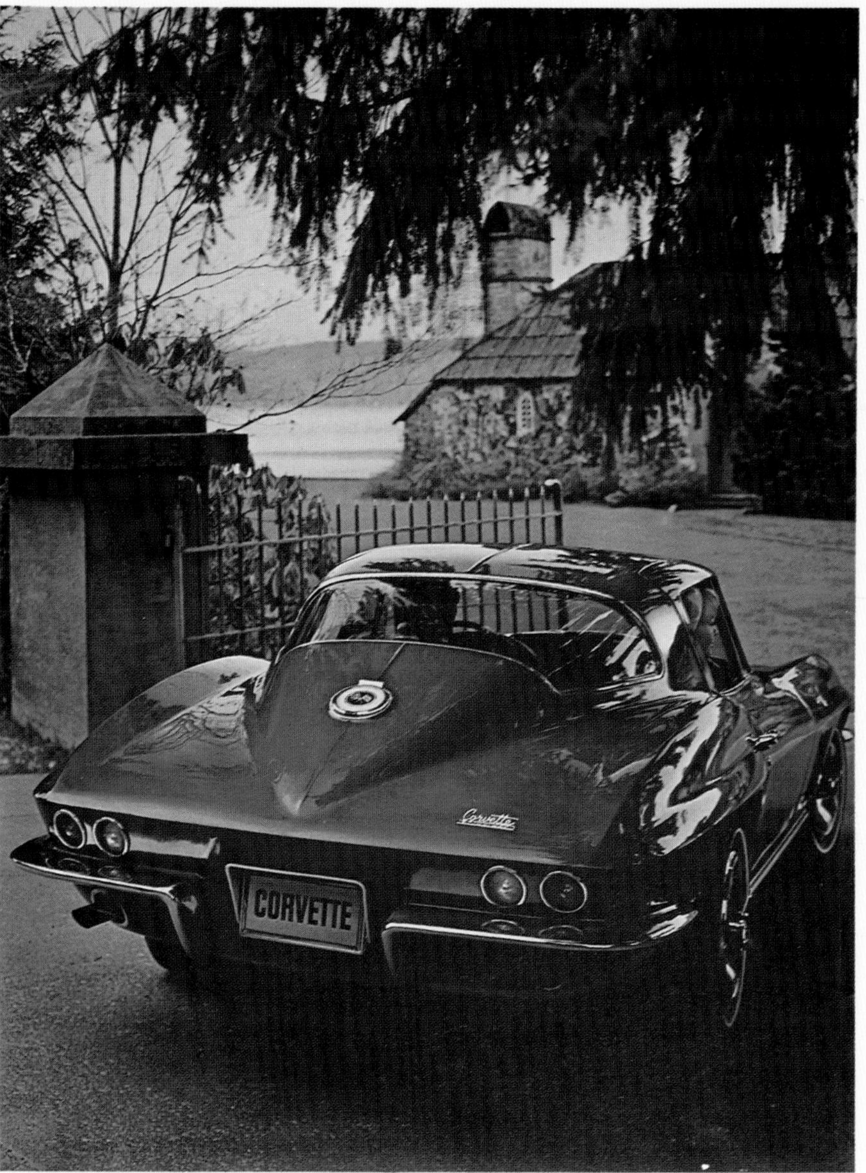

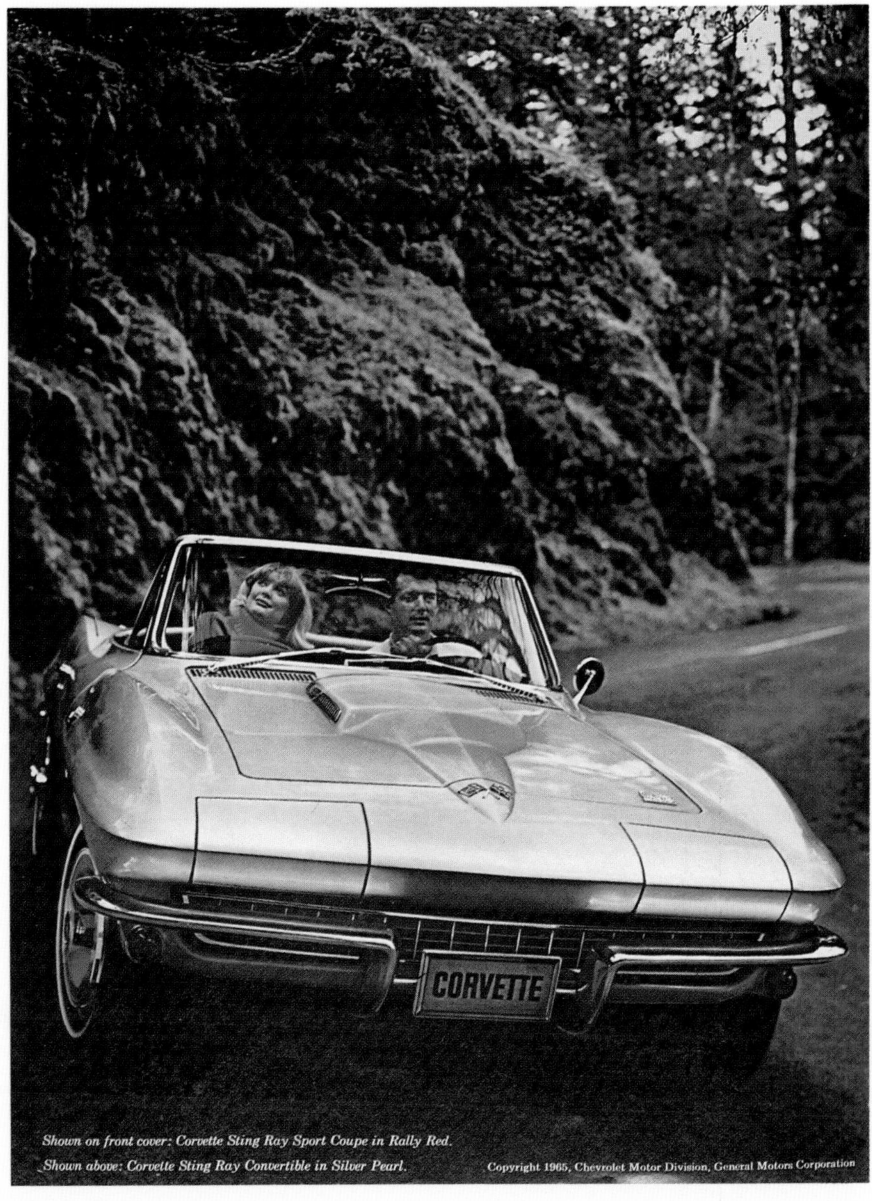

CORVETTE
Shown on front cover: Corvette Sting Ray Sport Coupe in Rally Red.
Shown above: Corvette Sting Ray Convertible in Silver Pearl.
Copyright 1965, Chevrolet Motor Division, General Motors Corporation

LEFT *The initial furor over the Sting Ray hardtop was diminishing by 1966 and convertible Corvettes were the top sellers by far. Roadsters accounted for 17,762 sales, compared to just 9,958 for the still stunning hardtop. In either form, the Corvette was an awesome performer. Though sales catalogues did not give performance figures, the Corvette with the top-rated 427 could reach 60 mph (97 kph) in just 4.8 seconds and top speed was in excess of 140 mph (225 kph).*

THE 1966 CORVETTE STING RAY BY CHEVROLET
Features and Options and all that's new
CORVETTE

ABOVE *There was nothing much new on the interior of the 1966 Corvette. Emphasis was on comfort and the availability of leather seats.*

RIGHT *Styling changes were minor for 1966 with the removal of the air vents on the hardtop and an egg-crate style front grill. Serial numbers for coupes began with the prefix 194376S, convertibles with 194676S.*

ABOVE *Not quite a rainbow but the colour chart for the 1966 Corvette was impressive with 10 exterior colours and 8 interior choices. Some of the rarer colours were Mosport Green and Sunfire Yellow.*

The sport coupe's fully carpeted luggage area
Right: Enthusiast's delight: 4-Speed box
Seat belts with retractors are standard
Pushbutton AM/FM all-transistor radio

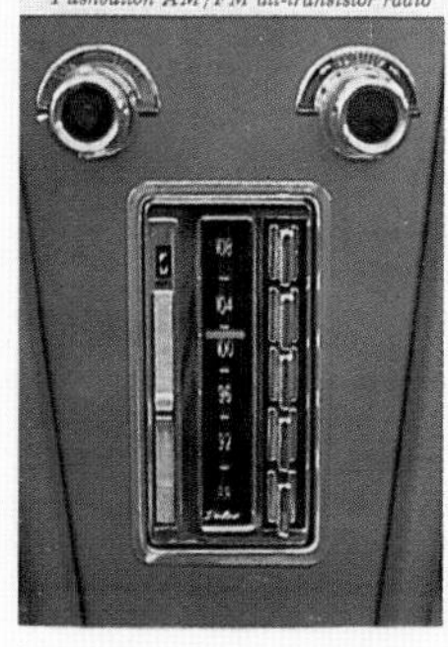

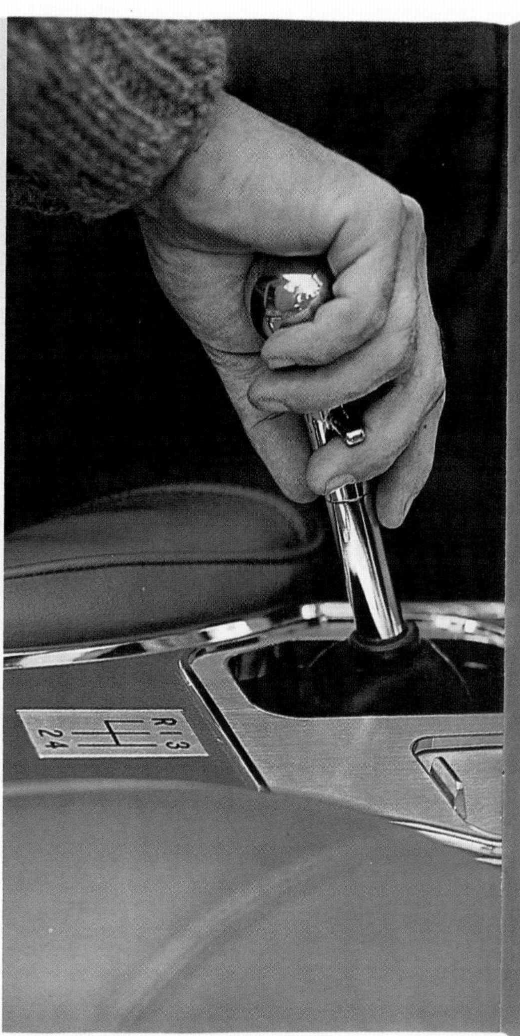

RIGHT *The four-speed transmission, available in close or wide ratio form, was the gearbox of choice in the Corvette. Seatbelts were touted as standard equipment and catalogues noted the availability of an AM-FM radio and the large amount of luggage space in the coupe.*

RIGHT *If all had gone according to plan, 1967 would have seen the catalogues talking about an all-new body and interior for the Corvette. But development took longer than expected, and 1967 saw the familiar Sting Ray styling back with a host of small but significant refinements. On the outside, the side fender vents expanded from three to five and the power bulge on the hood of 427-equipped Corvettes was redesigned to resemble a manta ray. A two-tone hood paint scheme further accentuated the bulge.*

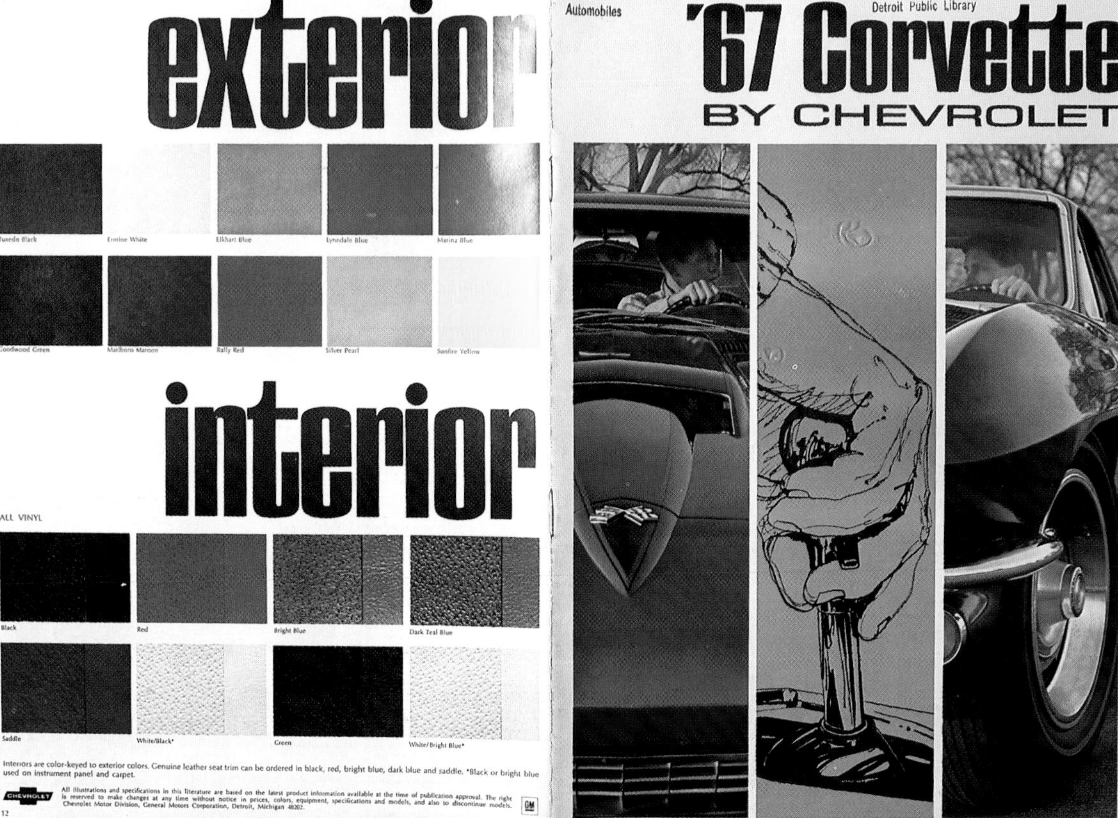

RIGHT *Convertibles continued to outsell coupes in 1967 with 14,436 roadsters being built compared to 8,504 hardtops. Sales were down from the previous year, which can be attributed to buyers awaiting the all-new body style that would appear in 1968. Other changes to the 1967 model including the replacement of standard hubcaps with slotted 'Rally' wheels. The expensive but beautiful cast aluminium wheels were dropped from the option list.*

Your first venture inside a '67 Corvette will convince you that here's a cockpit luxuriously rigged for two. All-vinyl bucket seats have the grain look of real leather; backrests and foam-cushioned seats are bordered by narrow front and side bolsters that let you ride deep and comfortably. Backrest tops and sides as well as cushion side panels are trimmed with bright metal moldings. For an elegant flair, order genuine leather seat trim which is available in five colors—black, red, bright blue, dark blue or saddle, depending on exterior color selected.

Corvette's instrument panel is a devotee's delight. Safety-padded, vinyl-covered and replete with those instruments so important to the serious driver. The large speedometer and tachometer are front and center; so's the trip odometer that runs to 999.9 miles. Ammeter, oil pressure gauge and electrically operated temperature and fuel level gauges round out the engine performance indicators. Two panel indicator lights guard against oversights. One flashes red when the parking brake is set and the ignition on (it also monitors hydraulic pressure balance when foot brakes are applied); the other indicator light warns you if headlights are on but not fully rotated to the open position. And newly styled controls are capped by smooth contoured knobs. There are many other safety engineered items built into every '67 Corvette. See page 11 for a more complete list.

Convenience is another measure of true luxury. That's why special attention has been given to standard interior details in the '67 Corvette. The hood release handle and door locks are in new convenient positions; sliding air vent controls are located on either side of the vertical

luxurious

center console so both driver and passenger can regulate air flow; positive latches help keep folding seat backs secured; and seat belts with retractors and push-button buckles release quickly, clip to the side of the center console when not in use. Other convenience features you wouldn't want to be without; crank-operated ventipanes; blended-air heater-defroster with 3-speed blower; bright metal door grips and pulls; locking glove box door that doubles as a handy tray; cigarette lighter; and rally-type electric clock which features sweep second hand.

Elsewhere in Corvette's interior, color-keyed deep-twist carpeting covers every inch of exposed floor area. Anchors for front seat shoulder belts, you can order, are located in the body inner quarter panel. And the steering wheel has the rich look of walnut wood.

Put the finishing touches on all this sporting luxury, inside and out, by specifying such Options and Custom Features as Four-Season air-conditioning system for year-around comfort, AM-FM radio with a new 31-inch fixed-height antenna for best reception, telescopic steering wheel, dual side-mounted off-road exhaust system with bright metal casings, Strato-ease headrests, power brakes, power steering, power windows, special cast-aluminum wheels and whitewall or red-stripe tires.

No need to ask whether Corvette for '67 is a luxury car or a sports car. You can see for yourself it's both.

Red-stripe tires and special cast-aluminum wheels

Telescopic steering wheel

Whitewall tires and dual side-mounted off-road exhausts

Turn to page 9 for a comprehensive list of extra-cost Options and Custom Features available for '67 Corvette.

7

LEFT *The option list continues to grow in the 1967 catalogue. Among the most popular are a telescoping steering wheel, air-conditioning and side-mounted 'off-road' exhaust pipes. Basic price for the coupe was $4,353 with the convertible starting at $4,141.*

individual

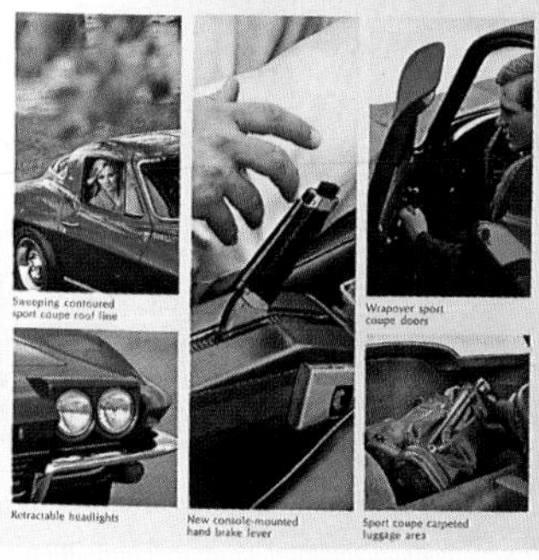

Sweeping contoured sport coupe roof line

Wrapover sport coupe doors

Retractable headlights

New console-mounted hand brake lever

Sport coupe carpeted luggage area

When sports car enthusiasts talk about Corvette, certain words, like "individual," crop up often. That's because both the Sting Ray Sport Coupe and Convertible possess a rareness that sets them apart. You can see at a glance that no *one* attribute gives Corvette its exclusive character; rather, it's a combination of many features. Like retractable headlights that hide away at the flick of a switch, weather-wise fiber glass body and protective wraparound bumpers. And for '67, Corvettes ordered with 427 Turbo-Jet V8s sport a special hood with a cutaway bubble, ornamentation and 427 numerals giving it the dash of the power plant it caps.

Other new touches that accent Corvette's '67 personality: bright wheel trim rings and center caps; a new front fender louver design; wide back-up lights centered in the rear panel; and many new standard safety features (see page 11 for a comprehensive list).

If you search for fastback individuality, consider the Corvette Sport Coupe with its sweeping, contoured roof line. Doors extend well into the top to help ease entry and exit. Inside, you'll find just as much singularity. A fully carpeted luggage area (plus a secret space for valuables and tools) spreads out behind the front bucket seats. In true sports car fashion, the newly designed parking brake lever stands ready at hand on the center console. And overhead, there's a new vinyl-covered foam-and-fiber-cushioned headlining with special niches for the padded sun visors.

All this and more make Corvette for '67 the kind of "individual" you're sure to like.

See page 9 for more extra-cost Options and Custom Features.

3

LEFT *The major change to the interior in 1967 was the changing of the emergency brake from a pedal system to a lever mounted between the bucket seats. Production numbers ran from 100001 to 122940 with coupes getting the prefix 194377S and convertibles being assigned 194677S.*

BELOW *Wider six-inch rims and a list of safety features marked the 1967 Corvette. Under the hood power choices remained the same as the previous year with one exception. For only 20 special customers – racers mostly – Chevrolet offered a 430-horsepower version of the 427 V8 designated by the code L-88. In fact, this racing engine produced in excess of 500 horsepower and an L-88 1967 Corvette is one of the most collectible Corvettes ever.*

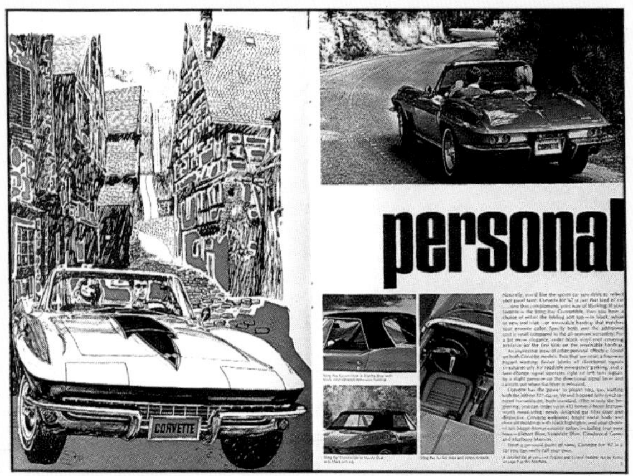

LEFT *As a reflection of trends elsewhere in the American automobile industry, the 1967 Corvette catalogue offered the option of a vinyl-covered removable hardtop for the convertible. Few chose the trendy top.*

RIGHT *When the new shape first debuted on a 1965 show Corvette it was called the Mako Shark. When it made production in 1968 it was called simply Corvette. The Sting Ray designation dropped from the line-up that year.*

Pick a paint!
Here's a tough one. Try to select just one of these ten luxurious Magic-Mirror colors. Eight of them are brand new.
(Tuxedo Black and Rally Red are popular choices we kept from last year's selection.) The fabric top for the Convertible can be specified in black, white or beige. You can also order a black vinyl cover for the removable hardtop.
Tuxedo Black
International Blue
Silverstone Silver
Corvette Bronze
Cordovan Maroon
British Green
Polar White
Rally Red
Safari Yellow
Le Mans Blue
Choose a vinyl!
One more decision. Try to settle on the one color you like best from this excellent selection.
Interiors are color-keyed to exterior colors with deep-twist carpeting also hued to match. The textured vinyl looks like leather, but if you like, genuine hide can be ordered in black, red, medium blue, dark orange or tobacco.

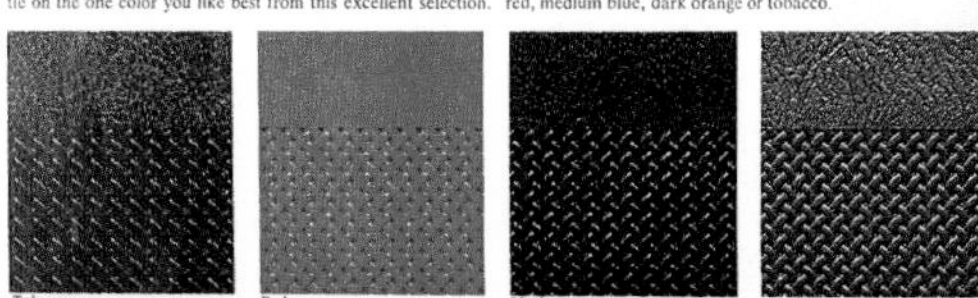

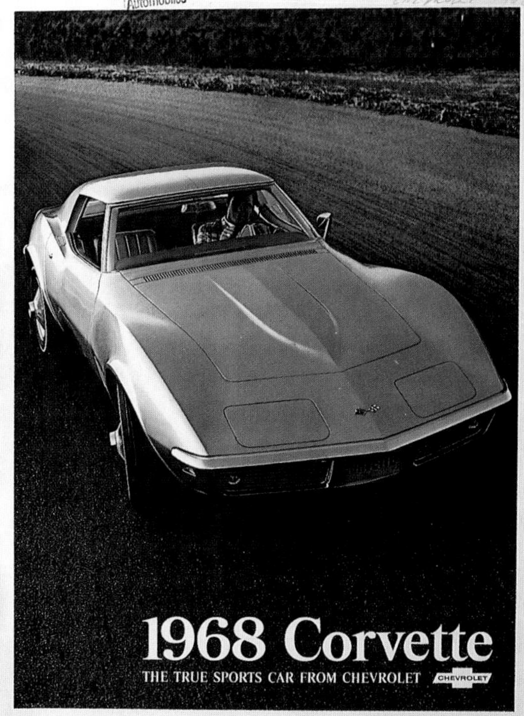

Automobiles
1968 Corvette
THE TRUE SPORTS CAR FROM CHEVROLET
CHEVROLET

No need to beware of substitutes. There aren't any.
CORVETTE
GM

LEFT *Although not as pure as the Sting Ray, the Mako Shark look of the Corvette was an instant hit in 1968. Corvette catalogues were full of details on the avant garde design.*

LEFT *While the Corvette was in its heyday in 1968, another car that Chevrolet had high hopes for – the Corvair – wasn't and efforts to have the success of the Corvette rub off by somehow linking the two in catalogues failed. The Corvair was discontinued after 1969.*

RIGHT *Although the chassis was largely unchanged from 1967 to 1968, almost nothing else was the same. The styling was eye-catching but the automotive press of the day disliked it immensely, calling it excessive and cumbersome. Still, the public loved it, with sales reaching a record 28,566. Convertibles still outsold coupes by two-to-one but 1968 was the last year that would happen. Basic prices rose to $4,663 for the hardtop and $4,230 for the convertible.*

The Corvette Sting Ray Convertible sans top.

Corvette Convertible with folding soft top.

Convertible with vinyl covered removable hardtop you can order.

Hide-A-Way windshield wiper-washer system closed . . . and open.

Uncap it! The Corvette Convertible takes the same basic Sting Ray idea with the lid off and turns in top-down driving for two. And there are three different ways to put the top on it. Soft top (in black, white or beige) or removable hardtop – pick either one as standard or order them together at extra cost. Black vinyl covering clads the hard one if specified.

There's a big story in glass for the '68 Corvette Convertible. Like the Coupe, and like Corvettes since '53, a rustless fiber glass body is basic. Full door glass styling aids visibility as well as appearance and the Convertible's removable hardtop has a glass rear window for the first time. The basic idea is good looks.

Both the Coupe and Convertible start off with a 300-hp Turbo-Fire 327 V8 standard along with a fully synchronized 3-Speed box. Four other engines are available, and with 427 V8's there's a special high-domed hood. Additional transmission choices are 4-Speed, close-ratio 4-Speed and Turbo Hydra-Matic – which breaks into the Corvette power team lineup this year.

For comfort, air flows through Corvette with full door windows closed, thanks to the new Astro Ventilation system with vent-ports in the driver and passenger sides of the instrument panel. For protection, there are safety features like never before (some are listed on page 11). For long-lasting good looks, choose from ten Magic-Mirror finishes. *Corvette '68 . . . all different all over.*

4

RIGHT *Unlike the Sting Ray, the new coupe would not be a true closed vehicle. The body design allowed for two roof panels and the rear window to be removed making it close to a convertible.*

Corvette simulated wood steering wheel and instrumentation.

Three-section stowage compartment behind the seats.

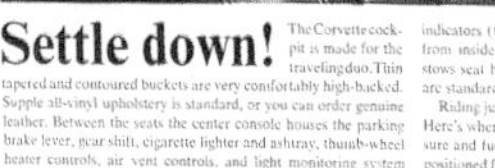

Settle down! The Corvette cockpit is made for the traveling duo. Thin tapered and contoured buckets are very comfortably high-backed. Supple all-vinyl upholstery is standard, or you can order genuine leather. Between the seats the center console houses the parking brake lever, gear shift, cigarette lighter and ashtray, thumb-wheel heater controls, air vent controls, and light monitoring system indicators (to check operation of important outside running lights from inside through space-age fiber optics). The console also stows seat belt buckle straps—twin sets with pushbutton buckles are standard. Coupe equipment also includes twin shoulder belts.

Riding just above the console is the recessed instrument cluster. Here's where the engine tale is told. Water temperature, oil pressure and fuel gauges along with an ammeter and rally clock are positioned for easy reading. Windshield wiper-washer controls are also in console. And if you order an AM/FM radio—available with or without FM Stereo multiplex—controls are mounted here horizontally. Joining in are new features like door ajar flasher and seat belt reminder light. Directly in front of the driver are the speedometer, tachometer, trip odometer, light controls, ignition lock, high beam indicator, turn signal indicator, brake system warning light—and a 3-spoke steering wheel that looks like wood.

Luxurious deep-twist carpeting looks and feels great. It even floors the luggage area behind the seats. Also back there is a stowage area housing the battery, one for the jack and tools and a glove box with pushbutton key lock.

There's a great deal more to like inside Corvette. One small example is a new ignition alarm system to remind you to take the key when you leave the car. It's activated when driver's door is opened with the key in "accessory" or "off" ignition position. *The Corvette interior . . . most luxurious and sporty ever.*

6

7

Shown on cover: Corvette Sting Ray Coupe

Corvette Sting Ray Coupe with roof sections in place.

Two-piece removable roof section.

Detachable glass rear window.

There's a special hood for 427's.

Go hardtop! The Corvette Sting Ray is for those who appreciate the true sports kind of car – and even for those who don't right now. It's that special kind of an automobile that comes along about once every generation to totally arrest the imagination of car buffs. In 15 years of Corvettes the car has not only driven into prominence in the sports car field, but has also been a forerunner of some exciting and practical automobile innovation. For 1968, the mechanics of Sting Ray have been improved and refined (it's still basically made for people who feel that the best part of living is driving), and this, obviously, is a most inspiring year for design.

Consider: the '68 Sting Ray Coupe is a hardtop and more. Uncommon removable sections over pilot and navigator lift out for open air moving. A nearly vertical glass rear window tucks out of the way into a neat compartment in the luggage area. The effect is a flow-through cochère roof that's never been seen on an American production sports car until now.

Long, low profile with blunt styling brings up the rear per the continental GT tradition. The aerodynamic design features a spoiler back there, too. Behind front wheels, functional louvers help keep the horses cool. Wraparound front and rear bumpers plus line-smoothing hideaway features help make Corvette a trim one style-wise. On the nose end, vacuum-operated headlights glide open automatically when lights are turned on. Windshield wipers aren't around when they shouldn't be. They're hidden under a power-operated panel which actuates when wipers are turned on or off. Below beltline, wheel trim rings and center caps cover big 7-inch-wide wheels. Special tuck-in treatment goes to the bright metal body sill between the wheels as you can see. Front and rear marker lights add a special touch to the Corvette from the sidelines. *Corvette Sting Ray Coupe . . . a driving new design.*

Consult your Chevrolet Dealer regarding specific availability of the Corvette Sting Ray Coupe, start of production of which will be a little later. There are a number of Corvette extra-cost Options and Custom Features featured throughout this book. For a complete rundown see Page 11.

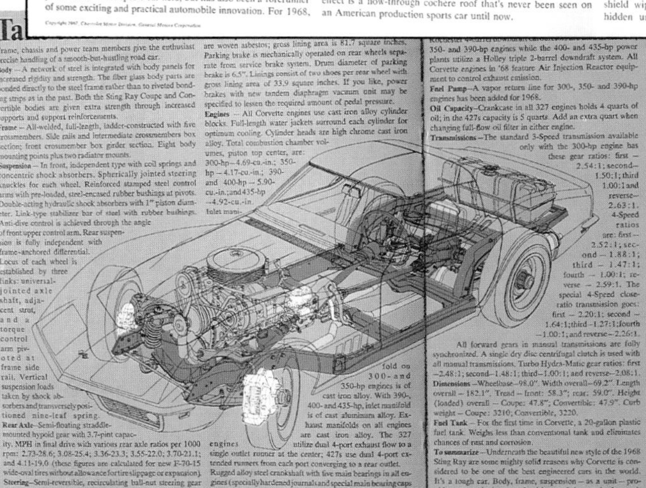

Ta

Frame, chassis and power team members give the enthusiast precise handling of a smooth-but-hustling road car.

Body – A network of steel is integrated with body panels for increased rigidity and strength. The fiber glass body parts are bonded directly to the steel frame rather than to riveted bonding strips as in the past. Both the Sting Ray Coupe and Convertible bodies are given extra strength through increased supports and support reinforcements.

Frame – All-welded, full-length, ladder-constructed with five crossmembers. Side rails and intermediate crossmembers box section; front crossmember box girder section. Eight body mounting points plus two radiator mounts.

Suspension – In front, independent type with coil springs and concentric shock absorbers. Spherically jointed steering knuckles for each wheel. Reinforced stamped steel control arms with pre-loaded, steel-encased rubber bushings at pivots. Double-acting hydraulic shock absorbers with 1" piston diameter. Link-type stabilizer bar of steel with rubber bushings. Anti-dive control is achieved through the angle of front upper control arm. Rear suspension is fully independent with frame-anchored differential. Locus of each wheel is established by three links: universal-jointed axle shaft, adjacent strut, and a torque control arm pivoted at frame side rail. Vertical suspension loads taken by shock absorbers and transversely positioned nine-leaf spring.

Rear Axle – Semi-floating straddle-mounted hypoid gear with 3.7-pint capacity. MPH in final drive with various rear axle ratios per 1000 rpm: 2.73-28.6; 3.08-25.4; 3.36-23.3; 3.55-22.0; 3.70-21.1; and 4.11-19.0 (these figures are calculated for new F-70-15 wide-oval tires without allowance for tire slippage or expansion).

Steering – Semi-reversible, recirculating ball-nut steering gear with GM-developed energy absorbing column. Steering damper between frame and relay rod mounted on the tie rod. Dual-mounting steering arm tie rod connection permits a choice between street or fast ratio. Turning diameter curb to curb – 39.9 ft. Number of turns lock to lock with street steering – 3.4; fast – 2.92. Power steering is a pump-powered hydraulic cylinder assisting the parallelogram linkage. Number of turns lock to lock with power steering – 2.92.

Brakes – First American production car to use disc brakes at all four wheels. Dual circuit master cylinder with warning light. are woven asbestos; gross lining area is 81.7 square inches. Parking brake is mechanically operated on rear wheels separate from service brake system. Drum diameter of parking brake is 6.5". Linings consist of two shoes per rear wheel with gross lining area of 33.9 square inches. If you like, power brakes with new tandem diaphragm vacuum unit may be specified to lessen the required amount of pedal pressure.

Engines – All Corvette engines use cast iron alloy cylinder blocks. Full-length water jackets surround each cylinder for optimum cooling. Cylinder heads are high chrome cast iron alloy. Total combustion chamber volumes, piston top center, are: 300-hp—4.69-cu.-in.; 350-hp – 4.17-cu.-in.; 390- and 400-hp – 5.90-cu.-in.; and 435-hp – 4.92-cu.-in. Inlet manifold on 300- and 350-hp engines is of cast iron alloy. With 390-, 400- and 435-hp, inlet manifold is of cast aluminum alloy. Exhaust manifolds on all engines are cast iron alloy. The 327 engines utilize dual 4-port exhaust flow to a single outlet runner at the center; 427s use dual 4-port extended runners from each port converging to a rear outlet. Rugged alloy steel crankshaft with five main bearings in all engines (specially hardened journals and special main bearing caps with four bolt attachment per cap in 435-hp version). Crank arm length: 327–1.625; 427–1.88. There are 6 counterweights on all cranks. Rubber mounted inertia torsional damper. Steel sprocket and chain timing gear. Camshaft in all engines is cast iron alloy with 5 steel-backed babbitt bearings. Valve train in each engine includes stamped individually mounted overhead rocker arms, push rods actuated with hydraulic lifters (except the 435-hp which has solid lifters). Intake valves are steel alloy. Overall head diameter of intake valves in 300-hp engine is 1.935-1.945; 350-hp–2.017-2.023; 390- and 400-hp mills

350- and 390-hp engines while the 400- and 435-hp power plants utilize a Holley triple 2-barrel downdraft system. All Corvette engines in '68 feature Air Injection Reactor equipment to control exhaust emission.

Fuel Pump – A vapor return line for 300-, 350- and 390-hp engines has been added for 1968.

Oil Capacity – Crankcase in all 327 engines holds 4 quarts of oil; in the 427s capacity is 5 quarts. Add an extra quart when changing full-flow oil filter in either engine.

Transmissions – The standard 3-Speed transmission available only with the 300-hp engine has these gear ratios: first – 2.54:1; second – 1.50:1; third 1.00:1 and reverse – 2.63:1. 4-Speed ratios are: first – 2.52:1; second – 1.88:1; third – 1.47:1; fourth – 1.00:1; reverse – 2.59:1. The special 4-Speed close-ratio transmission goes: first – 2.20:1; second – 1.64:1; third – 1.27:1; fourth – 1.00:1; and reverse – 2.26:1.

All forward gears in manual transmissions are fully synchronized. A single dry disc centrifugal clutch is used with all manual transmissions. Turbo Hydra-Matic gear ratios: first – 2.48:1; second – 1.48:1; third – 1.00:1; and reverse – 2.08:1.

Dimensions – Wheelbase – 98.0". Width overall – 69.2". Length overall – 182.1". Tread – front: 58.3"; rear: 59.0". Height (loaded) overall – Coupe: 47.8"; Convertible: 47.9". Curb weight – Coupe: 3210; Convertible, 3220.

Fuel Tank – For the first time in Corvette, a 20-gallon plastic fuel tank. Weighs less than conventional tank and eliminates chances of rust and corrosion.

To summarize – Underneath the beautiful new style of the 1968 Sting Ray are some mighty solid reasons why Corvette is considered to be one of the best engineered cars in the world. It's a tough car. Body, frame, suspension – as a unit – provide an empathy between the driver and the terrain that can't really be appreciated until you "do it" yourself. Power teams can be tailored to your inclinations. Having disc brakes all around wraps up the total Corvette package very smartly. And for this year a refined rear suspension with a lower rear roll center, plus a lower center of gravity – combined with the reduced camber effect resulting from wider 7" rims and wide-oval tires – *adds* to the already proven handling potential of America's only true production sports car. Outside, inside and deep down, the '68 Corvette Sting Ray is a special way to go.

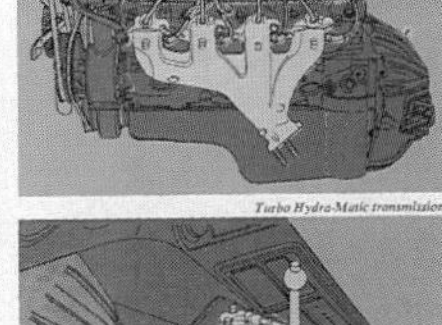

Turbo Hydra-Matic transmission

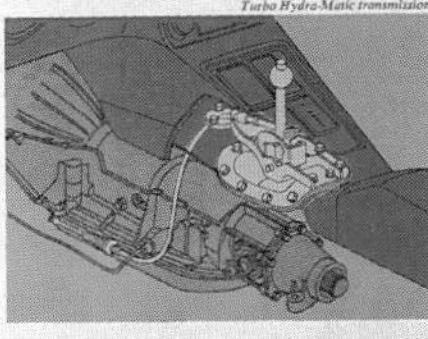

1968 Corvette Power Teams

Engine Bore & Stroke	HP & Torque at RPM	Carb. & Induction	Comp. Ratio	Cam & Lifters	Transmission	Axle Ratios Std.	Axle Ratios Opt.*
Standard Engine							
327-cu.-in. Turbo-Fire V8 4.00 x 3.25	300 @ 5000; 360 @ 3400	4-Barrel; High-Flow	10.0:1	General Performance; Hydraulic	3-Speed (2.54:1 Low); 4-Speed (2.52:1 Low)	3.36:1	3.08:1
					Turbo Hydra-Matic	3.08:1*	—
Extra-Cost Engines							
327-cu.-in. Turbo-Fire V8 4.00 x 3.25	350 @ 5800; 360 @ 3600	4-Barrel; High-Flow	11.0:1	High Performance; Hydraulic	4-Speed (2.52:1 Low)	3.36:1	3.55:1
					Special 4-Speed (2.20:1 Low)	3.70:1	4.11:1
427-cu.-in. Turbo-Jet V8 4.251 x 3.76	390 @ 5400; 460 @ 3600	4-Barrel; High-Flow	10.25:1	High Performance; Hydraulic	4-Speed (2.52:1 Low)	3.08:1*	3.36:1
					Special 4-Speed (2.20:1 Low)	3.36:1*	3.08:1; 3.55:1; 3.70:1
					Turbo Hydra-Matic	3.08:1*	2.73:1
427-cu.-in. Turbo-Jet V8 4.251 x 3.76	400 @ 5400; 460 @ 3600	Triple 2-Barrel; High-Flow	10.25:1	High Performance; Hydraulic	4-Speed (2.52:1 Low)	3.08:1*	3.36:1
					Special 4-Speed (2.20:1 Low)	3.36:1*	3.08:1; 3.55:1; 3.70:1
					Turbo Hydra-Matic	3.08:1*	2.73:1
427-cu.-in. Turbo-Jet V8 4.251 x 3.76	435 @ 5800; 460 @ 4000	Triple 2-Barrel; High-Flow	11.0:1	Special Performance; Mechanical	Special 4-Speed (2.20:1 Low)	3.55:1*	3.36:1; 3.70:1; 4.11:1

*Available only with Positraction. All engines available with air conditioning except 435-hp. All axle ratios available with air conditioning except 3.08:1 with standard engine and Turbo Hydra-Matic.

LEFT *The idea of removable T-Tops, as they came to be called, would inspire designers for decades to come. As convertibles became more rare, cars were offered with the T-top option. Unfortunately, the 1968 T-Top Corvette was plagued with rain leaks and the car overall got very poor marks for workmanship. The post mortem verdict was that Chevrolet tried to cram too many new features into the Corvette all at once. Serial numbers in 1968 ran from 400001 to 428566. Coupes carried the prefix 194378S, and convertibles were designated 194678S.*

LEFT *High-horsepower engines were at the heart of the Corvette for 1968. The catalogue listed three versions of the 427 V8 and a smart buyer could order the race-bred L-88 version if they knew the right code, since it was not mentioned in a brochure. Fewer than 100 were built. Also new to the line-up was the three-speed Turbo Hydramatic automatic transmission, which was a quantum improvement over the Powerglide that had been with the Corvette since its debut in 1953.*

RIGHT *In addition to the plethora of factory-installed options, Chevrolet dealers had additional options they could offer a Corvette buyer in 1968 from floor mats to luggage racks.*

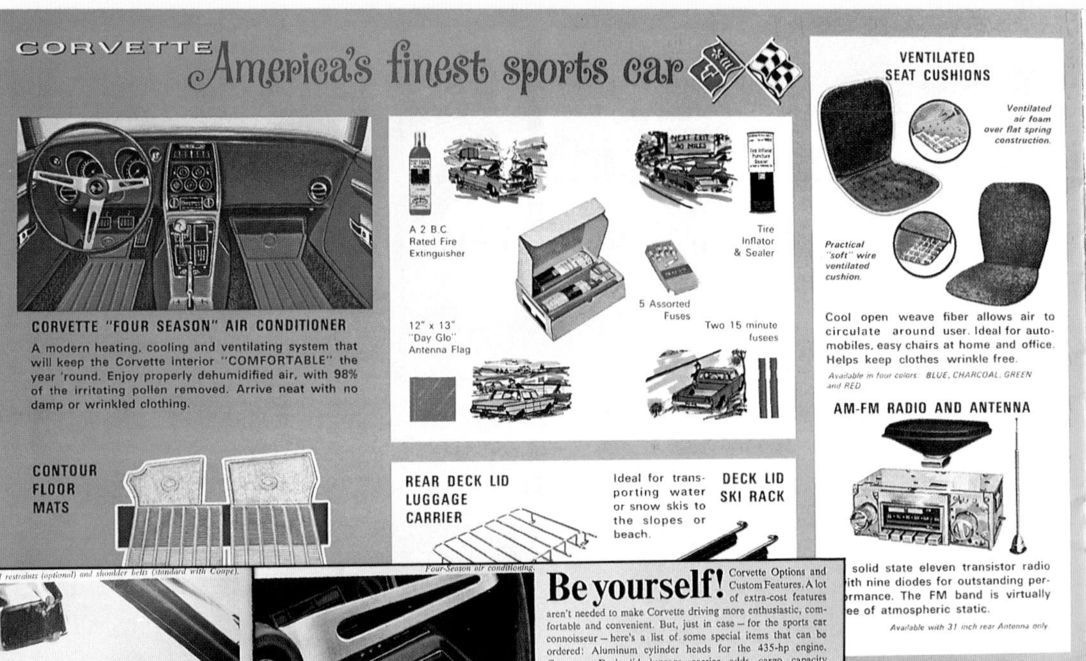

CORVETTE America's finest sports car
CORVETTE "FOUR SEASON" AIR CONDITIONER
A modern heating, cooling and ventilating system that will keep the Corvette interior "COMFORTABLE" the year 'round. Enjoy properly dehumidified air, with 98% of the irritating pollen removed. Arrive neat with no damp or wrinkled clothing.
A 2 B C Rated Fire Extinguisher
Tire Inflator & Sealer
5 Assorted Fuses
12" x 13" "Day Glo" Antenna Flag
Two 15 minute fusees
CONTOUR FLOOR MATS
REAR DECK LID LUGGAGE CARRIER
Ideal for transporting water or snow skis to the slopes or beach.
DECK LID SKI RACK
VENTILATED SEAT CUSHIONS
Ventilated air foam over flat spring construction.
Practical "soft" wire ventilated cushion.
Cool open weave fiber allows air to circulate around user. Ideal for automobiles, easy chairs at home and office. Helps keep clothes wrinkle free.
Available in four colors: BLUE, CHARCOAL, GREEN and RED
AM-FM RADIO AND ANTENNA
solid state eleven transistor radio
diodes for outstanding per-
The FM band is virtually
of atmospheric static.
Available with 31 inch rear Antenna only
AUTO COMPASS
LOCKING GASOLINE TANK CAP
Prevents gasoline from being contaminated or siphoned from the tank.

Strato-ease head restraints (optional) and shoulder belts (standard with Coupe).

4-Speed fully synchronized transmission.

Special wheel covers and nylon red-stripe tires.

Four-Season air conditioning.

AM/FM radio.

Power windows.

Be yourself! Corvette Options and Custom Features. A lot of extra-cost features aren't needed to make Corvette driving more enthusiastic, comfortable and convenient. But, just in case – for the sports car connoisseur – here's a list of some special items that can be ordered: Aluminum cylinder heads for the 435-hp engine. Compass. Deck lid luggage carrier adds cargo capacity and sporty looks. Deck lid ski carrier. Deluxe shoulder belts for the Convertible (standard with the Coupe). Emergency road kit with fire extinguisher, tire inflator and sealer, trouble flag, two flares, assorted fuses. Optional engines: 350-hp Turbo-Fire 327 V8; 390-, 400- or 435-hp Turbo-Jet 427 V8 (Special high-domed hood is included when 427-cu.-in. engine is specified). Fire extinguisher. Floor mats of clear vinyl to keep deep-twist carpeting looking new. Folding vinyl-coated soft top for Convertible (black is standard, beige and white available). Four-Season air conditioning, built into Corvette's heater-defroster system, cleans, dehumidifies and blends air to the temperature you desire. Full-transistor ignition system (not available with 300-hp Turbo-Fire 327 V8). Gas cap lock. Hand portable spotlight. Strato-ease head restraints. Genuine leather seat trim. Off-road exhaust system. Positraction rear axle, on slippery or irregular surfaces, sends power to the wheel that has the most traction. Power brakes to reduce braking effort about one-third. Power steering to assist in handling corners and twisting roads. Power windows. Pushbutton AM/FM radio with twin speakers and fixed height rear antenna. Rear window defroster. Removable hardtop for Convertible (may be specified as standard in lieu of folding convertible top). Special purpose front and rear suspension with 435-hp engine. Speed warning indicator – determine your speed limit and set control, then buzz reminds you when you exceed pre-set speed. Special bright metal wheel covers. FM Stereo multiplex. Adjustable steering column for individual driving comfort. Soft-Ray tinted window glass and/or windshield. Transmissions: 4-Speed fully synchronized (2.52:1 low); special 4-Speed fully synchronized close-ratio (2:20:1 low); Turbo Hydra-Matic which operates automatically unless you want to shift it – through three forward gears up to 65 mph. Black vinyl covering for removable hardtop. Visor vanity mirror. Nylon cord wide-oval red stripe or white stripe tires.

Safety Features Standard for the 1968 Corvette: Energy-absorbing steering column; Seat belts with pushbutton buckles for driver and passenger positions; Shoulder belts for driver and passenger with pushbutton buckles and convenient stowage provision on the Coupe; Passenger-guard door locks; Four-way hazard warning flasher; Dual master cylinder brake system with warning light and corrosion-resistant brake lines; Latches on folding seat backs; Dual-speed windshield wipers and washer; Outside rearview mirror; Back-up lights; New side marker lights and parking lights that illuminate with headlights; Padded instrument panel, sun visors, windshield pillars; Reduced-glare instrument panel top, inside windshield moldings, horn button, steering wheel hub, and windshield wiper arms and blades; Inside day-night mirror with deflecting base; Lane-change feature in direction signal control; Safety armrests; Thick-laminate windshield; Soft, low-profile window control knobs; Yielding window control handles; Energy-absorbing instrument panel; Tire safety rim; Safety door latches and hinges; Uniform shift quadrant; Snag-resistant steering wheel hardware; Fuel tank and filler pipe security.

10 11

LEFT *Corvette's interior was all-new for 1968 and it sported high-back bucket seats that contained integral shoulder harnesses. Also, the catalogue mentions a fibre-optic system that monitored the exterior lights.*

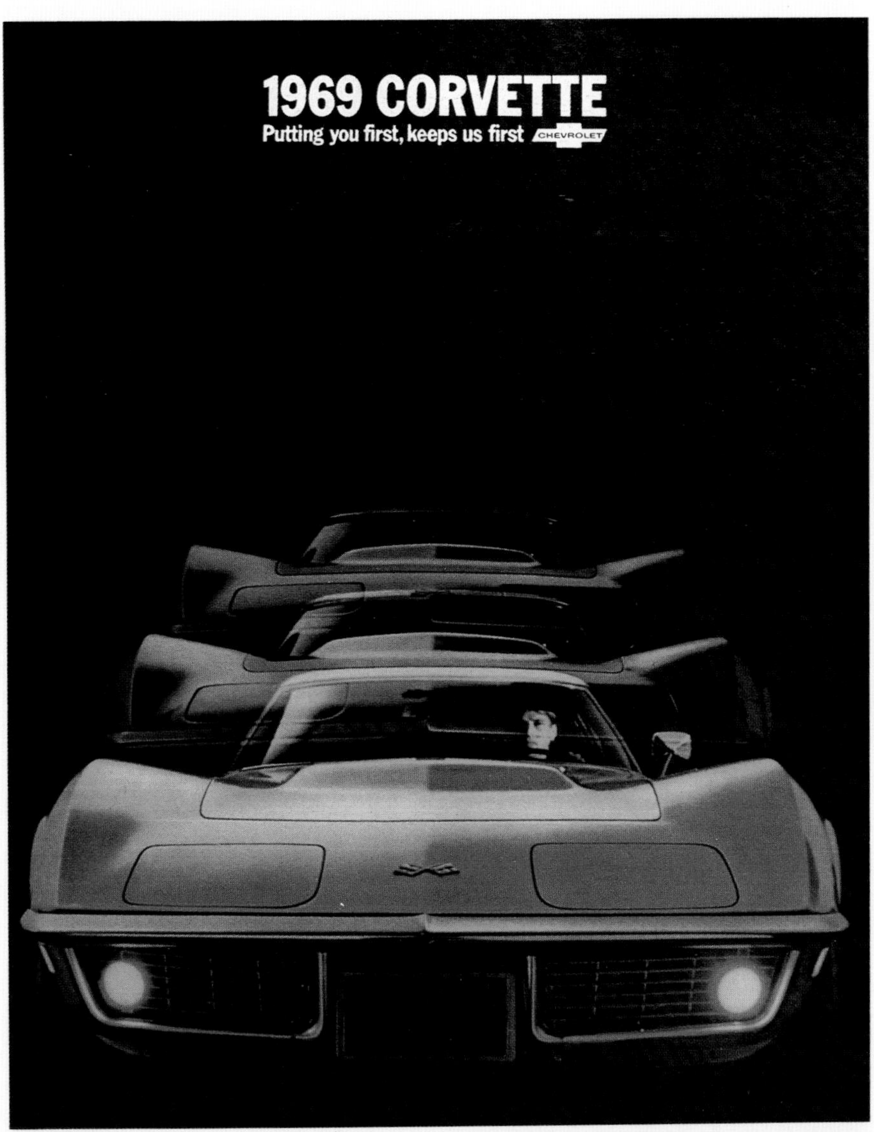

1969 CORVETTE
Putting you first, keeps us first
CHEVROLET

LEFT *When the 1969 Corvette was unveiled, it was still growing in popularity, thanks to the redesign a year earlier. Changes to the exterior were minimal, with the most noticeable being the reappearance of the designation Stingray, now as one word instead of the two that appeared on the car between 1963 and 1967. Elsewhere, there were some changes made to the side fender vents and the door handles were redesigned. Inside, more shoulder room was made available through redesigned door panels and the steering wheel shrank an inch in diameter.*

LEFT *As proof of the Corvette's popularity, a record 38,762 were sold in 1969 – a mark that would stand for seven years. Serial numbers ran from 700001 to 738762, with coupes carrying the prefix 194379S and roadsters getting the designation 194679S. Coupes outsold convertibles for the first time, 22,154 to 16,608. That trend continues today.*

The aerodynamic lines of America's original sports car make it the one automobile nobody mistakes for anything else. In Coupe or Convertible this is the genuine article, designed and engineered without compromise. Corvette stands proudly alone, because nobody but Chevrolet can turn out a car like this on a production line.
And it's as honest as it is beautiful. As you've learned to expect, Corvette goes, stops and handles like nothing else. The basic engine this year is a very healthy 350 CID 300-hp V8 (plenty enough for most, but if you like, you can order one with up to 435-hp). Of course, Corvette is still the stopper, too, with disc brakes at all four wheels. Road-grabbing 15-inch wide ovals plus new 8-inch wide wheels and wider tread give Stingray a better grip . . . and an even bolder appearance. Other subtle but significant refinements include a stronger, more rigid frame for improved ride and handling, new maximum security 3-way locking system on the steering column and unique headlight washers that even clean in motion with jets of water.
Shown here are the ways you can get it: Coupe with removable hardtop sections; Convertible with soft top or removable hardtop. For a more complete list of Corvette extra-cost Options and Custom Features illustrated or described throughout this book, see Page 11.
Corvette Stingray Coupe.
Coupe with roof sections removed.
Convertible with top down.
Vinyl-covered removable hardtop.
Headlight washers.
CORVETTE

RIGHT *New to the engine compartment was the 350 cubic-inch V8, the last enlargement of the Chevrolet small block engine. It came in 300 and 350 horsepower versions and it would be the workhorse engine throughout the 1970s. Also new in 1969 were low-profile tyres, called 'Wide Ovals', and 8-inch-wide wheels to accommodate the new rubber.*

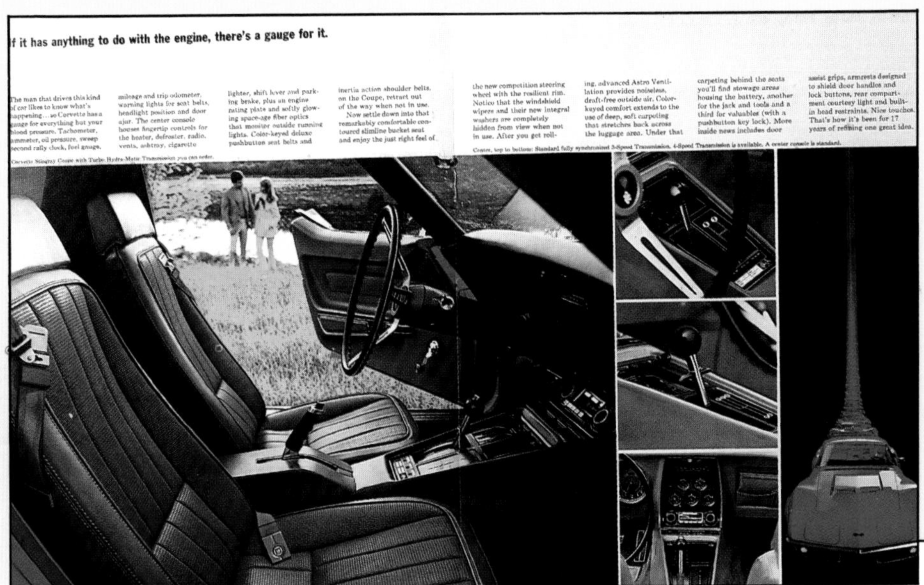

LEFT *The new interior introduced in 1968 carried over largely intact except for some noticeable efforts to improve interior room through slimmer door panels. As a reminder of what a particular Corvette had under the hood, an engine rating plate was affixed to the centre console, just below the shift lever.*

BELOW *As the decade closed, Chevrolet was selling in its Corvette brochures the theme that it could be both a sports car and a touring car. 'It's just a useless old idea about sports cars being generally uncomfortable,' says the catalogue. As the power of the Corvette dropped in the 1970s, the luxury would have to rise. But in 1969, a customer could order both a luxurious and powerful Corvette.*

RIGHT *Model year 1969 would be the last year for the 427 V8, which could be had in a variety of power-transmission combinations, though the use of air-conditioning with the big blocks was limited. Interestingly, the catalogue now mentions the L-88 option, though it points out it's for off-road use. Another 427 that didn't make any catalogue was the all-aluminium ZL-1. Producing more than 600 horsepower, only two ZL-1 Corvettes were built and sold to special customers.*

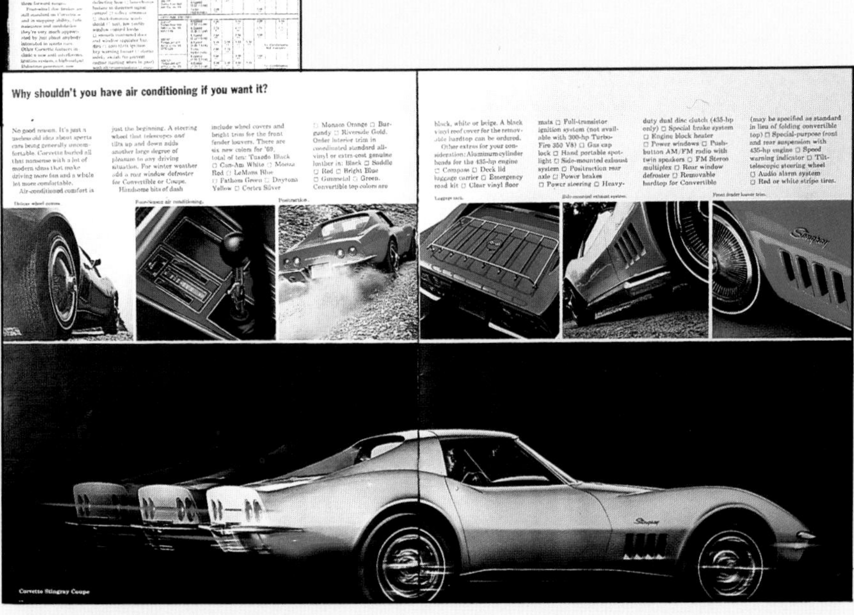

CHAPTER 3
THE 1970S: A DECADE OF CHALLENGES

Mission Control Center '70.

Cape Kennedy hasn't got anything on us. Corvette's cockpit is as heavy on instrumentation as it is on comfort.

First, you sit yourself down in one of the high-backed contoured bucket seats featuring our new integrated head restraints. The shoulder belts (standard on coupe) are guided through a slot in each seatback for neat, secure positioning.

You rest your feet on soft carpeting that not only stretches wall to wall but over the entire rear stowage area with its hidden compartments for valuables, battery and tools.

You check out the central command console before your countdown. Tach, ammeter, water temp, oil pressure, fuel gauge, brake warning light, running light monitors—you name it, it's there.

Once under way, you can enjoy Astro Ventilation, which routes outside air in, through your choice of high or low vents. A rear deck vent exhausts stale air, for a constant flow, even with the windows closed.

New for '70 is a Custom Interior you can order with black or saddle leather seats, plush cut-pile carpeting and the rich look of wood on door panels and console.

The standard all-vinyl interior comes in black, saddle, dark brown, dark green, blue and red.

No matter if your mission's only a trip to the drive-in, the interior of the 1970 Corvette is designed to put you in complete control.

Chevrolet Corvette Custom Interior and Tilt-Telescopic steering column.

RIGHT *Corvette literature reflects the oil crisis of the 1970s, with options limited to the luxurious interior.*

Never has there been a more trying time for the automobile industry and the Corvette in particular than the 1970s. As the decade started off, some of the signs of trouble began to appear. Regulations to cut down on automobile emissions also began to cut into engine horsepower. On the Corvette, the 1970s were a time of diminishing results when it came to raw acceleration. At no time during the period did Corvette performance again duplicate that of the awesome models of the 1950s and 1960s. Big-block engines disappeared, and horsepower fell to 165 at the darkest of times.

As almost a throwback to the Corvette's debut, the automatic transmission dominated production, threatening to push the four-speed manual gearbox into extinction. With performance de-emphasized, there was little need for the manual transmission.

Catalogues talked instead about luxury and creature comforts such as air-conditioning, leather seats and stereos. The once lengthy list of options dwindled as engine choices and special performance goodies disappeared.

In styling, the Corvette changed little in the 1970s. The Mako Shark styling, hailed by many as stunning, aged well.

It easily accepted new demands for energy-absorbing bumpers and it received a fresh new look with the addition of a glass fastback in 1978. But in 1975, the Corvette roadster disappeared, due mainly to lower sales and fears about safety standards.

Behind the scenes, the two men who had the most impact on the Corvette – chief stylist William Mitchell and chief engineer Zora Arkus-Duntov – retired from Chevrolet by the late 1970s. They turned over their car to engineer Dave McLellan and stylist Jerry Palmer. Together, these two men struggled to keep the car relevant at the end of the decade while developing a new generation Corvette for the 1980s and beyond.

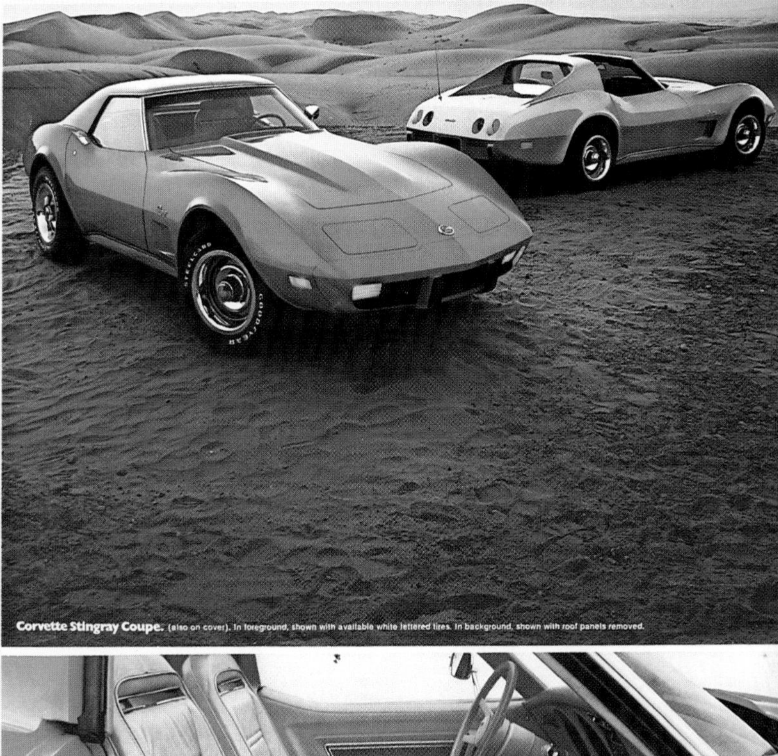

Corvette Stingray Coupe. (also on cover). In foreground, shown with available white lettered tires. In background, shown with roof panels removed.

ABOVE *1976: Little changed in the styling of Corvette exteriors.*

1958-62 Corvette's stylists really began to show their stuff during this period. The '58 'Vette was the first designed with dual headlights. In the cockpit, the horizontal gauge arrangement was replaced by a control panel which put all of the running instruments directly in front of the driver. And a center console was built in between driver and passenger. This feature, along with Corvette's original bucket seats and floor shift, started a trend that has made these items regulars on performance cars.

8

RIGHT *Brochures promoted Corvette history, and emphasized options over performance.*

If there is one bright spot to the 1970s, it is in the fact that the Corvette weathered the decade better than almost all of its competitors. Sales zoomed to record levels, in part because the Corvette was, in many respects, all alone as America's performance car. The hearty sales were also a tribute to the basic spirit of the car, which survived the 1970s and emerged at the other end poised for true automative greatness.

Corvette
EU·9262
Chevrolet. Building a better way to see the U.S.A.

ABOVE *An egg-crate grill design, larger, angular parking lamps and square exhaust tips were the outside changes made to the 1970 Corvette, which appeared in showrooms late due to a strike against General Motors. Under the hood more became less in the Corvette. Although the top engine displaced 454 cubic inches, horsepower was down to 390 in the most popular version. A 460-horsepower version was available, though it was not as wild as previous 427 engines. There was a fiercer version of the 454 cubic-inch engine available though it was not listed in any catalogue. Known by the code LS-7, it was a 454 V8 that produced 465 horsepower through the use of solid lifters and aluminium cylinder heads. Yet this was a competition item, and none are known to have been installed in regular production cars.*

'70 Corvette: Superstructure.

If you respect exquisite machinery, you'll find the new Corvette as beautiful underneath as it is on top. Put one on a hoist and the first thing you see is the frame—two steel side rails running the full length of the body. These are braced with five cross-members into a rigid structure. Corvette's body is then mounted solidly to the frame for increased torsional rigidity.

Corvette's unusually low center of gravity is due partly to the fact that the frame rails run outside of the seating area. And the front/rear weight distribution (47/53% with 350 CID engines) results in benefits in traction, braking and reduced steering effort.

Corvette's front suspension uses upper and lower A-shaped arms, with anti-dive geometry built into the upper control arm. Variable-rate coil springs up front cushion small bumps, yet maintain firm control on rough roads. A hefty front stabilizer bar reduces roll.

Out back is where you find one of Corvette's real handling secrets—a fully independent rear suspension with Positraction rear axle. Its key feature is a transverse-mounted variable-rate leaf spring which soaks up loads from the two axle shafts, which are joined to the differential by universal joints. This design allows each rear wheel to react independently to changes in road surface without affecting the other wheel.

The standard steering ratio is 3.4 turns lock to lock, or you can order Corvette's power steering for even quicker response.

A lot of sports cars may look good on top. None look as refined as Corvette underneath. And it's what's underneath that counts when it comes to performance.

Chevrolet Corvette Stingray Coupe wi

1963-67 The first Stingray came in '63. The fresh new look of its fastback coupe started the fastback trend. Also new were disappearing headlights. Underneath, there was news, too—with the improved handling characteristics of an independent rear suspension. By '65, 4-wheel discs were standard and a prized option became the famed "porcupine head" Turbo-Jet 396-cu.-in. V8. This is basically the same engine you can now order in the Chevelle SS or Camaro SS—two other entries from Chevy's Sports Department.

10

Windshield wipers. Headlights. Door handles. Coupe roof panels. Everything tucks away but the landing gear.

We call the '70 Corvette "Body Beautiful." But it's also an application of pure design—the most extensively aerodynamically tested model we've ever offered.

Every facet of its design, from the front and rear spoilers to the flush-fitting door handles, has been wind-tunnel tested and refined.

For those who have trouble deciding between a coupe and a convertible, we have some alternatives. Every convertible comes with a soft top. You can order a removable hardtop, too. In the coupe model, the roof panels lift off to let the sunshine in. So, any way you work it—you've still got a convertible feel for '70. And no matter which way you go, tinted glass is standard.

Convertible tops can be ordered in white, black or sandalwood, while a grained black vinyl roof cover is available for the convertible's removable hardtop.

For '70, there's a new grille of precision-cast metal. In the outboard corners of the grille, you'll find Corvette's new larger parking lights with their parabolic reflectors.

Complementing the change up front are new chromed louvers and new stainless steel body sill moldings on each side. The hidden headlights come with their own washing system for the outer units. The new look in the rear includes high-visibility taillights and rectangular exhaust extensions.

You'll also notice a flare to the wheelwells on the '70 Corvette for extra body protection from flying stones and debris from the road. Standard tires are F70 x 15 wide-ovals mounted on 8-in.-wide wheels. This combination makes for the best traction, handling and tire mileage characteristics ever offered on Corvette. You can opt for your choice of white lettering or white stripes, too.

Chevrolet Corvette Coupe with roof sections removed.

BELOW *For the first time, the Chevrolet advertising crew began to try to capitalize on the history of the Corvette. This brochure juxtaposes the 1970 Corvette against the original Sting Ray model.*

LEFT *Although the big-block Corvette was on the decline, chief engineer Zora Arkus-Duntov offered in 1970 the option of a high-winding version of the stock 350-cubic-inch V8. Called the LT-1, it produced 370 horsepower using a solid-lifter valve system. It could not be ordered with an automatic transmission or any other comfort items, such as air-conditioning. At $447, it was an option only a few hundred die-hard performance fans chose.*

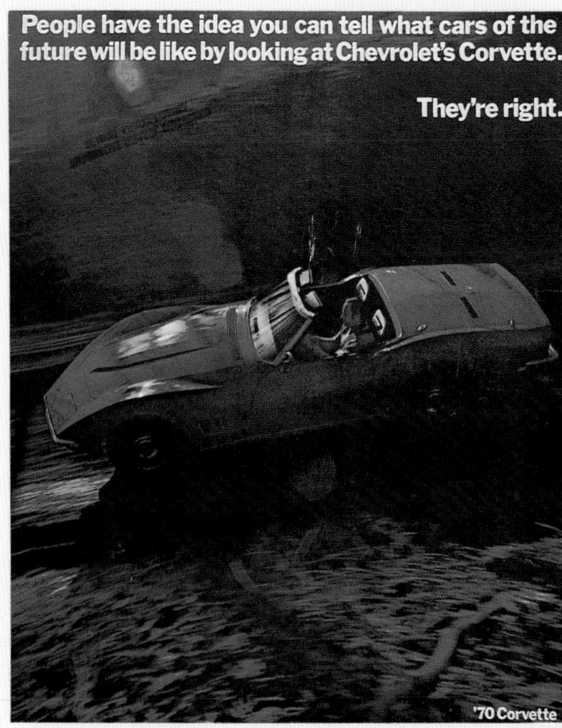

People have the idea you can tell what cars of the future will be like by looking at Chevrolet's Corvette.
They're right.
'70 Corvette

ABOVE *Because of a strike against General Motors, brochures for the 1970 Corvette appeared long before any of the cars did. In fact, 1970 Corvettes did not become generally available until February of 1970, a full three months late. That accounted for the dismal sales figures for that model.*

When you buy a Corvette, you buy a lot more than a

You buy an image.

A car that looks all hood and wheels. A car that's eager for the open road. A car with no compromises like jump seats for the kiddies. A car that says, "I believe in engines and gears and feel of the road." A car whose form follows its function.

You buy a pacesetter. A representation of what could come in automotive design. From the very begin

1970 Chevrolet Corvette Stingray Co

2

vette pioneered. It hasn't stopped. When Chevrolet introduces something new—from disc brakes to a
len headlight system—it usually debuts on Corvette.
ou buy an environment. It's an automobile, sure, but you'll find yourself knowing more about it than
thing you've ever driven. It's got gauges galore for the ultimate in feedback.
uy any other sports car and all you get is today's car. Buy a Corvette and you buy a piece of tomorrow.
YNJ 037
any of the items pictured on these cars are extra-cost Options and Custom Features. For a complete listing, see your dealer.
pyright 1970, Chevrolet Motor Division, General Motors Corporation

LEFT *The convertible remained a popular version of the Corvette, accounting for 6,648 of the 17,316 cars sold that year. Convertibles carried the prefix 194670S, while hardtops carried the prefix 194370S. Serial numbers ran from 400001 to 417316.*

ABOVE *The interior of the 1970 Corvette was decidedly more comfortable than it was in the late 1950s. The catalogues for 1970 boasted about how the seats had been reshaped to give more lateral support and there was the option of fake wood trim on the doors and transmission console. Price for a basic Corvette coupe was $5,192. A convertible cost $4,849.*

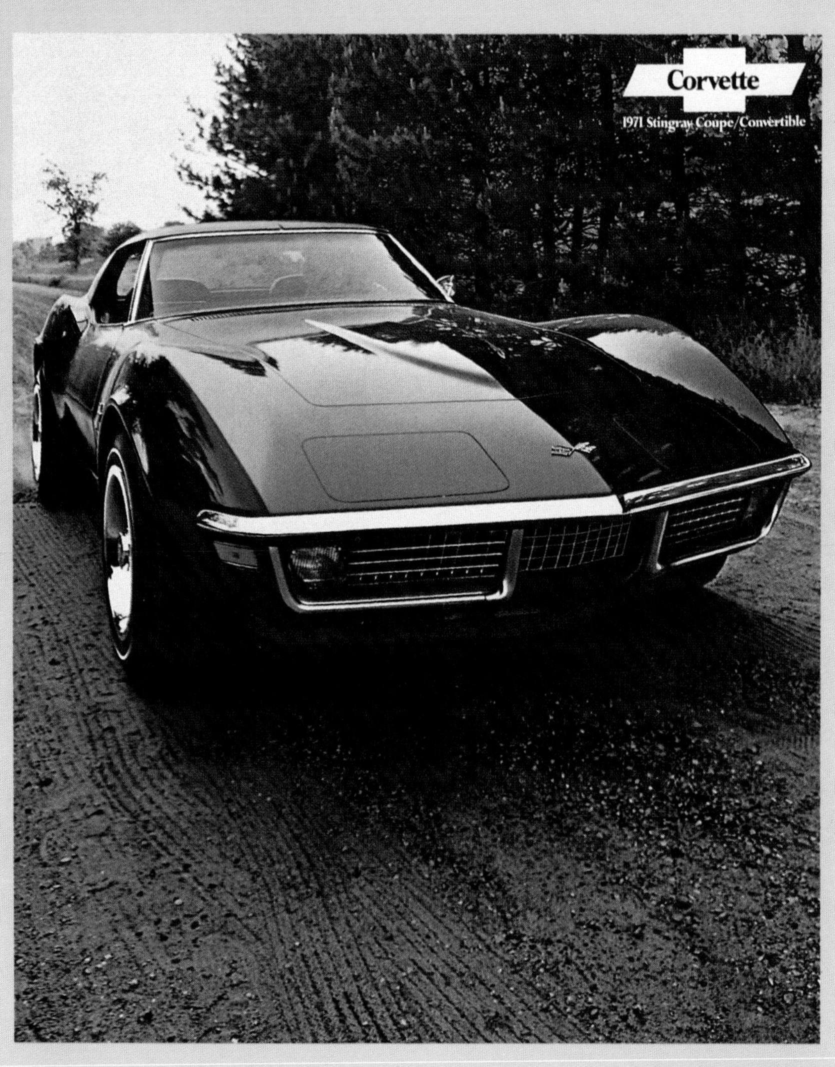

LEFT *Because the labour strike against General Motors shortened the 1970 model year, the 1971 Corvette carried over unchanged on the outside. Also, most of the development money was being spent to bring engines into compliance with new emission laws and develop new safety items that would appear in coming years. Sales, however, rebounded from 1970, to 21,801. Coupes received the serial prefix 194371S, with convertibles tagged 194671S. Serial numbers ran from 100001 to 121801. Basic prices increased in 1971 with the coupe costing $5,536 and the roadster costing $5,299.*

BELOW *A Corvette buyer in 1971 still had a plethora of options to wade through, though the powertrain list was shrinking from its peak in 1969. And the base car was filled with features that did not come on other cars, such as flush door handles, pop-up headlights and lift-off roof panels.*

RIGHT *Chevrolet went to great lengths by the 1971 model year to stress that beauty was more than skin deep on the Corvette. The chassis was as sophisticated as any sports car of the day, with a fully independent suspension in the rear, and upper and lower A-arms up front. Front/rear weight ratio was an optimum 48/52 percent.*

Windshield wipers. Headlights. Door handles. Coupe roof panels. Everything tucks away but the landing gear.
We call the 1971 Corvette "Body Beautiful." But it's also an application of pure design—the most extensively aerodynamically tested model we've ever offered.
Every facet of its design, from the front and rear spoilers to the flush-fitting door handles, has been wind-tunnel tested and refined.
For those who have trouble deciding between a coupe and a convertible, we have some alternatives. Every convertible comes with a soft top. You can order a removable hardtop, too. In the coupe model, the roof panels lift off to let the sunshine in. So, any way you work it—you've still got a convertible feel for 1971. And no matter which way you go, tinted glass is standard.
Convertible tops can be ordered in white or black, while a black vinyl roof cover is available for the convertible's removable hardtop.
And while we're speaking about colors, have you seen our new firemist hues for 1971? Deep, lustrous finishes applied in a way to make the paint look exceedingly rich. With tiny flecks of metallic color that highlight innate Corvette beauty. You can choose firemist colors in Ontario Orange, Steel Cities Gray or War Bonnet Yellow.
The big things we haven't changed. Like Corvette's styling. We've continued those husky-looking larger parking lights. The precision-cast grille. Ditto the chromed louvers and stainless steel body sill moldings, the rectangular exhaust bezels and high visibility taillights.
The body shape stays the same. We like it that way, and you'll like the fender flares that keep stones from pecking away at the paint. Standard tires are F70 x 15 wide ovals mounted on 8"-wide wheels. You get the best traction, handling and tire mileage characteristics ever offered for Corvette. If you like, opt for either white lettering or white stripes.
Chevrolet Corvette Stingray Coupe with roof sections removed.
11

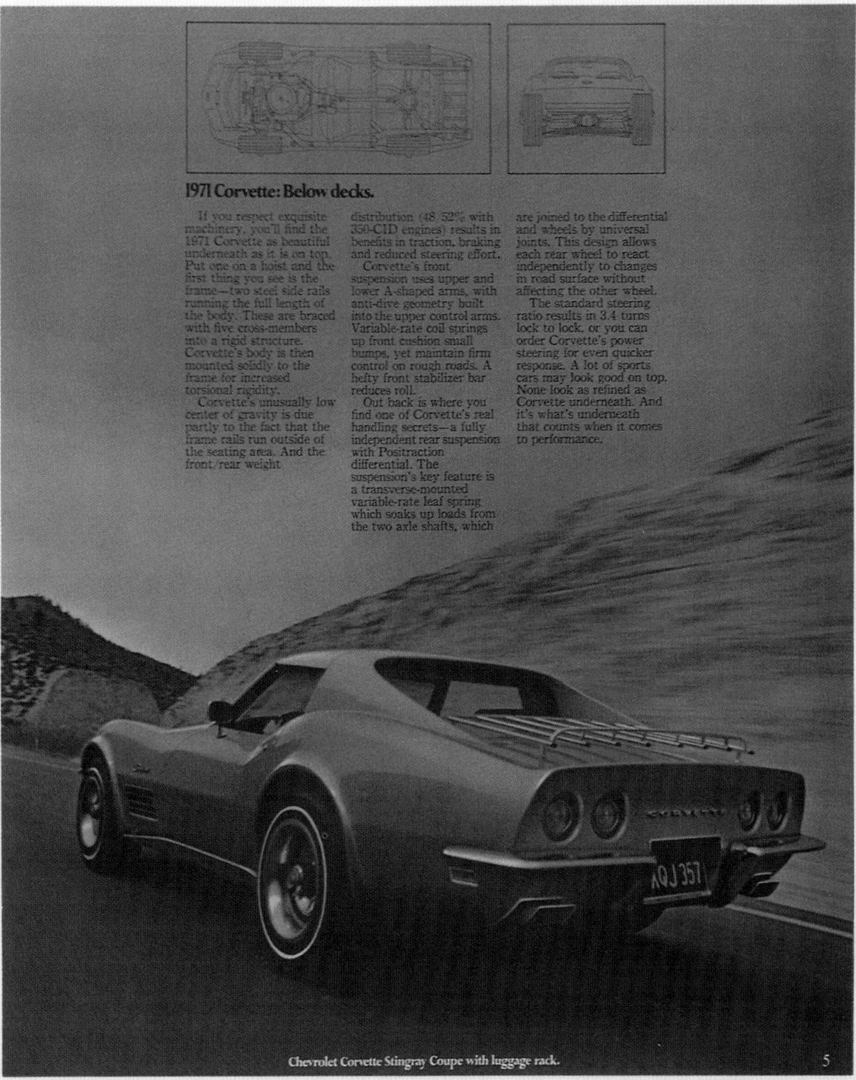

Our Corvette Coupe has two removable roof panels.

Should your choice be a Corvette Coupe, a lot comes with it as standard equipment. Like the two removable roof panels shown in the picture. In addition, the rear window is also removable. With both top sections and the rear window taken out and stowed neatly behind you, the joys of open-air driving are yours. In minutes, both sections can be reinstalled for complete closed-car comfort.

Standard wheels include bright trim rings along with a ribbed center hub on each wheel. A lock, visible on the stern above the name, turns the new standard audio alarm system on and off. When activated, any attempt to force doors or hood open is greeted by a loud, raucous hooting from somewhere under the car. How long does it blast? Until you turn it off or the battery wears down. The Corvette has a very strong battery.

Corvette's fiberglass body features an advanced "low profile" resin for smoother surfaces, and a strong steel "birdcage" surrounding the passenger area. The result is a very rigid structure with less weight than a comparable steel copy.

1972 Corvettes are available in 10 colors, four new: Pewter Silver, Targa Blue, Bryar Blue, Elkhart Green. Plus: Steel Cities Gray, Sunflower Yellow, Mille Miglia Red, Classic White, War Bonnet Yellow, Ontario Orange.

Of the ten, three—Steel Cities Gray, War Bonnet Yellow and Ontario Orange—are firemist colors with metallic flakes in the paint.

Corvette exterior options

Luggage carrier. Many owners like this convenience available from your dealer. Adds to your vacationing pleasure.

We've shown you *white-stripe tires*, which are available; blackwall tires are standard.

Custom wheel covers. Distinctive appearance, available to dress up your wheels.

LEFT *Development money continued to be tight at General Motors and there were no funds to redesign the Corvette in 1972. Although not mentioned in the catalogue, 1972 would be the last year that the rear window on the coupe could be removed.*

The convertible's folding top is standard. The hardtop is well worth the price.
If you've a bent to enjoy driving with nothing but nature around you, the Corvette Convertible must be your choice. In seconds you can unlatch the top, raise the deck lid, drop the top into the compartment and snap the deck cover down without leaving the driver's seat. One person can raise it back, too. The folding top may be ordered in either black or white.
For owners considering a Corvette in colder climes, or if you just like the appearance of the available hardtop, you should specify it. In winter, the hardtop gives you a warm, snug feeling against the icy winds. Saves the folding top, too. You can specify the hardtop with an available black vinyl roof cover.
Like the coupe shown above, the convertible carries the classic bumper, grille and parking light motif forward from previous models.
We've retained the great basic body shape, with fender flares to help protect the paint behind the wheels against the ravages of stones. You survey all you see through Soft-Ray tinted glass. Plus, high visibility taillights, stainless steel body sill moldings, rectangular exhaust bezels and square die-cast body side louvers. Everything works. It all has a purpose. One of the finest driving experiences the Western Hemisphere has to offer, enjoyed the world over.
More exterior options
Removable hardtop. For appearance, extra-snug cold weather driving.
Vinyl roof cover. On the extra-cost hardtop. Black, to accent the top.
Tires. White-stripe or white lettered. Both in F70 x 15 sizes.
Locking gas cap. Non-vented type.
Rear window defroster. Helps keep the back window clear.
Heavy-duty battery. Extra starting power.
Door edge guards. In vinyl to help protect your doors.
Compass. Helps keep you on the straight and narrow.
OOP 635

RIGHT *Convertible sales continued to slip, with the roadster accounting for about a third of overall sales of 26,992. Roadster serial numbers ran from 1Z67K2S500001 to 1Z67K2S506508. Coupe numbers ran from 1Z37K2S500001 to 1Z37K2S520486.*

LEFT *Horsepower numbers were way down in the 1973 Corvette catalogues. The fine print said the lower numbers were net horsepower in which the engine is rated with all the accessories connected. Although a more realistic way of judging power, this helped obscure the fact that emission standards were sapping Corvette engines. The once awesome list of available engines had shrunk to just three. The top 454-cubic-inch engine could only propel the car through the quarter-mile (.402 km) in 15 seconds.*

Exterior Dimensions.

Wheelbase	98"
Length (overall)	184.7"
Width (overall)	69.0"
Height (loaded) Coupe	47.7"
Convertible	47.9"
Tread—Front	58.7"
Tread—Rear	59.5"

Exterior Colors.
Corvette Medium Blue Metallic (New)
Corvette Dark Blue Metallic (New)
Corvette Blue/Green Metallic (New)
Corvette Orange Metallic (New)
Corvette Silver Metallic (New)
Corvette Yellow (New)
Corvette Yellow Metallic (New)
Mille Miglia Red
Elkhart Green
Classic White

Safety and Security Features:

Occupant Protection Features. Single-buckle seat belts and shoulder belts (except convertible) with push-button buckles and retractors for driver and passenger (with reminder light and buzzer). Built-in head restraints. Energy-absorbing steering column. Passenger-guard door locks. Safety door latches and hinges. Folding seat back latches. Energy-absorbing padded instrument panel. Contoured windshield header (except convertible). Thick-laminate windshield. Padded sun visors. Safety armrests. Safety steering wheel. Side-guard beams.

Accident Prevention Features. Side marker lights and reflectors (front side marker lights flash with direction signal). Parking lights that illuminate with headlights. Four-way hazard warning flasher. Backup lights. Lane-change feature in direction signal control. Windshield defroster, washers and dual-speed wipers. Wide-view inside day-night mirror (vinyl-edged, shatter-resistant glass and deflecting support). Outside rearview mirror. Dual master cylinder brake system with warning light. Starter safety switch. Improved bumper system.

Anti-Theft Features. Anti-theft ignition key warning buzzer. Anti-theft steering column lock. Anti-theft audio alarm system.

1973 CORVETTE
Building a better way to see the U.S.A.
STINGRAY COUPE/STINGRAY CONVERTIBLE
Chevrolet

RIGHT *In lieu of genuine performance options, the list of extra-cost goodies ran to stereo sound systems, thicker carpeting and leather seats.*

1. Removable roof panels on the coupe lift off and tuck away in the luggage area to let the sunshine in. Soft-Ray tinted glass is standard on both coupe and convertible models. It's like looking at the world through Corvette-colored glasses.

2. Corvette power teams are known for their efficient performance. For '73, all engines operate on regular, no-lead or low-lead fuels. All feature valve-in-head design and exhaust valve rotators. There's an Air Injection Reactor and new Exhaust Gas Recirculation system. New mufflers are larger for quieter operation. Also included as standard equipment with all power teams: A fully synchronized 4-Speed transmission. Positraction rear axle. Full dual exhaust system. A high-output Delcotron generator. And a sealed side-terminal energizer-type battery.

3. The new stronger front bumper (which surrounds the new die-cast aluminum grille) has a special mounting. The bumper outer cover is the same color as the body and is made of resilient urethane to resist dents and prevent rust.

4. New GR70-15 steel-belted radial ply blackwall tires are standard. White stripe radials are also available. (White lettered radials will be available at mid-year.) Radials run cooler for improved durability. They help give a softer, quieter ride at highway speed.

5. The new domed air induction hood improves high-output engine operation. It hides the wiper blades, too. Just between the hood and the windshield.

6. Corvette's 4-wheel independent suspension includes new shocks and springs to shrug off bumps. Body mounts are new for a smoother, quieter ride with reduced noise, vibration and harshness. Improved acoustical materials and applications make for quieter riding. All in all, the '73 Vette is a "tuned" vehicle. With sound levels that have been reduced.

Also standard: Steel-reinforced fiberglass body. All-welded ladder-type frame. Four-wheel disc brakes. Four-wheel independent suspension. Front and rear air spoilers.

1

2

3

Available Features. You get a lot without asking when you ask for a Corvette. But there's also a lot you can do to custom tailor it. For example:

1. Removable hardtop for convertible models. If you're having trouble deciding between open-air summer fun and buttoned-up winter practicality, why not have the best of both worlds? The available hardtop gives you a warm feeling during cold weather, while you make it easy on your folding top. Neat looking, too. Order to match the exterior color. Or there's an available black vinyl roof cover you can order.

2. Power windows. Let your finger do the window raising and lowering. Switches are mounted on the center console.

3. Custom wheel covers. Distinctive appearance, available to dress up your wheels.

4. Tilt-telescoping steering wheel. Ideal for long trips and drivers of any shape or size. Just get in, flick the lever and slide the wheel in front of you. Then you lock it into any one of seven positions that feels most comfortable.

5. Air conditioning/heating/ventilating system. One of the most sophisticated systems available in any sports car.

6. AM/FM/Stereo radio. Receives FM Stereo broadcasts for long distances with its 16-transistor 9-diode circuitry. AM monaural, plus FM monaural. Two speakers, fixed height rear antenna. Full ignition shielding.

AM/FM radio. Monaural AM and FM. Same features as above, but without FM Stereo.

3-range Turbo Hydra-matic transmission can be ordered with all engines.

Power steering. With fast steering ratio for quick response.

Power brakes. Retain excellent disc brake feel while lessening effort.

Rearview mirror and maplight combination.

Also available, factory installed: Rear window defogger. Heavy-duty battery (included with 454-cu.-in. engine). Custom Deluxe shoulder belts (standard on coupe).

Available from your dealer: Non-vented locking gas cap. Compass. Infant safety carrier. Rear deck luggage carrier. Front antenna. Right-hand mirror. Hand spotlight. Fire extinguisher.

LEFT *Corvette got its first real styling change in five years, thanks to government-mandated safety regulations. New cars in 1973 had to have energy-absorbing front bumpers and the urethane-covered nose on the Corvette did the job nicely. It also looked good. Sales were also good, with more than 30,000 Corvettes sold. Coupe serial numbers ran from 1Z37K3S400001 to 1Z37K3S424372. Convertible numbers ran from 1Z67K3S400001 to 1Z67K3S406093.*

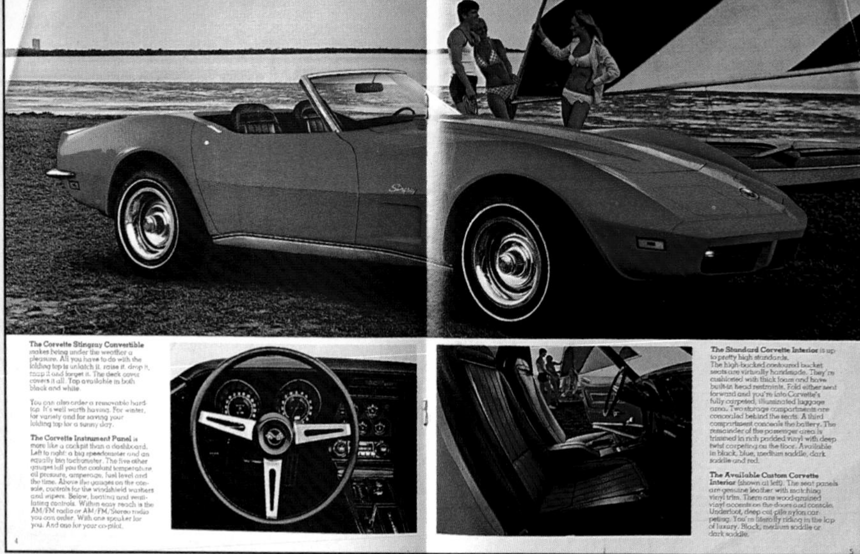

RIGHT *By 1973 the trend was to automatic transmissions in Corvettes. With horsepower for the base engine down to 190, and even the huge 454 V8 down to 275 horsepower, cruising was the primary mission.*

IF YOU ARE CONSIDERING YOUR FIRST CORVETTE...

We know what you feel.

We know what it's like to possess (and be possessed by) a car so exciting to look at that it makes the scene wherever it stops. Or turns heads wherever it goes.

And we know the feeling of a friendly wave of the hand (or flick of the lights) when you meet another Corvette on the road . . . of being a part of a whole new and exciting life style.

We *know* because we've been there.

But there's more. You can't really appreciate a Corvette until you look past the image to the car, itself. So, for the next few pages, we'd like to show you what's behind this dramatically styled car that captivates owners and onlookers alike. To what's outside, inside and underneath that makes Corvette the sought-after sports car it's been for over 20 years.

It's a great trip. Getting to know a Corvette has got to be one of the great pleasures in life.

And anyone who truly loves the road and where it goes deserves that pleasure at least once in his life. Or hers.

IF YOU HAVE ALREADY OWNED A CORVETTE...

Who knows better than you that the basic Corvette formula is too good to mess with. Right?

Relax! The same people who brought you *your* Corvette are still running the store and keeping the faith. The '74 isn't a totally new Corvette, just better.

Take the styling. We wouldn't just change it for the sake of change. But when we made the rear bumper stronger, we made Corvette's entire rear styling look different. And, we think, better. (You can see it beautifully on page 4.)

Take another example. Remember last year? When we tuned the body and chassis for steel belted radials? It made the interior quieter. Quiet enough that the exhaust sounds, which had been a pleasant part of the background, seemed to be too prominent.

So, this year, we did some more tuning—in the dual exhaust system. We added a pair of resonators . . . mini-mufflers. *Voilà!* The '74 Corvette still delivers the growl of performance you know and like, but at a level that now lets you enjoy Corvette's available FM stereo radio to its hilt.

So be reassured. The 1974 Corvette still represents what it set out to be: A car that combines the road-holding and handling qualities of a true sports car with the grace and refinement of a personal luxury car. After all, that's why Corvette is so much in demand. And who would want to change that? Not us. Not you.

ABOVE *The Corvette catalogues in 1974 had changed their tune, from one of all-out performance to civilized yet stylish cruising. A line from the catalogue espousing the new exhaust resonators that enabled the driver to hear the stereo better would have been unthinkable in 1969. Elsewhere, the rear of the car benefited from the energy absorbing bumper rule, giving both ends of the car a nice rounded look.*

STANDARDS

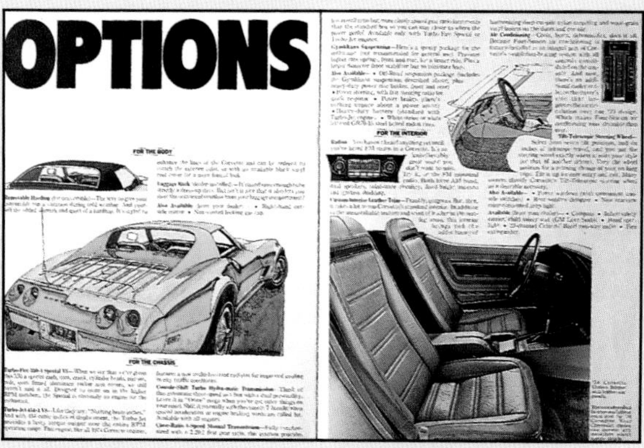
OPTIONS

RIGHT *Though buyers would have had no way of knowing, 1974 was the last year a big-block V8 could be ordered. The 454-cubic-inch V8 was just too thirsty for the energy conscious times.*

ABOVE *The standard equipment list grows in the 1974 Corvette catalogue. An AM-FM radio comes with the basic price of $6,372 for the coupe, $6,156 for the convertible. Coupes were designated 1Z37J4S400001 through 1Z37J4S432028. Roadsters were coded 1Z67J4S400001 through 1Z67J4S404629.*

RIGHT *A smart buyer could find a real bargain on the option list when it came to the Gymkhana Suspension. Code FE7, the option gave the buyer special springs and shock absorbers that dramatically improved handling. It cost $7.*

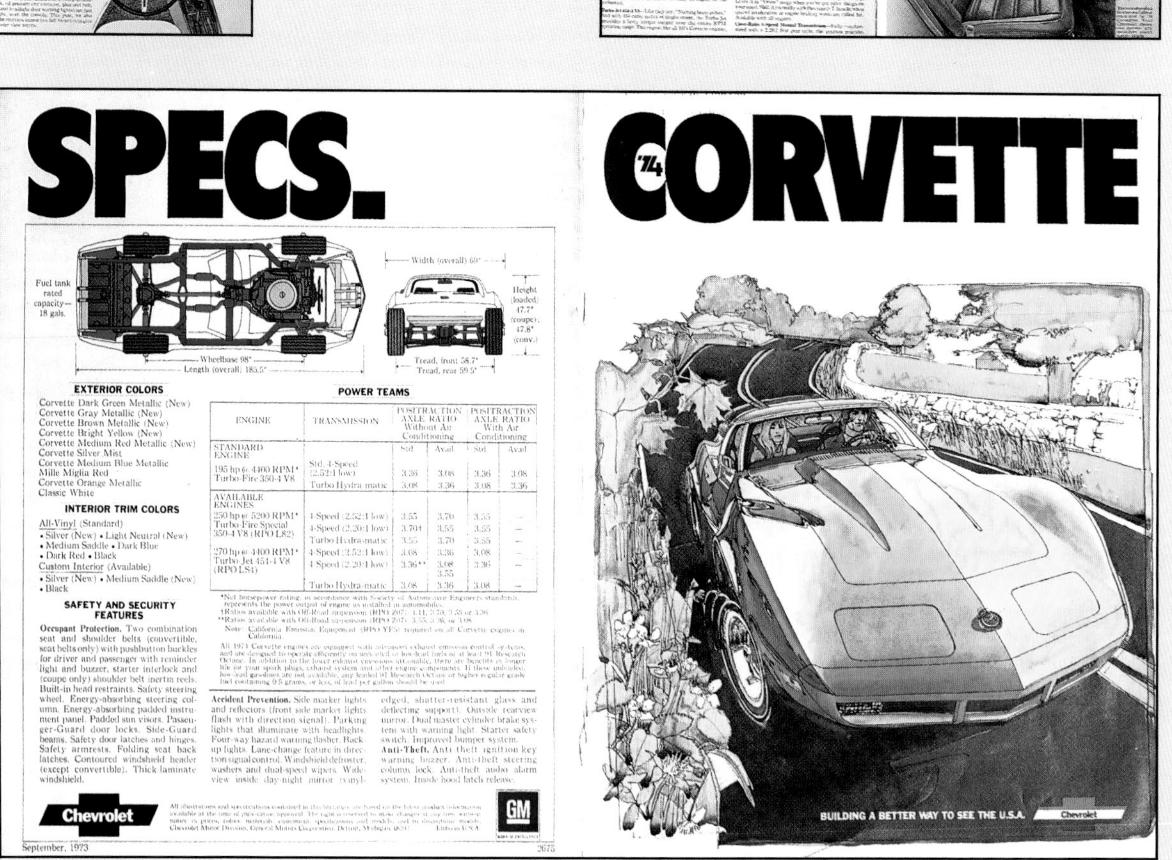

SPECS.

EXTERIOR COLORS

Corvette Dark Green Metallic (New)
Corvette Gray Metallic (New)
Corvette Brown Metallic (New)
Corvette Bright Yellow (New)
Corvette Medium Red Metallic (New)
Corvette Silver Mist
Corvette Medium Blue Metallic
Mille Miglia Red
Corvette Orange Metallic
Classic White

INTERIOR TRIM COLORS

All-Vinyl (Standard)
• Silver (New) • Light Neutral (New)
• Medium Saddle • Dark Blue
• Dark Red • Black

Custom Interior (Available)
• Silver (New) • Medium Saddle (New)
• Black

SAFETY AND SECURITY FEATURES

Occupant Protection. Two combination seat and shoulder belts (convertible, seat belts only) with pushbutton buckles for driver and passenger with reminder light and buzzer, starter interlock and (coupe only) shoulder belt inertia reels. Built-in head restraints. Safety steering wheel. Energy-absorbing steering column. Energy-absorbing padded instrument panel. Padded sun visors. Passenger-Guard door locks. Side-Guard beams. Safety door latches and hinges. Safety armrests. Folding seat back latches. Contoured windshield header (except convertible). Thick laminate windshield.

POWER TEAMS

ENGINE	TRANSMISSION	POSITRACTION AXLE RATIO Without Air Conditioning		POSITRACTION AXLE RATIO With Air Conditioning	
		Std.	Avail.	Std.	Avail.
STANDARD ENGINE 195 hp @ 4400 RPM* Turbo-Fire 350-4 V8	Std. 4-Speed (2.52:1 low)	3.36	3.08	3.36	3.08
	Turbo Hydra-matic	3.08	3.36	3.08	3.36
AVAILABLE ENGINES 250 hp @ 5200 RPM* Turbo-Fire Special 350-4 V8 (RPO L82)	4-Speed (2.52:1 low)	3.55	3.70	3.55	—
	4-Speed (2.20:1 low)	3.70†	3.55	3.55	—
	Turbo Hydra-matic	3.55	3.70	3.55	—
270 hp @ 4400 RPM* Turbo-Jet 454-4 V8 (RPO LS4)	4-Speed (2.52:1 low)	3.08	3.36	3.08	—
	4-Speed (2.20:1 low)	3.36**	3.08 3.55	3.36	—
	Turbo Hydra-matic	3.08	3.36	3.08	—

*Net horsepower rating, in accordance with Society of Automotive Engineers standards, represents the power output of engine as installed in automobiles.
†Ratios available with Off-Road suspension (RPO Z07): 4.11, 3.70, 3.55 or 3.36
**Ratios available with Off-Road suspension (RPO Z07): 3.55, 3.36, or 3.08
Note: California Emission Equipment (RPO YF5) required on all Corvette engines in California.

All 1974 Corvette engines are equipped with advanced exhaust emission control systems, and are designed to operate efficiently on unleaded or low-lead fuels of at least 91 Research Octane. In addition to the lower exhaust emissions attainable, there are benefits in longer life for your spark plugs, exhaust system and other engine components. If these unleaded, low-lead gasolines are not available, any leaded 91 Research Octane or higher regular grade fuel containing 0.5 grams, or less, of lead per gallon should be used.

Accident Prevention. Side marker lights and reflectors (front side marker lights flash with direction signal). Parking lights that illuminate with headlights. Four-way hazard warning flasher. Back-up lights. Lane-change feature in direction signal control. Windshield defroster, washers and dual-speed wipers. Wide-view inside day-night mirror (vinyl-edged, shatter-resistant glass and deflecting support). Outside rearview mirror. Dual master cylinder brake system with warning light. Starter safety switch. Improved bumper system.

Anti-Theft. Anti-theft ignition key warning buzzer. Anti-theft steering column lock. Anti-theft audio alarm system. Inside hood latch release.

Chevrolet

GM

September, 1973

2675

BELOW *In 1975, there were a lot of firsts and lasts. The catalogue now talked about such things as catalytic converters and the mandatory use of unleaded fuel. The only changes to the exterior of the car was the addition of small rubber bumper tips fore and aft. And the 1975 Corvette would be the last of the open cars, with the roadster going away for the next 11 years. Horsepower would also take another nose-dive, with the disappearance of the big-block engine and only one upgraded engine available.*

48.0" (conv.)
58.7"
47.9" (coupe)
59.5"
69.0"
185.2"
98.0"

Interior dimensions.

Head room. . . . 36.2" (coupe) 37.1" (conv.)
Leg room. . . . . . 42.1"
Shoulder room. . . . . . 47.9"
Hip room. . . . . 48.8"

Fuel capacity: 18 gallons.
Battery: 3250 watts, side terminal.

Safety and Security Features.

Occupant Protection. Two combination seat and (coupe only) shoulder belts with pushbutton buckles, reminder light and buzzer, starter interlock and (coupe only) shoulder belt inertia reels. Built-in head restraints. Safety steering wheel. Energy-absorbing steering column. Energy-absorbing padded instrument panel. Padded sun visors. Passenger-guard door locks. Side-guard beams. Safety door latches and hinges. Safety armrests. Folding seat back latches. Contoured windshield header (coupe only). Thick-laminate windshield.

Accident Protection. Side marker lights and reflectors (front side marker lights flash with direction signal). Parking lights that illuminate with headlights. Four-way hazard warning flasher. Back-up lights. Lane-change feature in direction signal control. Windshield defrosters, washers and dual-speed wipers. Wide-view inside day-night mirror (vinyl-edged, shatter-resistant glass and deflecting support). Outside rearview mirror. Dual master cylinder brake system with warning light. Starter safety switch.

Anti-Theft. Anti-theft ignition key reminder buzzer. Anti-theft audio alarm system. Anti-theft steering column lock. Inside hood latch release.

Chevrolet

All illustrations and specifications contained in this literature are based on the latest product information available at the time of publication approval. The right is reserved to make changes at any time without notice in prices, colors, materials, equipment, specifications and models, and to discontinue models. Chevrolet Motor Division, General Motors Corporation, Detroit, Mich. 48202. Litho in U.S.A.

GM
MARK OF EXCELLENCE

September, 1974

3015

Automobiles

CORVETTE '75

Here's this year's version of last year's "Best All-Around Car," as selected by readers of *Car and Driver* magazine. Corvette makes excitement make sense.

CHEVROLET MAKES SENSE FOR AMERICA.

With Corvette, it's hard to know where to start. That's because a Corvette has the ability to become exactly what its owner hopes it will be: A superb road car; a stunning style anywhere; a means to good times, good places, good things. Obviously, we can't hope to discuss all of the many possible Corvettes-to-be. Instead, we can talk about the '75 Corvette only as it is: The exceptional assembly of standard systems, features and available options. From this, we know you'll be able to put together your kind of Corvette.
How are you at building a dream?
CORVETTE
cover and in foreground above: '75 Corvette Stingray Coupe. Background above: '75 Corvette Stingray Convertible. Many Options and Custom
available for Corvette. Some are illustrated or described in this catalog. Copyright 1974, Chevrolet Motor Division, General Motors Corporation.

LEFT *The coupe was the Corvette of choice by 1975. In that year, 33,836 of the coupes would be sold, compared to just 4,629 roadsters. The open car was killed off because of lagging sales and the mistaken notion that federal crash standards would outlaw ragtops.*

ABOVE *Under the hood, the Corvette was hurting in 1975. The base 350-cubic-inch engine produced a measly 165 horsepower, while the optional L-82 managed only 205. Yet the price of the Corvette was still rising. A coupe commanded a basic price of $7,117, up nearly $2,500 from the 1968 Corvette.*

LEFT *A headlight-on warning system and the advent of an electronic ignition system were the big news in the 1975 catalogues. Coupe serial numbers ran from 1Z37J5S400001 to 1Z37J5S433836. Roadsters carried the tag 1Z67J5S400001 through 1Z67J5S404629.*

Corvette Stingray Coupe. (also on cover). In foreground, shown with available white lettered tires. In background, shown with roof panels removed.

LEFT *On the inside, the Corvette got a new steering wheel design but enthusiasts were dismayed to find that it was the same wheel offered in the economy Chevy Vega GT. Some refinements were made to keep the cockpit cooler by use of new heat shielding and air vents were rerouted to keep the cockpit quieter.*

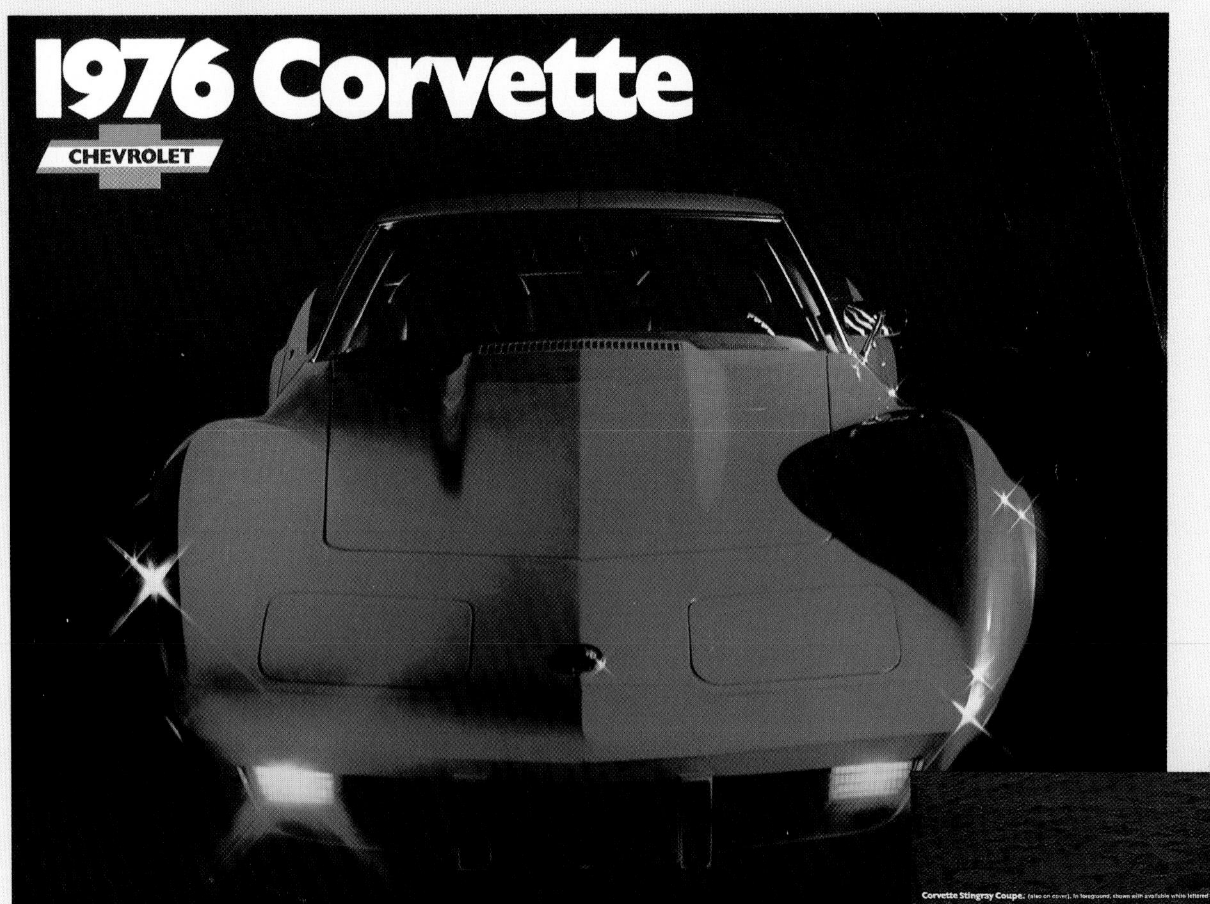

LEFT *The 1976 Corvette carried over mostly unchanged from the previous year. Although the convertible was gone, and there were no power changes, sales continued strong. More than 46,000 Corvettes were sold that year. Serial numbers ran from 1Z67J6S400001 to 1Z67J6S446558. The basic price was up to $7,605.*

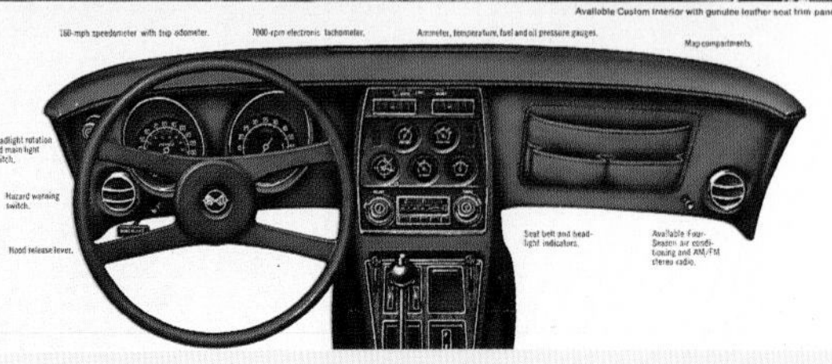

RIGHT *The Corvette in 1976 was a leading example of a car that had a user-friendly cockpit. Big gauges dominated the view in front of the driver, though any hopes that the car could hit the 160 mph (256 kph) top speed indicated on the speedometer were pure fantasy.*

BELOW *By 1977, the Corvette had become a true boulevard car, steeped more in comfort and prestige than performance. The catalogues were long on talk about plush interiors and styling, rather than engines and transmissions. As almost an admission that the car was a shadow of its former self, the name 'Stingray' was removed. Still, a record 49,213 Corvettes were sold in 1977, a tribute to the car's initial design and appeal. Serial numbers run from 1Z67J7S100001 to 1Z67J7S149213.*

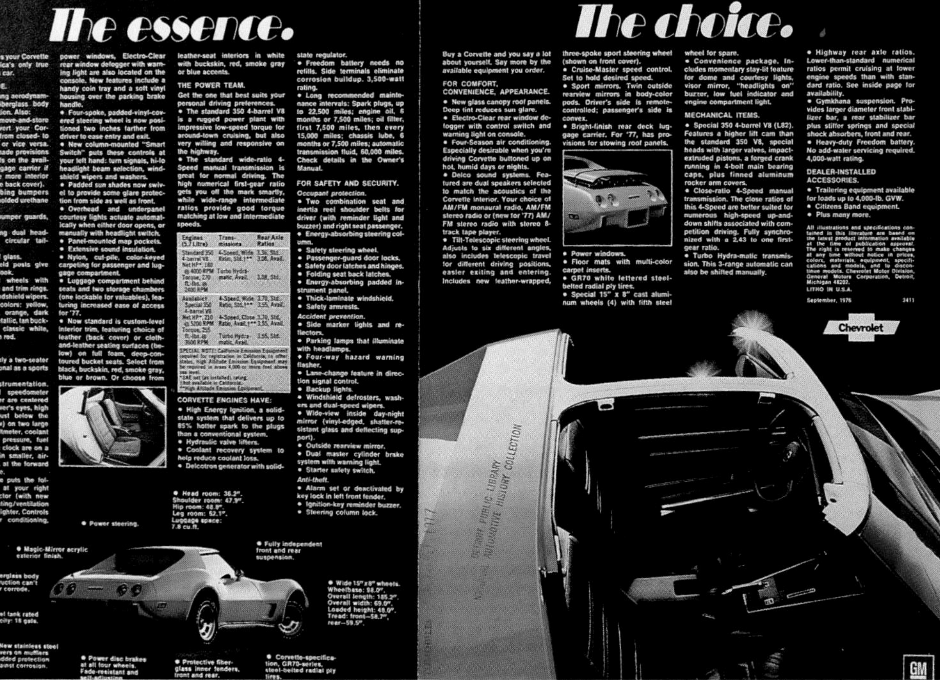

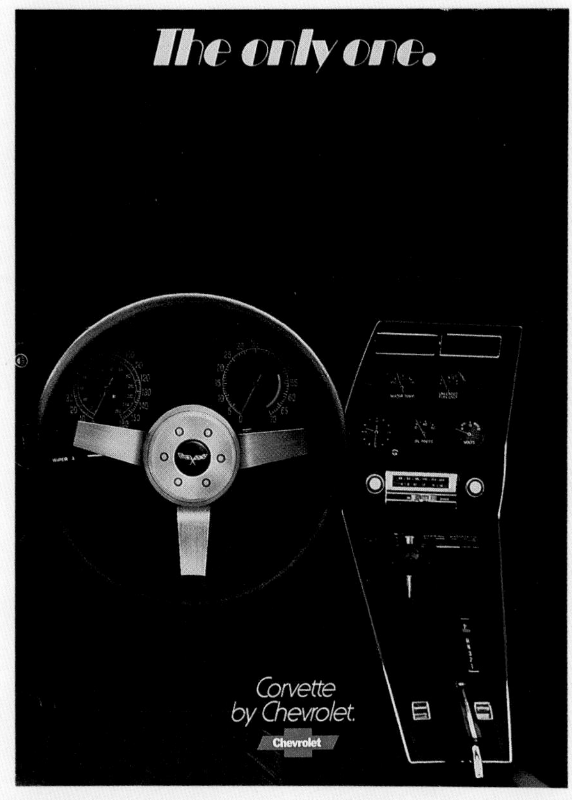

ABOVE *All the news was about the Corvette's interior. Leather seats, power steering and power brakes became standard equipment. Cloth-and-leather seats were available at extra cost. The centre console was redesigned to accommodate a new AM-FM stereo cassette player which was on the option list. Also, glass T-Tops are listed as options, but a dispute with an outside supplier limits their availability. The new standard equipment pushes the basic price up $1,000 over the previous year to $8,648.*

LEFT *In 1978, the Corvette passed its 25th birthday. The car was restyled with a sharp glass fastback which created a lot of needed luggage space. Corvette catalogues also offered a Silver Anniversary Package, which included a two-tone paint scheme, with silver on top and dark grey on the bottom, divided by a pinstripe. Otherwise, it was a stock Corvette. The other special car offered that year was the Indy Pace Car Corvette. Included were alloy wheels, chin and rear deck spoilers, special silver leather seats, glass liftoff roof panels and a host of standard equipment, including air-conditioning. Basic price for the 6,200 Pace Car Corvettes was $13,653, compared to $9,351 sticker price for a stock Corvette. All the Pace Cars were sold at prices ranging from $15,000 to $75,000 in the belief they would become collector's items. Overall, 47,667 were sold. Serial numbers ran from 1Z67J8S100001 through 1Z67J8S147667. Pace Car Corvettes carried the designation Z78.*

ABOVE *Many of the items that were rushed into production for the 1978 Pace Car Corvette appeared in the 1979 catalogue. The most notable items were the bucket seats, which were standard, and the front and rear spoilers, which were optional. The optional L-82 engine was now generating 220 horsepower. That put zero-to-60 mph times back in the sub 7-second range.*

ABOVE RIGHT *Despite the fact that the Corvette had been unchanged since 1968 – sales set a record in 1979. 53,807 cars were sold that year. Serial numbers ran from 1Z87A400001 to 1Z87A453807.*

RIGHT *Two changes in 1979 included the use of Tungsten-halogen headlights and the return of the crossed-flags insignia to the nose and sides.*

CHAPTER 4

THE 1980S AND BEYOND: CORVETTE HITS ITS PRIME

When the 1980s began, the Corvette had almost nowhere to go but up. Although sales were still strong – more than 40,000 a year on average – inflation was pushing up prices and the current design had been taken about as far as possible. Catalogues contained more Corvette history than highlights of improvements,but in the works was an all-new car that would offer no apologies for its performance.

Some of the new technology would make its way into the models of the early 1980s, a lightweight composite suspension spring and electronic fuel injection to name but two. A new state-of-the-art assembly plant was built to accommodate these changes.

When the next generation Corvette made its debut as a 1984 model, it was a giant step for the car and the sales catalogues were filled with enthusiasm and new features. The styling was slick and, perhaps, a bit understated. Handling was top-notch,unlike any other Corvette offered since the car's original debut in 1953,while engine performance was on the upgrade.

The engineers were committed to a programme of making each succeeding Corvette even better. Every year some new and significant improvement was made in the car. By the

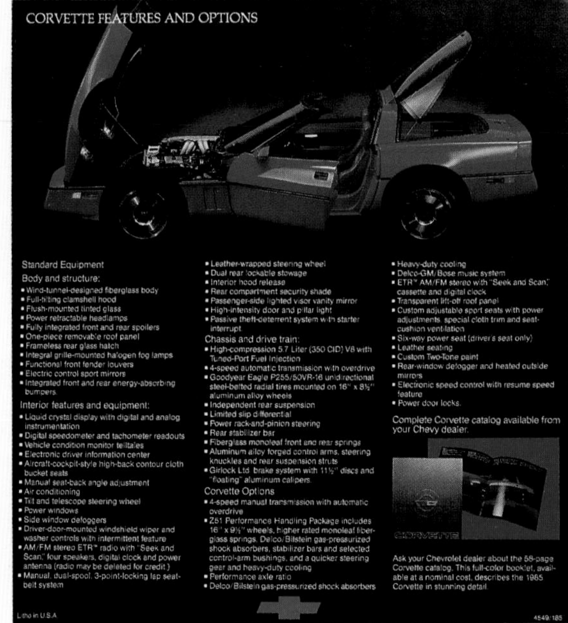

CORVETTE FEATURES AND OPTIONS

Standard Equipment

Body and structure:
- Wind-tunnel-designed fiberglass body
- Full-tilting clamshell hood
- Flush-mounted tinted glass
- Power retractable headlamps
- Fully integrated front and rear spoilers
- One-piece removable roof panel
- Frameless rear glass hatch
- Integral grille-mounted halogen fog lamps
- Functional front fender louvers
- Electric control sport mirrors
- Integrated front and rear energy-absorbing bumpers.

Interior features and equipment:
- Liquid crystal display with digital and analog instrumentation
- Digital speedometer and tachometer readouts
- Vehicle condition monitor telltales
- Electronic driver information center
- Aircraft-cockpit-style high-back contour cloth bucket seats
- Manual seat-back angle adjustment
- Air conditioning
- Tilt and telescope steering wheel
- Power windows
- Side window defoggers
- Driver-door-mounted windshield wiper and washer controls with intermittent feature
- AM/FM stereo ETR™ radio with "Seek and Scan," four speakers, digital clock and power antenna (radio may be deleted for credit.)
- Manual, dual-spool, 3-point-locking lap seat-belt system
- Leather-wrapped steering wheel
- Dual rear lockable stowage
- Interior hood release
- Rear compartment security shade
- Passenger-side lighted visor vanity mirror
- High-intensity door and pillar light
- Passive theft-deterrent system with starter interrupt.

Chassis and drive train:
- High-compression 5.7 Liter (350 CID) V8 with Tuned-Port Fuel Injection
- 4-speed automatic transmission with overdrive
- Goodyear Eagle P255/50VR-16 unidirectional steel-belted radial tires mounted on 16" x 8½" aluminum alloy wheels
- Independent rear suspension
- Limited slip differential
- Power rack-and-pinion steering
- Rear stabilizer bar
- Fiberglass monoleaf front and rear springs
- Aluminum alloy forged control arms, steering knuckles and rear suspension struts
- Girlock Ltd. brake system with 11½" discs and "floating" aluminum calipers.

Corvette Options
- 4-speed manual transmission with automatic overdrive
- Z51 Performance Handling Package includes 16" x 9½" wheels, higher rated monoleaf fiberglass springs, Delco/Bilstein gas-pressurized shock absorbers, stabilizer bars and selected control-arm bushings, and a quicker steering gear and heavy-duty cooling
- Performance axle ratio
- Delco/Bilstein gas-pressurized shock absorbers
- Heavy-duty cooling
- Delco-GM/Bose music system
- ETR™ AM/FM stereo with "Seek and Scan," cassette and digital clock
- Transparent lift-off roof panel
- Custom adjustable sport seats with power adjustments, special cloth trim and seat-cushion ventilation
- Six-way power seat (driver's seat only)
- Leather seating
- Custom Two-Tone paint
- Rear-window defogger and heated outside mirrors
- Electronic speed control with resume speed feature
- Power door locks.

Complete Corvette catalog available from your Chevy dealer.

CORVETTE

Ask your Chevrolet dealer about the 58-page Corvette catalog. This full-color booklet, available at a nominal cost, describes the 1985 Corvette in stunning detail.

Litho in U.S.A.

4549/185

RIGHT *Automotive technology is once again to the fore after the slump in the 1970s.*

mid-1980s top speed was 150 mph (241 kph) and zero to 60 mph (97 kph) times were approaching 5 seconds. Innovation was everywhere from the special uni-directional tyres to the anti-lock brakes.

As an acknowledgment that the fun had returned to stay,the Corvette roadster reappeared in 1986.

Into the late 1980s, the Corvette received more power, better ride characteristics and better quality control. Yet as good as the basic Corvette had become by 1989, the engineers were not satisfied with making what is arguably the best mass-produced sports car in the world. They were intent on making sure that their baby could do battle with the best exotic cars the world could offer. Towards that end they introduced in 1990 the ZR-1 Corvette, the most potent Corvette ever built. With a top speed approaching 180 mph (290 kph) and a basic price of about $60,000, the 380 hp ZR-1 was an amazing improvement.

Now new styling taken from the ZR-1 marks the latest model which appears ready for a long run into the 1990s as a true supercar.

RIGHT *Brochures of the 1980s begin to promote the Corvette as cultural icon.*

ABOVE *Corvette moves into the 1990s, able to compete with the world's best.*

1980 CORVETTE.

How many other cars can you name at a single glance? That should tell you something about the continuing uniqueness of Corvette. It could very well be the most recognizable car on the road today. It has a host of imitators. But none of them catch your eye with such striking authority. Because Corvette remains what they can only aspire to be. A legend. Still the only true American production sports car.

Since 1953, Corvette has claimed a special place in the hearts of those who love cars. It has captured that fine line between dreams and reality.

Corvette for 1980. The legend lives on.

As you can see, Corvette engineers have been successful once again in refining this legendary classic.

The new, aerodynamically designed front bumper cover now features an integral air dam and deeply recessed grille and parking lights. And functional air exhaust louvers were added to the front fender air vents. They're black in keeping with many other styling accents.

Other exterior highlights include a new hood with a lower profile. New rear bumper cover with integral rear spoiler. New flag emblems. New rear lights. And cornering lights, new to Corvette as well as being standard, are fully automatic. The lights are illuminated by the turn signal when the headlights are on . . . and are turned off when the signal is cancelled.

Inside there's a new rich, ribbed pattern cloth interior. And for the driver, a standard sliding sun shield to help cut down on side sun for added comfort.

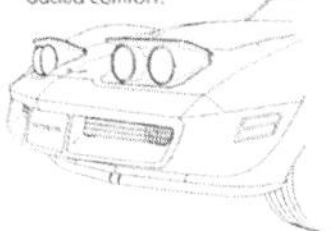

And there's good news for those who like their Corvettes luxury equipped. For 1980, the Corvette comes complete with air conditioning, dual Sport mirrors, power windows, Tilt-Telescopic steering wheel, and a convenience group which consists of comforting items like time-delay dome and courtesy lights and intermittent windshield wipers. (Check below for a more complete listing of standard 1980 Corvette features.)

But don't get the idea that the Corvette is dedicated only to comfort and convenience. It's still one great sports machine. In fact, an extensive weight reduction program has lowered the 1980 Corvette's weight by hundreds of pounds compared to last year. With a 5.7 Liter 4-Bbl. V8 still the standard engine (5.0 Liter in California). Result? Better weight efficiency.

For 1980, Corvette remains one trim machine — with enough comfort and convenience features to add pleasure to the sport. Its list of standards speaks for itself.

NEW STANDARDS FOR 1980

Air conditioning • Cornering lights • Power windows • Tilt-Telescopic steering wheel • Dual, remote-control Sport mirrors • Convenience group (includes time-delay dome and courtesy lights, headlight warning buzzer, underhood light, low fuel warning light, color-keyed floor mats, intermittent windshield wipers and a passenger-side illuminated visor vanity mirror).

MORE STANDARDS

5.7 Liter (5.0 Liter in California) 4-Bbl. V8 engine • Automatic transmission or Four-Speed fully synchronized transmission (except California) • AM/FM radio • High Energy Ignition system • Steel-belted radial ply tires • Power disc brakes at all four wheels • Limited slip rear axle • Fully independent four-wheel suspension system • Power steering • Exhaust valve rotators for even wear • Delco Freedom battery never needs refilling. Sealed side terminals help prevent corrosion buildup • Delcotron generator with built-in solid-state regulator • Hydraulic valve lifters • Large-diameter front stabilizer bar • Wide 15" × 8" wheels • Removable roof panels • Tinted glass in all windows • Heavy-gage frame structure with corrosion-resistant coating • Energy-absorbing honeycomb cushion front bumper system • Energy-absorbing rear bumper system with twin hydraulic cylinders • Hide-A-Way windshield wipers with integral washers in wiper arms • Power-operated retractable headlights • High-rise front fenders with functional louvers • Corrosion-resistant steel-reinforced fiberglass body with a steel partial-frame underbody • Built-in anti-theft audio alarm system control switch integral with driver's door lock • Special

Custom Interior with choice of cloth/leather or all-leather seating surfaces • Day/night inside rearview mirror • Sport-styled 3-spoke steering wheel • Aircraft-style center console • Tachometer (7000 rpm) • Electric clock • Ammeter, oil pressure, fuel and temperature gages • Separate trip odometer • Console-mounted parking brake control • Cut-pile carpeting • Color-keyed seat belts • Folding seat back latches • Roof courtesy light with automatic door switches • Underfloor stowage compartment.

A WORD ABOUT THIS CATALOG:

We have tried to make this catalog as comprehensive and factual as possible. And we hope you find it helpful. However, since the time of printing, some of the information you'll find here may have been updated. Also, some of the equipment shown or described throughout this catalog is available at extra cost. Your dealer has details and, before ordering, you should ask him to bring you up to date.

The right is reserved to make changes at any time, without notice, in prices, colors, materials, equipment, specifications and models, and to discontinue models. Check with your Chevrolet dealer for complete information.

LEFT *Cornering lights were added features in 1980 and air-conditioning and the tilt/telescoping steering wheel were made standard equipment. The basic price rises to $13,956. Serial numbers run from 1Z87A100001 to 1Z87A140614.*

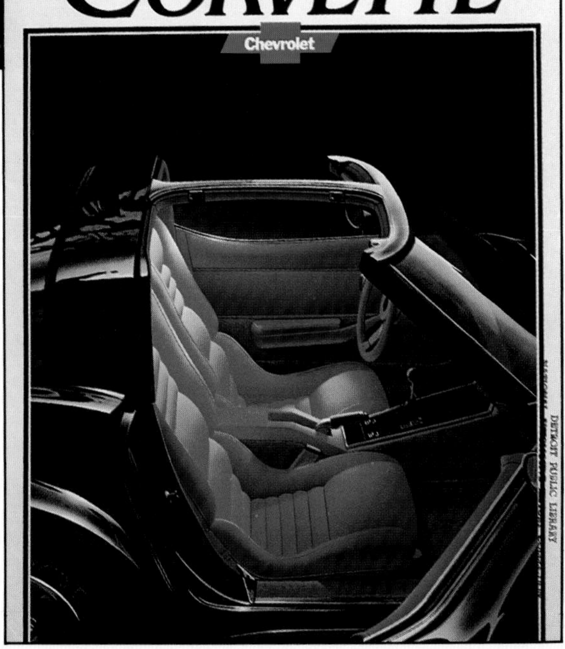

RIGHT *The 1980 Corvette catalogue offered buyers both less and more. It was a time when government mandates on fuel economy went into effect and new air-pollution rules took effect in California. The Corvette was put on a diet, to reduce weight and improve mileage, and the standard equipment list grew.*

LEFT *The realities of a changing world begin to encroach on the aging Mako Shark design of the Corvette. Due to emission standards, power of the basic L-48 engine drops to 190 horsepower, with the optional L-82 engine producing 230 horsepower. Catalogues give California buyers some bad news: neither the L-48 nor the L-82 350-cubic-inch engines can pass that state's new smog rules. So California, a crucial market for the Corvette, gets a 180-horsepower, 305-cubic-inch V8 Corvette and it's available only with the automatic transmission. But improvements are made elsewhere on the Corvette. Weight is down by 250 lb (90 kg) to about 3,550 lb (1610 kg) and new spoilers reduce wind resistance, dropping the drag coefficient from .503 to .443.*

BELOW *In an effort to save weight – and experiment with new technology – the 1981 catalogue talks about a new 8-lb (4-kg) monoleaf rear suspension spring that reduced weight by 33 lb (45 kg). It is the first new suspension component that will make up the all-new Corvette due in 1984. Inflation pushes the Corvette's basic price to $16,259.*

RIGHT *Although to the casual reader of Corvette catalogues 1981 may have seemed just like 1980, there were significant changes that heralded the beginning of the new era. The first effort at computer controls in the engine compartment helps the car make its emission goals.*

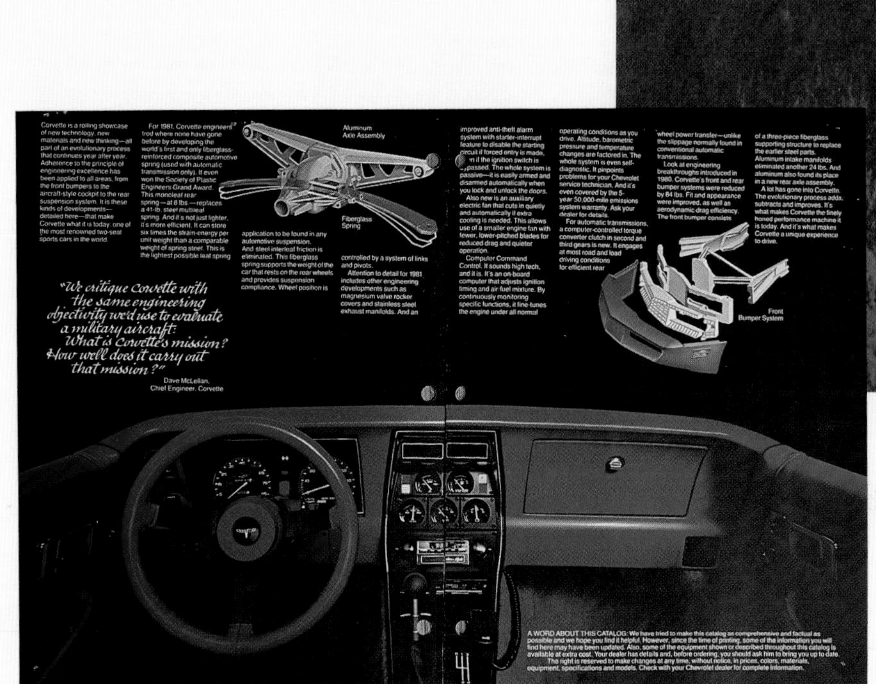

Corvette is a rolling showcase of new technology, new materials and new thinking—all part of an evolutionary process that continues year after year. Adherence to the principle of engineering excellence has been applied to all areas, from the front bumpers to the aircraft-style cockpit to the rear suspension system. It is these kinds of developments—detailed here—that make Corvette what it is today: one of the most renowned two-seat sports cars in the world.

For 1981, Corvette engineers trod where none have gone before by developing the world's first and only fiberglass-reinforced composite automotive spring (used with automatic transmission only). It even won the Society of Plastic Engineers Grand Award. This monoleaf rear spring—at 8 lbs.—replaces a 41-lb. steel multileaf spring. And it's not just lighter, it's more efficient. It can store six times the strain-energy per unit weight than a comparable weight of spring steel. This is the lightest possible leaf spring application to be found in any automotive suspension. And steel interleaf friction is eliminated. This fiberglass spring supports the weight of the car that rests on the rear wheels and provides suspension compliance. Wheel position is controlled by a system of links and pivots.

Attention to detail for 1981 includes other engineering developments such as magnesium valve rocker covers and stainless steel exhaust manifolds. And an improved anti-theft alarm system with starter-interrupt feature to disable the starting circuit if forced entry is made, even if the ignition switch is bypassed. The whole system is passive—it is easily armed and disarmed automatically when you lock and unlock the doors.

Also new is an auxiliary electric fan that cuts in quietly and automatically if extra cooling is needed. This allows use of a smaller engine fan with fewer, lower-pitched blades for reduced drag and quieter operation.

Computer Command Control. It sounds high tech, and it is. It's an on-board computer that adjusts ignition timing and air/fuel mixture. By continuously monitoring specific functions, it fine-tunes the engine under all normal operating conditions as you drive. Altitude, barometric pressure and temperature changes are factored in. The whole system is even self-diagnostic. It pinpoints problems for your Chevrolet service technician. And it's even covered by the 5-year 50,000-mile emissions system warranty. Ask your dealer for details.

For automatic transmissions, a computer-controlled torque converter clutch in second and third gears is new. It engages at most road and load driving conditions for efficient rear wheel power transfer—unlike the slippage normally found in conventional automatic transmissions.

Look at engineering breakthroughs introduced in 1980. Corvette's front and rear bumper systems were reduced by 84 lbs. Fit and appearance were improved, as well as aerodynamic drag efficiency. The front bumper consists of a three-piece fiberglass supporting structure to replace the earlier steel parts. Aluminum intake manifolds eliminated another 24 lbs. And aluminum also found its place in a new rear axle assembly.

A lot has gone into Corvette. The evolutionary process adds, subtracts and improves. It's what makes Corvette the finely honed performance machine it is today. And it's what makes Corvette a unique experience to drive.

"We critique Corvette with the same engineering objectivity we'd use to evaluate a military aircraft: What is Corvette's mission? How well does it carry out that mission?"

Dave McLellan, Chief Engineer, Corvette

A WORD ABOUT THIS CATALOG: We have tried to make this catalog as comprehensive and factual as possible and we hope you find it helpful. However, since the time of printing, some of the information you will find here may have been updated. Also, some of the equipment shown or described throughout this catalog is available at extra cost. Your dealer has details and, before ordering, you should ask him to bring you up to date.

The right is reserved to make changes at any time, without notice, in prices, colors, materials, equipment, specifications and models. Check with your Chevrolet dealer for complete information.

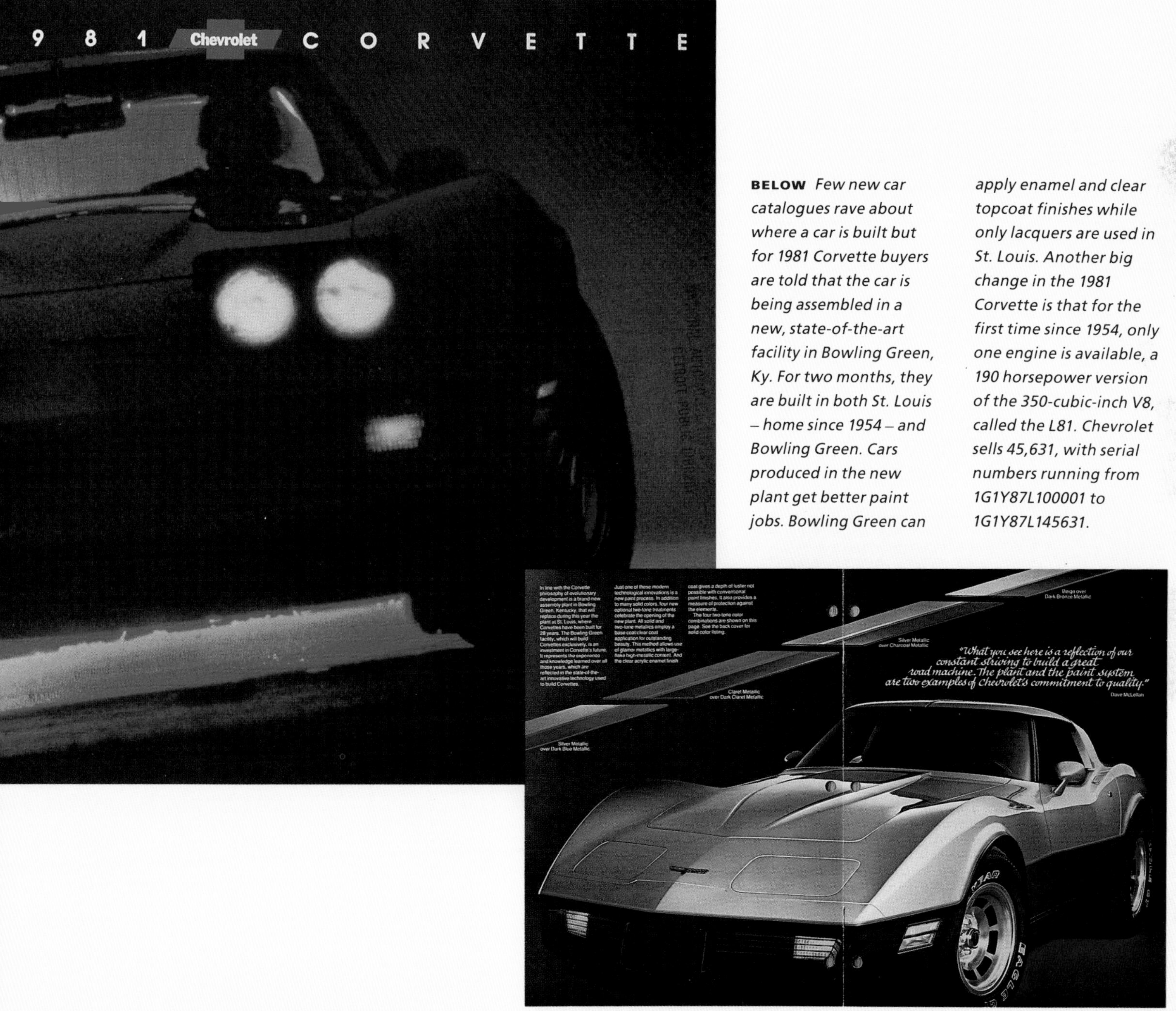

BELOW *Few new car catalogues rave about where a car is built but for 1981 Corvette buyers are told that the car is being assembled in a new, state-of-the-art facility in Bowling Green, Ky. For two months, they are built in both St. Louis – home since 1954 – and Bowling Green. Cars produced in the new plant get better paint jobs. Bowling Green can apply enamel and clear topcoat finishes while only lacquers are used in St. Louis. Another big change in the 1981 Corvette is that for the first time since 1954, only one engine is available, a 190 horsepower version of the 350-cubic-inch V8, called the L81. Chevrolet sells 45,631, with serial numbers running from 1G1Y87L100001 to 1G1Y87L145631.*

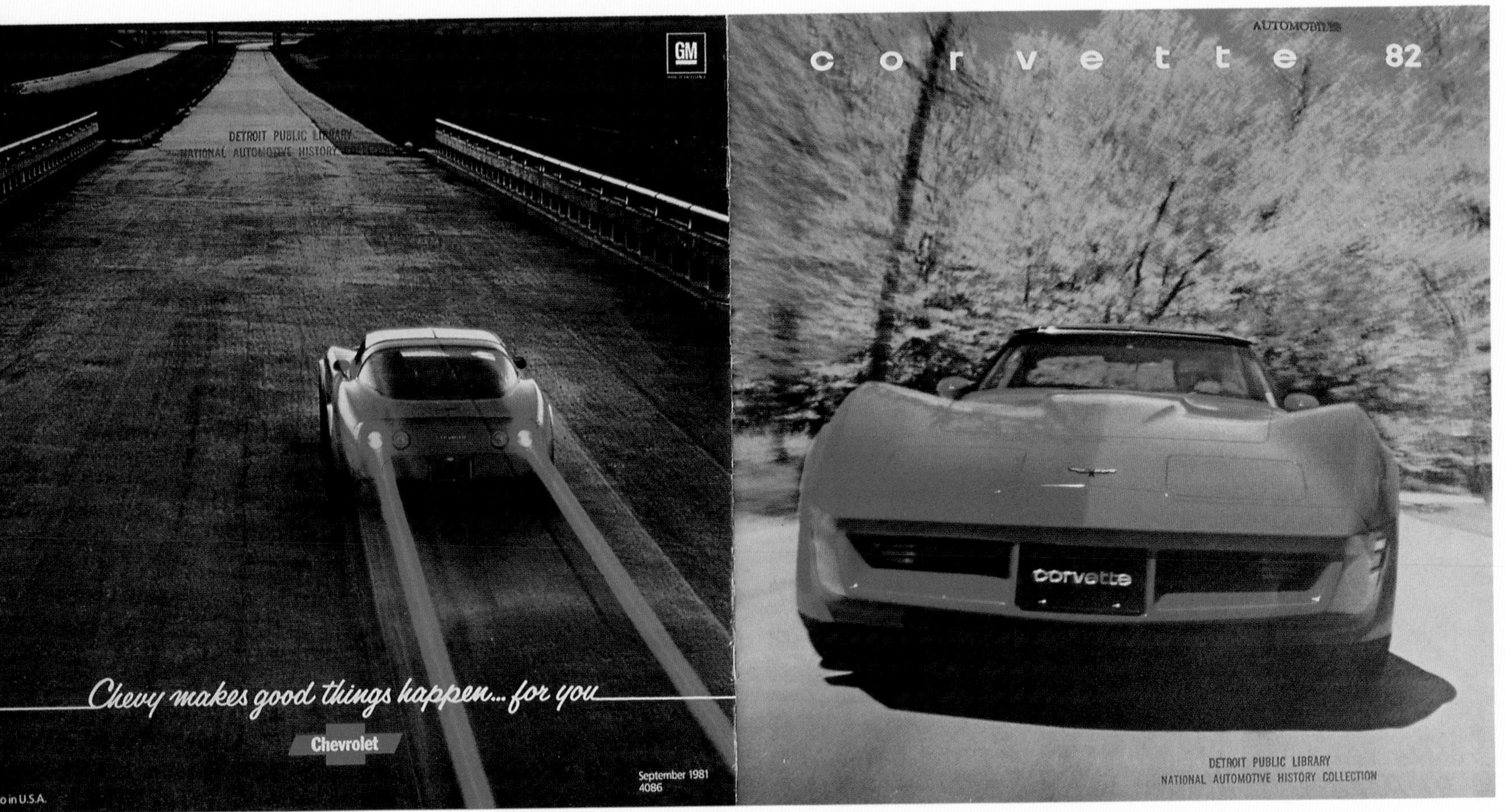

ABOVE *By 1982, the rumours that an all-new Corvette was on the horizon were in full bloom. As in 1981, Corvette literature was full of new items that would eventually add up to a new car. But for now, these new items would be available in the old chassis and body which had endured for 15 years. The big new item for 1982 was the reintroduction of fuel injection. Unlike the old Ramjet mechanical fuel injection system, the 1982 catalogue proudly announced that the new L-83 350-cubic-inch V8 used electronics to deliver the fuel. Horsepower was up 10 to 200. Though performance was still moderate – 7.9 seconds to 60 mph (97 kph), it was a move in the right direction.*

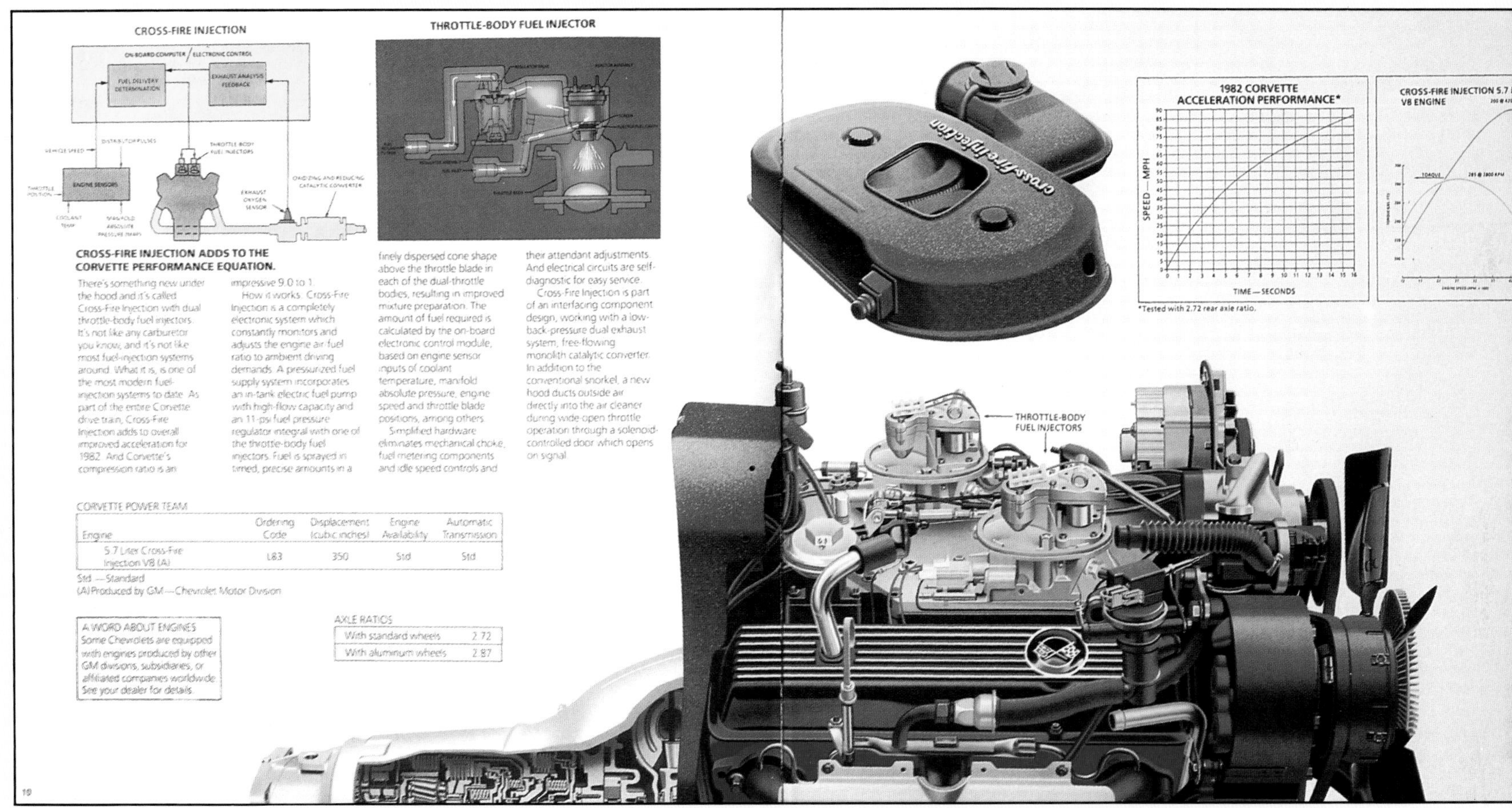

CROSS-FIRE INJECTION ADDS TO THE CORVETTE PERFORMANCE EQUATION.

There's something new under the hood and it's called Cross-Fire Injection with dual throttle-body fuel injectors. It's not like any carburetor you know, and it's not like most fuel-injection systems around. What it is, is one of the most modern fuel-injection systems to date. As part of the entire Corvette drive train, Cross-Fire Injection adds to overall improved acceleration for 1982. And Corvette's compression ratio is an impressive 9.0 to 1.

How it works: Cross-Fire Injection is a completely electronic system which constantly monitors and adjusts the engine air/fuel ratio to ambient driving demands. A pressurized fuel supply system incorporates an in-tank electric fuel pump with high-flow capacity and an 11-psi fuel pressure regulator integral with one of the throttle-body fuel injectors. Fuel is sprayed in timed, precise amounts in a finely dispersed cone shape above the throttle blade in each of the dual-throttle bodies, resulting in improved mixture preparation. The amount of fuel required is calculated by the on-board electronic control module, based on engine sensor inputs of coolant temperature, manifold absolute pressure, engine speed and throttle blade positions, among others.

Simplified hardware eliminates mechanical choke, fuel metering components and idle speed controls and their attendant adjustments. And electrical circuits are self-diagnostic for easy service.

Cross-Fire Injection is part of an interfacing component design, working with a low-back-pressure dual exhaust system, free-flowing monolith catalytic converter. In addition to the conventional snorkel, a new hood ducts outside air directly into the air cleaner during wide-open throttle operation through a solenoid-controlled door which opens on signal.

CORVETTE POWER TEAM

Engine	Ordering Code	Displacement (cubic inches)	Engine Availability	Automatic Transmission
5.7 Liter Cross-Fire Injection V8 (A)	L83	350	Std	Std

Std — Standard
(A) Produced by GM—Chevrolet Motor Division

A WORD ABOUT ENGINES
Some Chevrolets are equipped with engines produced by other GM divisions, subsidiaries, or affiliated companies worldwide. See your dealer for details.

AXLE RATIOS

With standard wheels	2.72
With aluminum wheels	2.87

ABOVE *Called Cross-Fire Injection, the L-83 engine used a computer-controlled system to deliver precise amounts of fuel to each cylinder. It accomplished two tasks: it delivered more power and helped make the exhaust cleaner.*

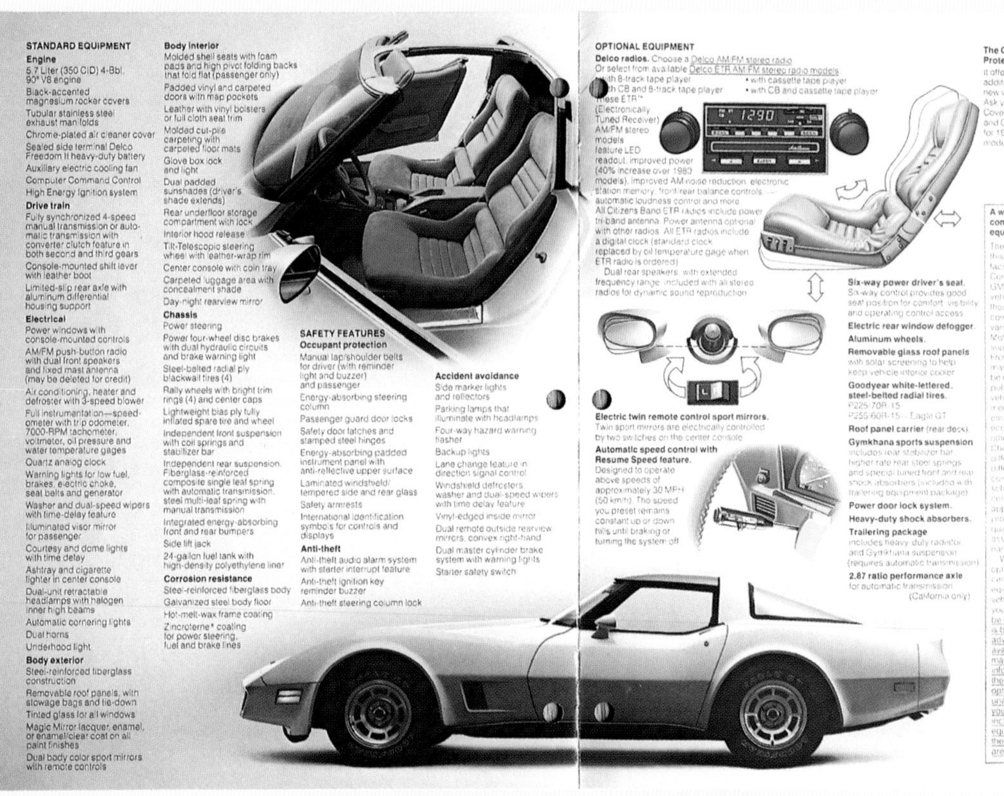

STANDARD EQUIPMENT

Engine
5.7 Liter (350 CID) 4-Bbl. 90° V8 engine
Black-accented magnesium rocker covers
Tubular stainless steel exhaust manifolds
Chrome-plated air cleaner cover
Sealed side terminal Delco Freedom II heavy-duty battery
Auxiliary electric cooling fan
Computer Command Control
High Energy Ignition system

Drive train
Fully synchronized 4-speed manual transmission or automatic transmission with converter clutch feature in both second and third gears
Console-mounted shift lever with leather boot
Limited-slip rear axle with aluminum differential housing support

Electrical
Power windows with console-mounted controls
AM/FM push-button radio with dual front speakers and fixed mast antenna (may be deleted for credit)
Air conditioning, heater and defroster with 3-speed blower
Full instrumentation—speedometer with trip odometer, 7000-RPM tachometer, voltmeter, oil pressure and water temperature gages
Quartz analog clock
Warning lights for low fuel, brakes, electric choke, seat belts and generator
Washer and dual-speed wipers with time-delay feature
Illuminated visor mirror for passenger
Courtesy and dome lights with time delay
Ashtray and cigarette lighter in center console
Dual-unit retractable headlamps with halogen inner high beams
Automatic cornering lights
Dual horns
Underhood light

Body exterior
Steel-reinforced fiberglass construction
Removable roof panels, with stowage bags and tie-down
Tinted glass for all windows
Magic Mirror lacquer, enamel, or enamel/clear coat on all paint finishes
Dual body color sport mirrors with remote controls

Body interior
Molded shell seats with foam pads and high pivot folding backs that fold flat (passenger only)
Padded vinyl and carpeted doors with map pockets
Leather with vinyl bolsters or full cloth seat trim
Molded cut-pile carpeting with carpeted floor mats
Glove box lock and light
Dual padded sunshades (driver's shade extends)
Rear underfloor storage compartment with lock
Interior hood release
Tilt-Telescopic steering wheel with leather-wrap rim
Center console with coin tray
Carpeted luggage area with concealment shade
Day-night rearview mirror

Chassis
Power steering
Power four-wheel disc brakes with dual hydraulic circuits and brake warning light
Steel-belted radial ply blackwall tires (4)
Rally wheels with bright trim rings (4) and center caps
Lightweight bias ply fully inflated spare tire and wheel
Independent front suspension with coil springs and stabilizer bar
Independent rear suspension. Fiberglass-reinforced composite single leaf spring with automatic transmission, steel multi-leaf spring with manual transmission
Integrated energy-absorbing front and rear bumpers
Side lift jack
24-gallon fuel tank with high-density polyethylene liner

Corrosion resistance
Steel-reinforced fiberglass body
Galvanized steel body floor
Hot-melt-wax frame coating
Zincroterne* coating for power steering, fuel and brake lines

SAFETY FEATURES

Occupant protection
Manual lap/shoulder belts for driver (with reminder light and buzzer) and passenger
Energy-absorbing steering column
Passenger guard door locks
Safety door latches and stamped steel hinges
Energy-absorbing padded instrument panel with anti-reflective upper surface
Laminated windshield/tempered side and rear glass
Safety armrests
International identification symbols for controls and displays

Anti-theft
Anti-theft audio alarm system with starter interrupt feature
Anti-theft ignition key reminder buzzer
Anti-theft steering column lock

Accident avoidance
Side marker lights and reflectors
Parking lamps that illuminate with headlamps
Four-way hazard warning flasher
Backup lights
Lane change feature in direction signal control
Windshield defrosters, washer and dual-speed wipers with time delay feature
Vinyl-edged inside mirror
Dual remote outside rearview mirrors, convex right-hand
Dual master cylinder brake system with warning lights
Starter safety switch

OPTIONAL EQUIPMENT

Delco radios. Choose a Delco AM/FM stereo radio. Or select from available Delco ETR AM/FM stereo radio models.
• with 8-track tape player • with cassette tape player
• with CB and 8-track tape player • with CB and cassette tape player
These ETR™ (Electronically Tuned Receiver) AM/FM stereo models feature LED readout, improved power (40% increase over 1980 models), improved AM noise reduction, electronic station memory, front/rear balance controls, automatic loudness control and more. All Citizens Band ETR radios include power tri-band antenna. Power antenna optional with other radios. All ETR radios include a digital clock (standard clock replaced by oil temperature gage when ETR radio is ordered).
Dual rear speakers, with extended frequency range, included with all stereo radios for dynamic sound reproduction.

Electric twin remote control sport mirrors. Twin sport mirrors are electrically controlled by two switches on the center console.

Automatic speed control with Resume Speed feature. Designed to operate above speeds of approximately 30 MPH (50 km/h). The speed you preset remains constant up or down hills until braking or turning the system off.

Six-way power driver's seat. Six-way control provides good seat position for comfort, visibility and operating control access.

Electric rear window defogger.

Aluminum wheels.

Removable glass roof panels with solar screening to help keep vehicle interior cooler.

Goodyear white-lettered, steel-belted radial tires.
P225/70R-15
P255/60R-15—Eagle GT

Roof panel carrier (rear deck).

Gymkhana sports suspension includes rear stabilizer bar, higher rate rear steel springs and special tuned front and rear shock absorbers (included with trailering equipment package).

Power door lock system.

Heavy-duty shock absorbers.

Trailering package includes heavy-duty radiator and Gymkhana suspension (requires automatic transmission).

2.87 ratio performance axle for automatic transmission (California only).

The GM Continuous Protection Plan
It offers service protection in addition to that provided by GM's new vehicle limited warranty. Ask your dealer about it. Coverage is limited to U.S.A. and Canada for 1981 model year.

A word about assembly, components and optional equipment in these Corvettes.
The Chevrolets described in this catalog are assembled at facilities of General Motors Corporation operated by the GM Assembly Division. These vehicles incorporate thousands of different components produced by various divisions of General Motors and by various suppliers to General Motors. From time to time during the manufacturing process, it may be necessary, in order to meet public demand for particular vehicles or equipment, or to meet federally mandated emissions, safety and fuel economy requirements, or for other reasons, to produce Chevrolet products with different components or differently sourced components than initially scheduled. All such components have been approved for use in Chevrolet products and will provide the quality performance associated with the Chevrolet name.
With respect to extra cost optional equipment, make certain you specify the type of equipment you desire on your vehicle when ordering it from your dealer. Some options may be unavailable when your car is built. Your dealer receives advice regarding current availability of options. You may ask the dealer for this information. GM also requests the dealer to advise you if an option you ordered is unavailable. We suggest that you verify that your car includes the optional equipment you ordered or, if there are changes, that they are acceptable to you.

LEFT *Standard equipment now outnumbered optional equipment on the Corvette, a trend that began in the 1970s. Power seats, air-conditioning and stereo radio were all included in the basic price of $18,290. One option not available for the first time since 1955 was a manual transmission. Since 85 per cent of all models were sold with the automatic transmission, Chevrolet decided to forego the manual gearbox for one year to concentrate on the new shifter for the next generation car.*

RIGHT *Perhaps it was because long-sighted buyers were awaiting the new Corvette – or more likely it was a reflection of boredom with the old Corvette styling and chassis – but only 25,407 Corvettes were sold in 1982. It was the lowest sales figure since 1967 and the 1982 sales benefited from a longer-than-usual selling time. Though initial plans called for introducing the new Corvette as an '83 model, sales did not begin until the spring of 1983, with the Corvette being introduced as a 1984 model.*

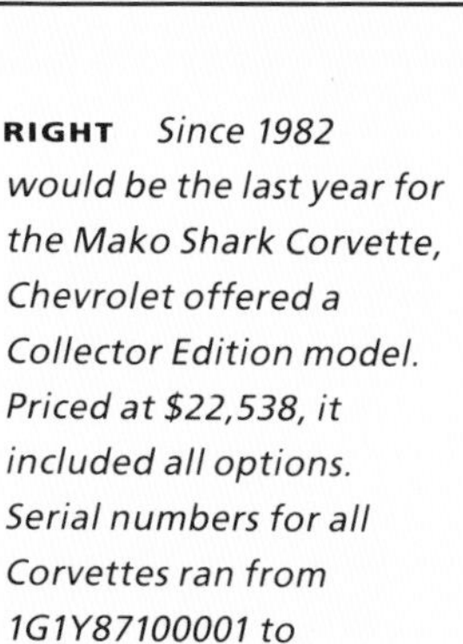

folded away clear out of sight, wire mesh headlight covers and a drive train featuring an overhead valve straight six, three 1-bbl. carbs and an automatic transmission.

It came in white, mostly with red interior, and the Corvette engineering team decided to label it a sports car. It sure didn't look like one of those things from Europe, though.

The buff book critics felt that maybe it was just too darn comfortable. They compared it with cars costing thousands more and assumed that it really didn't stand much of a chance in the 24 Hours of Le Mans.

A year later, Chevy hired a Belgian engineer who shoehorned a small block V8 into the existing body and frame and then backed that with a 4-speed transmission.

You could have a lot of fun with one of those Corvettes, especially if the guy next to you was driving a Jaguar XK120 Roadster or a 190SL Mercedes. And those cars, by golly, they *looked* European.

A few years later, along came a sleek apparition called a Stingray. A whole lot of amenities were provided. Windows winding up and down electrically, conditioned air, pop-off hardtop. There was even a coupe version.

And if that wasn't enough to cause quite a stir at the time, folks really took notice when a 427-cubic-inch engine was introduced for the Stingray along with a stiff suspension, a larger fuel tank and a few other tidbits.

Terrific, satisfying years.

Those Corvettes didn't look European at all and neither does the current model. It's an exciting kind of 'Vette that's coming on now. And sure the buffs still compare it with cars costing two to three times as much, only now European cars look like it. Almost.

IMPORTANT: A WORD ABOUT THIS CATALOG. We have tried to make this catalog as comprehensive and factual as possible and we hope you find it helpful. However, since the time of printing, some of the information you will find here may have been updated. Also, some of the equipment shown or described throughout this catalog is available at extra cost. Your dealer has details and, before ordering, you should ask him to bring you up to date. The right is reserved to make changes at any time, without notice, in prices, colors, materials, equipment, specifications and models. Check with your Chevrolet dealer for complete information.

LEFT *Seen from a historical perspective, the 1982 Corvette was the last of an era. As almost an admission of that, the brochures were heavy with historical references.*

RIGHT *Since 1982 would be the last year for the Mako Shark Corvette, Chevrolet offered a Collector Edition model. Priced at $22,538, it included all options. Serial numbers for all Corvettes ran from 1G1Y87100001 to 1G1Y8725407. Collector Cars carried the prefix 1G1Y07.*

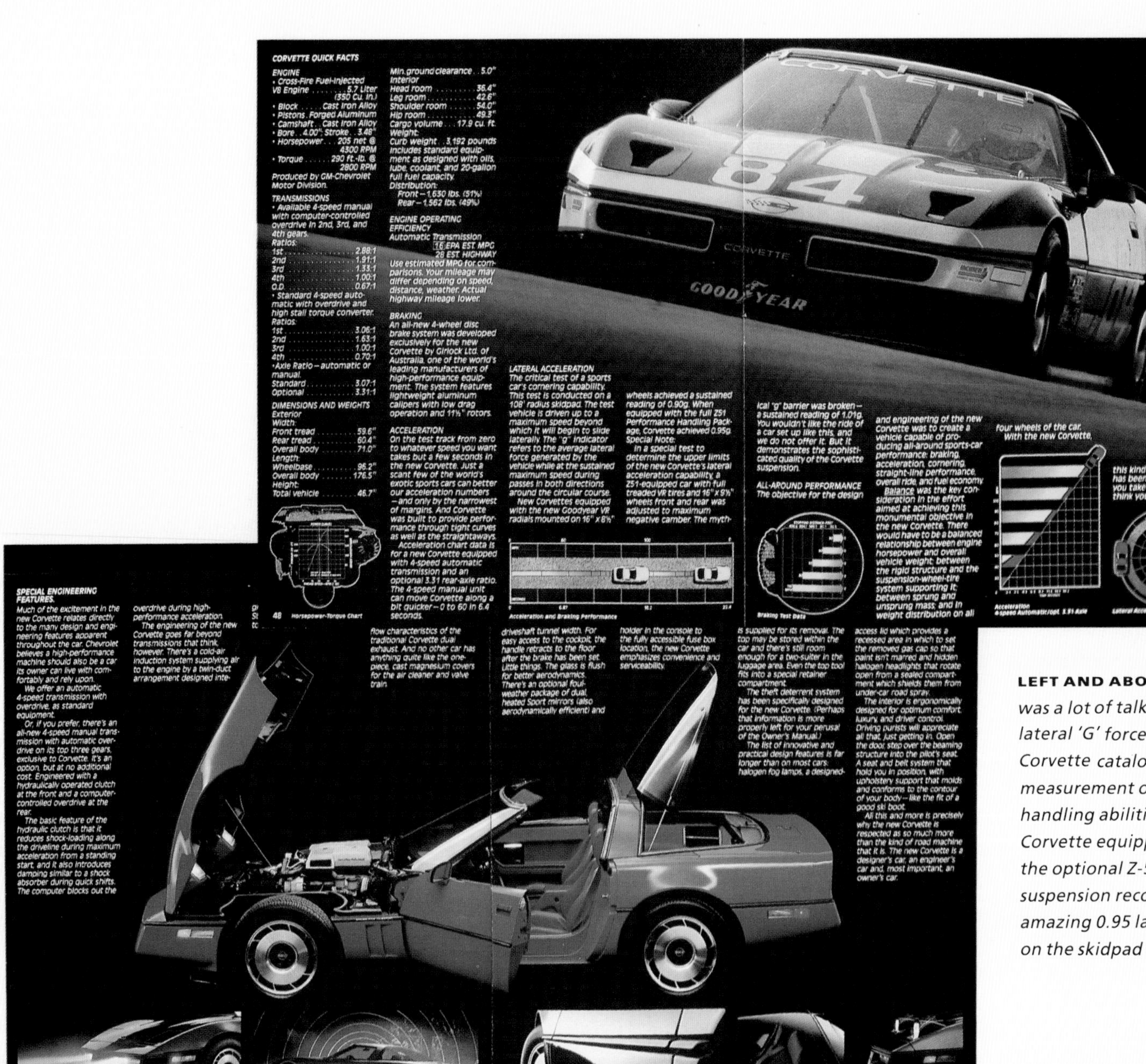

CORVETTE QUICK FACTS

ENGINE	
• Cross-Fire Fuel-Injected V8 Engine	5.7 Liter (350 Cu. In.)
• Block	Cast Iron Alloy
• Pistons	Forged Aluminum
• Camshaft	Cast Iron Alloy
• Bore	4.00"; Stroke. 3.48"
• Horsepower	205 net @ 4300 RPM
• Torque	290 ft.-lb. @ 2800 RPM

Produced by GM-Chevrolet Motor Division.

TRANSMISSIONS
• Available 4-speed manual with computer-controlled overdrive in 2nd, 3rd, and 4th gears.

Ratios:	
1st	2.88:1
2nd	1.91:1
3rd	1.33:1
4th	1.00:1
O.D.	0.67:1

• Standard 4-speed automatic with overdrive and high stall torque converter.

Ratios:	
1st	3.06:1
2nd	1.63:1
3rd	1.00:1
4th	0.70:1

•Axle Ratio—automatic or manual.

Standard	3.07:1
Optional	3.31:1

DIMENSIONS AND WEIGHTS

Exterior	
Width:	
Front tread	59.6"
Rear tread	60.4"
Overall body	71.0"
Length:	
Wheelbase	96.2"
Overall body	176.5"
Height:	
Total vehicle	46.7"
Min. ground clearance	5.0"
Interior	
Head room	36.4"
Leg room	42.6"
Shoulder room	54.0"
Hip room	49.3"
Cargo volume	17.9 cu. ft.
Weight:	
Curb weight	3,192 pounds
Includes standard equipment as designed with oils, lube, coolant, and 20-gallon full fuel capacity.	
Distribution:	
Front—1,630 lbs. (51%)	
Rear—1,562 lbs. (49%)	

ENGINE OPERATING EFFICIENCY

Automatic Transmission	
16	EPA EST MPG
28	EST. HIGHWAY
Use estimated MPG for comparisons. Your mileage may differ depending on speed, distance, weather. Actual highway mileage lower.	

BRAKING
An all-new 4-wheel disc brake system was developed exclusively for the new Corvette by Girlock Ltd. of Australia, one of the world's leading manufacturers of high-performance equipment. The system features lightweight aluminum calipers with low drag operation and 11½" rotors.

ACCELERATION
On the test track from zero to whatever speed you want takes but a few seconds in the new Corvette. Just a scant few of the world's exotic sports cars can better our acceleration numbers—and only by the narrowest of margins. And Corvette was built to provide performance through tight curves as well as the straightaways.
Acceleration chart data is for a new Corvette equipped with 4-speed automatic transmission and an optional 3.31 rear-axle ratio. The 4-speed manual unit can move Corvette along a bit quicker—0 to 60 in 6.4 seconds.

48 Horsepower-Torque Chart

LATERAL ACCELERATION
The critical test of a sports car's cornering capability. This test is conducted on a 108' radius skidpad. The test vehicle is driven up to a maximum speed beyond which it will begin to slide laterally. The "g" indicator refers to the average lateral force generated by the vehicle while at the sustained maximum speed during passes in both directions around the circular course.
New Corvettes equipped with the new Goodyear VR radials mounted on 16" x 8½" wheels achieved a sustained reading of 0.90g. When equipped with the full Z51 Performance Handling Package, Corvette achieved 0.95g.
Special Note:
In a special test to determine the upper limits of the new Corvette's lateral acceleration capability, a Z51-equipped car with full treaded VR tires and 16" x 9½" wheels front and rear was adjusted to maximum negative camber. The mythical "g" barrier was broken—a sustained reading of 1.01g. You wouldn't like the ride of a car set up like this, and we do not offer it. But it demonstrates the sophisticated quality of the Corvette suspension.

Acceleration and Braking Performance

ALL-AROUND PERFORMANCE
The objective for the design and engineering of the new Corvette was to create a vehicle capable of producing all-around sports-car performance: braking, acceleration, cornering, straight-line performance, overall ride, and fuel economy.
Balance was the key consideration in the effort aimed at achieving this monumental objective in the new Corvette. There would have to be a balanced relationship between engine horsepower and overall vehicle weight; between the rigid structure and the suspension-wheel-tire system supporting it; between sprung and unsprung mass; and in weight distribution on all four wheels of the car.
With the new Corvette, this kind of critical balance has been achieved. When you take to the road, we think you'll agree.

Braking Test Data

Acceleration
4-speed Automatic/opt. 3.31 Axle

Lateral Acceleration Test

49

SPECIAL ENGINEERING FEATURES.
Much of the excitement in the new Corvette relates directly to the many design and engineering features apparent throughout the car. Chevrolet believes a high-performance machine should also be a car its owner can live with comfortably and rely upon.
We offer an automatic 4-speed transmission with overdrive, as standard equipment.
Or, if you prefer, there's an all-new 4-speed manual transmission with automatic overdrive on its top three gears, exclusive to Corvette. It's an option, but at no additional cost. Engineered with a hydraulically operated clutch at the front and a computer-controlled overdrive at the rear.
The basic feature of the hydraulic clutch is that it reduces shock-loading along the driveline during maximum acceleration from a standing start, and it also introduces damping similar to a shock absorber during quick shifts. The computer blocks out the overdrive during high-performance acceleration.
The engineering of the new Corvette goes far beyond transmissions that think, however. There's a cold-air induction system supplying air to the engine by a twin-duct arrangement designed inte-

flow characteristics of the traditional Corvette dual exhaust. And no other car has anything quite like the one-piece, cast magnesium covers for the air cleaner and valve train.

driveshaft tunnel width. For easy access to the cockpit, the handle retracts to the floor after the brake has been set. Little things. The glass is flush for better aerodynamics. There's an optional foul-weather package of dual, heated Sport mirrors (also aerodynamically efficient) and

holder in the console to the fully accessible fuse box location, the new Corvette emphasizes convenience and serviceability.

is supplied for its removal. The top may be stored within the car and there's still room enough for a two-suiter in the luggage area. Even the top tool fits into a special retainer compartment.
The theft deterrent system has been specifically designed for the new Corvette. (Perhaps that information is more properly left for your perusal of the Owner's Manual.)
The list of innovative and practical design features is far longer than on most cars: halogen fog lamps, a designed-

access lid which provides a recessed area in which to set the removed gas cap so that paint isn't marred and hidden halogen headlights that rotate open from a sealed compartment which shields them from under-car road spray.
The interior is ergonomically designed for optimum comfort, luxury, and driver control. Driving purists will appreciate all that, just getting in. Open the door, step over the beaming structure into the pilot's seat. A seat and belt system that hold you in position, with upholstery support that molds and conforms to the contour of your body—like the fit of a good ski boot.
All this and more is precisely why the new Corvette is respected as so much more than the kind of road machine that it is. The new Corvette is a designer's car, an engineer's car and, most important, an owner's car.

Integral halogen fog lamps.

Parking brake on driver's left.

Multi-faceted anti-theft system is standard.

Protective molding also covers the only horizontal body seam.

A special tool to open the roof.

Removable transparent roof panel.

Powerful electric motors rotate the headlights.

40

41

LEFT AND ABOVE *There was a lot of talk about lateral 'G' forces in the Corvette catalogue. As a measurement of a car's handling abilities, a Corvette equipped with the optional Z-51 suspension recorded an amazing 0.95 lateral 'G' on the skidpad*

1968. *A leaner, sleeker Corvette with a completely new interior and exterior. For the first time, Corvette coupes had removable roof panels. The 3-speed Turbo Hydra-matic was introduced and a 427-cubic-inch V8 topped engine availabilities.*

1973. *The beginning of the transformation from street machine to international-class exotic car. Attention was directed to a totality of purpose—an integration of performance to design—as witnessed by the soft, body-colored front-end bumper assembly.*

1975. *The last convertible. Engine displacement stabilized at 350 cubic inches, with only the L-82 option offered in addition to the standard L-48. Corvette moved into the demanding realm of the grand-touring machine with a full range of luxury and comfort features.*

1978. *The 25th year. The Indy 500 Pace Car was the first box-stock, showroom-fresh car to pace the race in years. A Silver Anniversary Model was avidly sought after by collectors. The major styling change was a true fastback rear window design, which made for enhanced luggage capability.*

1982. *The first generation to be built in its entire production run in the all-new Corvette plant at Bowling Green, Kentucky. Increasing emphasis was placed on quality of construction and brilliance of paint. The fiberglass composite monoleaf spring was introduced in the '81 and '82 models, and in skidpad tests Corvette achieved 0.79g lateral acceleration with Gymkhana suspension. A 4-speed automatic with overdrive was introduced as standard equipment.*

TODAY. *A new-generation Corvette. Still the only American automobile designed as a driver's car rather than a passenger car. The culmination of 30 years of evolutionary engineering dedicated to perfecting the complete performance machine.*

1968

1978

1973

1982

1975

TODAY

7

LEFT AND RIGHT *When the all-new Corvette appeared in March 1983 as a 1984 model, it was only fitting that catalogues attempted to put it in some sort of historical perspective. In the 30 years since the first Corvette appeared, the car had many incarnations. It was at first America's best hope to combat the flow of sports cars coming from Europe. Then it became its own vehicle, a cross between a sports car and a dragster. In the 1970s, it was a luxury car with sporting pretensions. Now, as a 1984 model, it was on the road to becoming a world-class sports car that attempted to do every high-performance task well. Like a chart on evolution, this catalogue charts the many changes.*

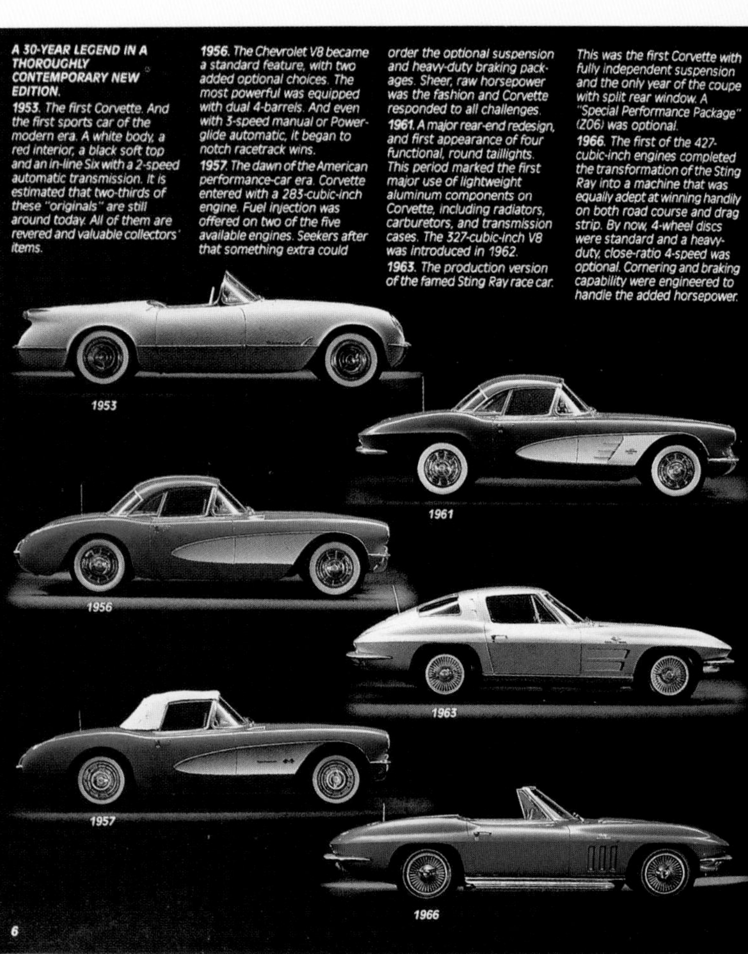

A 30-YEAR LEGEND IN A THOROUGHLY CONTEMPORARY NEW EDITION.

1953. *The first Corvette. And the first sports car of the modern era. A white body, a red interior, a black soft top and an in-line Six with a 2-speed automatic transmission. It is estimated that two-thirds of these "originals" are still around today. All of them are revered and valuable collectors' items.*

1956. *The Chevrolet V8 became a standard feature, with two added optional choices. The most powerful was equipped with dual 4-barrels. And even with 3-speed manual or Powerglide automatic, it began to notch racetrack wins.*

1957. *The dawn of the American performance-car era. Corvette entered with a 283-cubic-inch engine. Fuel injection was offered on two of the five available engines. Seekers after that something extra could order the optional suspension and heavy-duty braking packages. Sheer, raw horsepower was the fashion and Corvette responded to all challenges.*

1961. *A major rear-end redesign, and first appearance of four functional, round taillights. This period marked the first major use of lightweight aluminum components on Corvette, including radiators, carburetors, and transmission cases. The 327-cubic-inch V8 was introduced in 1962.*

1963. *The production version of the famed Sting Ray race car. This was the first Corvette with fully independent suspension and the only year of the coupe with split rear window. A "Special Performance Package" (Z06) was optional.*

1966. *The first of the 427-cubic-inch engines completed the transformation of the Sting Ray into a machine that was equally adept at winning handily on both road course and drag strip. By now, 4-wheel discs were standard and a heavy-duty, close-ratio 4-speed was optional. Cornering and braking capability were engineered to handle the added horsepower.*

1953

1961

1956

1963

1957

1966

6

RIGHT *Catalogues for the 1984 Corvette were chock full of news about the revolutionary car. From its smooth, aerodynamic lines to the lift-off roof panel, the car was the epitome of modern. Wheelbase was 96.2 in (2443 mm); overall length was 176.5 in (4503 mm); height was 46.7 in (1186 mm); and width was a fat 71 in (1778 mm). Weight was down to a relatively light 3,200 lb (1452 kgm). Price was a reasonable $21,800.*

PREPARE FOR LIFT-OFF.
A full-width, one-piece fiberglass roof section lifts off to create a true open-air feeling. There is no T-bar. And Corvette's advanced aerodynamics help to minimize cockpit turbulence. Available at extra cost is a transparent lift-off roof panel, impregnated with a solar screen to reduce glare.
26

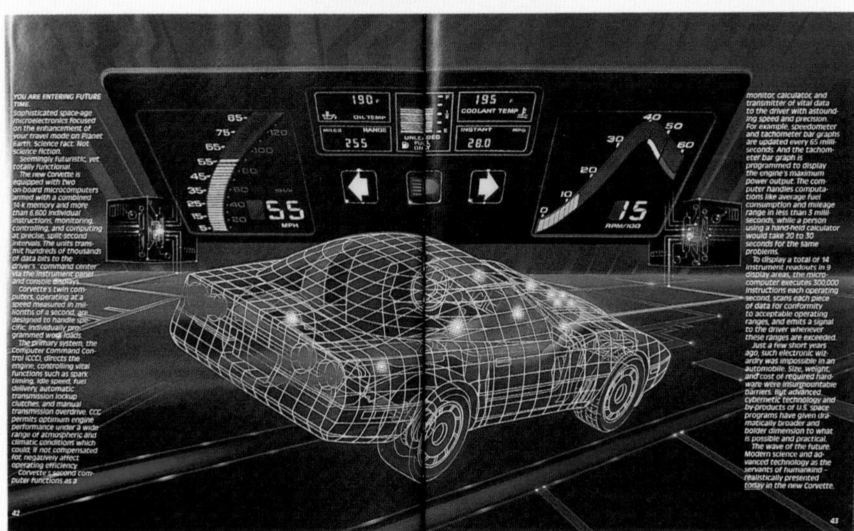

LEFT *Appearance of the new Corvette sparked as much debate as did the first Corvette in 1953. Chief target for complaint by some purists was the electronic dash display which used light bars to track speed and engine revolutions.*

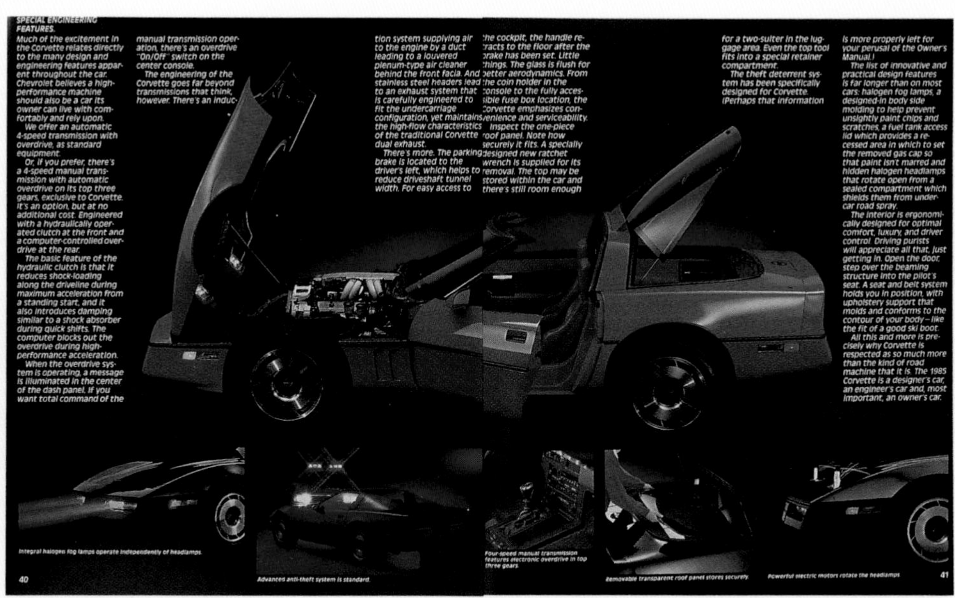

SPECIAL ENGINEERING FEATURES.

Much of the excitement in the Corvette relates directly to the many design and engineering features apparent throughout the car. Chevrolet believes a high-performance machine should also be a car its owner can live with comfortably and rely upon.

We offer an automatic 4-speed transmission with overdrive, as standard equipment.

Or, if you prefer, there's a 4-speed manual transmission with automatic overdrive on its top three gears, exclusive to Corvette. It's an option, but at no additional cost. Engineered with a hydraulically operated clutch at the front and a computer-controlled overdrive at the rear.

The basic feature of the hydraulic clutch is that it reduces shock-loading along the driveline during maximum acceleration from a standing start, and it also introduces damping similar to a shock absorber during quick shifts. The computer blocks out the overdrive during high-performance acceleration.

When the overdrive system is operating, a message is illuminated in the center of the dash panel. If you want total command of the manual transmission operation, there's an overdrive "On/Off" switch on the center console.

The engineering of the Corvette goes far beyond transmissions that think, however. There's an induction system supplying air to the engine by a duct leading to a louvered plenum-type air cleaner behind the front facia. And stainless steel headers lead to an exhaust system that is carefully engineered to fit the undercarriage configuration, yet maintains the high-flow characteristics of the traditional Corvette dual exhaust.

There's more. The parking brake is located to the driver's left, which helps to reduce driveshaft tunnel width. For easy access to the cockpit, the handle retracts to the floor after the brake has been set. Little things. The glass is flush for better aerodynamics. From the coin holder in the console to the fully accessible fuse box location, the Corvette emphasizes convenience and serviceability.

Inspect the one-piece roof panel. Note how securely it fits. A specially designed new ratchet wrench is supplied for its removal. The top may be stored within the car and there's still room enough for a two-suiter in the luggage area. Even the top tool fits into a special retainer compartment.

The theft deterrent system has been specifically designed for Corvette. (Perhaps that information is more properly left for your perusal of the Owner's Manual.)

The list of innovative and practical design features is far longer than on most cars: halogen fog lamps, a designed-in body side molding to help prevent unsightly paint chips and scratches, a fuel tank access lid which provides a recessed area in which to set the removed gas cap so that paint isn't marred and hidden halogen headlamps that rotate open from a sealed compartment which shields them from under-car road spray.

The interior is ergonomically designed for optimal comfort, luxury, and driver control. Driving purists will appreciate all that, just getting in. Open the door, step over the beaming structure into the pilot's seat. A seat and belt system holds you in position, with upholstery support that molds and conforms to the contour of your body—like the fit of a good ski boot.

All this and more is precisely why Corvette is respected as so much more than the kind of road machine that it is. The 1985 Corvette is a designer's car, an engineer's car and, most important, an owner's car.

Integral halogen fog lamps operate independently of headlamps.

40

Advanced anti-theft system is standard.

Four-speed manual transmission features electronic overdrive in top three gears.

Removable transparent roof panel stores securely.

Powerful electric motors rotate the headlamps.

41

LEFT *Turn the page in the 1984 Corvette catalogue and something new jumped out. The clamshell hood offered easy access to the engine compartment and the glass hatchback helped make the rear cargo area accessible. In the drivetrain was a new four-speed overdrive automatic transmission and an optional-at-no-cost four-speed manual gearbox that used an electric overdrive on the three top gears.*

LEFT *In past years, styling often overshadowed the engineering of the Corvette. In the 1984 version, that all changed. The sales catalogue was definitely orientated toward the technical side of the car. And there was a lot to talk about, from the special Goodyear 'Gatorback' uni-directional tyres to the 205-horsepower throttle-body fuel-injected engine. Zero-to-60 mph (97 kph) times dropped to 7 seconds.*

BELOW *Corvettes had a rich speed history. They always went fast in a straight line. The 1984 catalogue talked about a quantum leap in handling as well, thanks to an all-new chassis. Key to the handling were the Goodyear P255/50VR-16 tyres that were specially developed for the car. Huge four-wheel disc brakes also helped make sure the Corvette could stop from the estimated top speed of 140 mp (225 kph).*

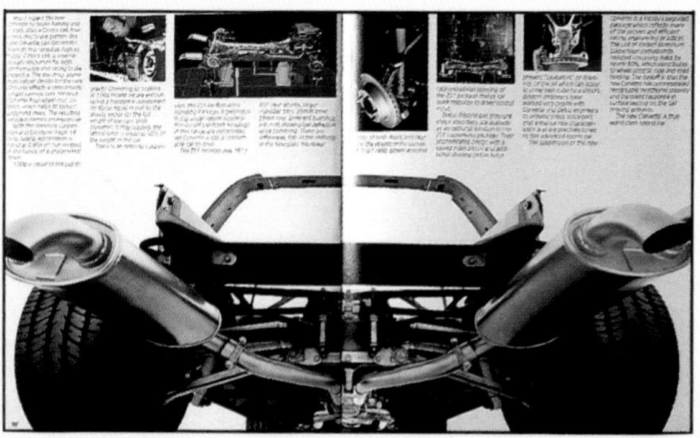

RIGHT *To achieve its racy looks and fine aerodynamics, the stylists tilted the Corvette windshield back to a 64-degree rake, a radical move on a production car.*

BELOW *Modern aerodynamic principals were applied to the Corvette in 1984, resulting in a 23 percent drop in drag coefficient to a very slick .341. Buyers loved the new Corvette, snapping up 51,547 of the cars. Serial numers run from 1G1AY0781E5100001 through 1G1AY0781E5151547.*

DESIGN HIGHLIGHTS.
A most acute windshield rake for a production car: 64 degrees. Hidden headlights tumble forward 162.5 degrees as they emerge, revealing a lean, aerodynamic shape. Clear, integrated halogen fog lamps. Front cornering lamps. Twin Sport mirrors are electrically adjusted and aerodynamically shaped. Body side rub strip is an integral part of the body design. Frameless glass rear window doubles as a hatch, with invisible hinge. Removable one-piece roof, with no T-bar, helps recreate the open-air feeling of sports cars past. Four functional circular taillights.

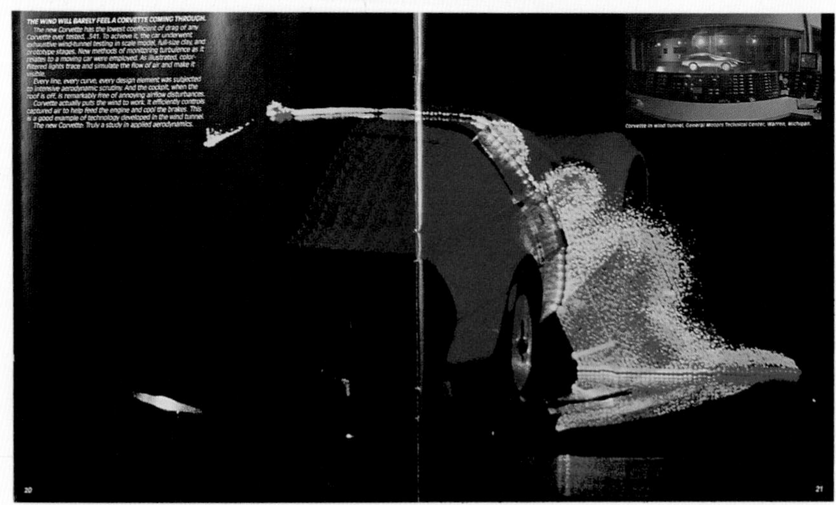

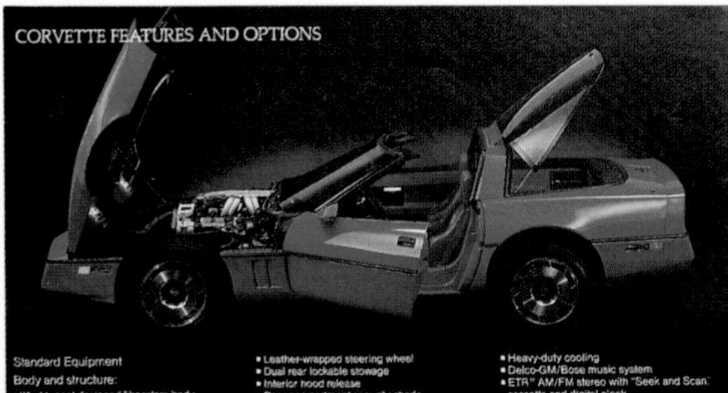

CORVETTE FEATURES AND OPTIONS

Standard Equipment

Body and structure:
- Wind-tunnel-designed fiberglass body
- Full-tilting clamshell hood
- Flush-mounted tinted glass
- Power retractable headlamps
- Fully integrated front and rear spoilers
- One-piece removable roof panel
- Frameless rear glass hatch
- Integral grille-mounted halogen fog lamps
- Functional front fender louvers
- Electric control sport mirrors
- Integrated front and rear energy-absorbing bumpers.

Interior features and equipment:
- Liquid crystal display with digital and analog instrumentation
- Digital speedometer and tachometer readouts
- Vehicle condition monitor telltales
- Electronic driver information center
- Aircraft-cockpit-style high-back contour cloth bucket seats
- Manual seat-back angle adjustment
- Air conditioning
- Tilt and telescope steering wheel
- Power windows
- Side window defoggers
- Driver-door-mounted windshield wiper and washer controls with intermittent feature
- AM/FM stereo ETR™ radio with "Seek and Scan," four speakers, digital clock and power antenna (radio may be deleted for credit.)
- Manual, dual-spool, 3-point-locking lap seat-belt system
- Leather-wrapped steering wheel
- Dual rear lockable stowage
- Interior hood release
- Rear compartment security shade
- Passenger-side lighted visor vanity mirror
- High-intensity door and pillar light
- Passive theft-deterrent system with starter interrupt.

Chassis and drive train:
- High-compression 5.7 Liter (350 CID) V8 with Tuned-Port Fuel Injection
- 4-speed automatic transmission with overdrive
- Goodyear Eagle P255/50VR-16 unidirectional steel-belted radial tires mounted on 16" x 8½" aluminum alloy wheels
- Independent rear suspension
- Limited slip differential
- Power rack-and-pinion steering
- Rear stabilizer bar
- Fiberglass monoleaf front and rear springs
- Aluminum alloy forged control arms, steering knuckles and rear suspension struts
- Girlock Ltd. brake system with 11½" discs and "floating" aluminum calipers.

Corvette Options
- 4-speed manual transmission with automatic overdrive
- Z51 Performance Handling Package includes 16" x 9½" wheels, higher rated monoleaf fiberglass springs, Delco/Bilstein gas-pressurized shock absorbers, stabilizer bars and selected control-arm bushings, and a quicker steering gear and heavy-duty cooling
- Performance axle ratio
- Delco/Bilstein gas-pressurized shock absorbers
- Heavy-duty cooling
- Delco-GM/Bose music system
- ETR™ AM/FM stereo with "Seek and Scan," cassette and digital clock
- Transparent lift-off roof panel
- Custom adjustable sport seats with power adjustments, special cloth trim and seat-cushion ventilation
- Six-way power seat (driver's seat only)
- Leather seating
- Custom Two-Tone paint
- Rear-window defogger and heated outside mirrors
- Electronic speed control with resume speed feature
- Power door locks.

Complete Corvette catalog available from your Chevy dealer.

Ask your Chevrolet dealer about the 58-page Corvette catalog. This full-color booklet, available at a nominal cost, describes the 1985 Corvette in stunning detail.

Litho in U.S.A. 4549/185

LEFT *So what did Chevrolet do for an encore in 1985? More power and refinements were the watchwords in the 1985 catalogues. The harsh ride of the 1984 car was softened somewhat by new spring rates and shock valves.*

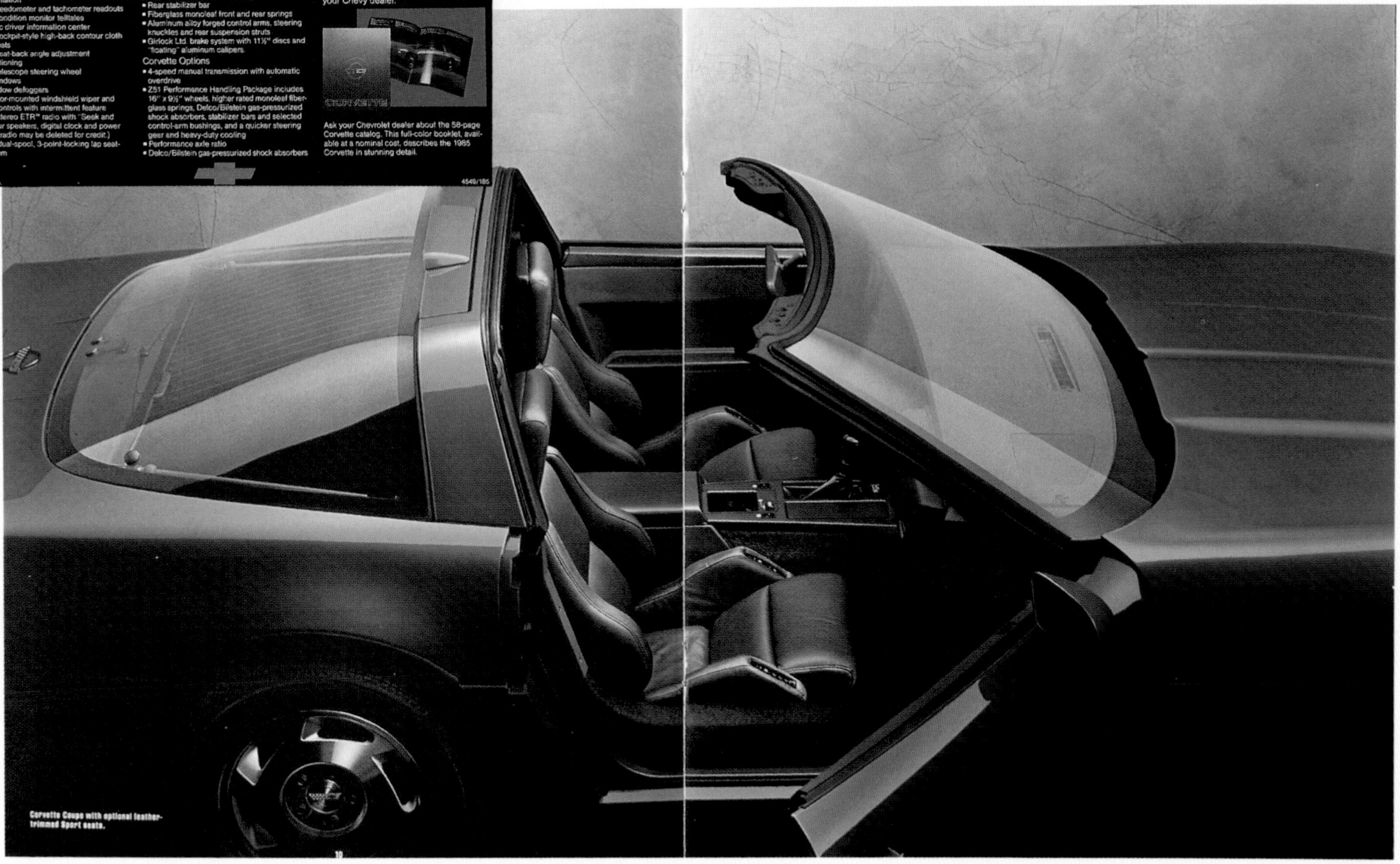

BELOW *With the optional multi-adjustable electric seats, the Corvette cockpit was indeed comfortable. Most buyers checked the option box next to the $895 Delco-Bose premium sound system, which was engineered for the Corvette's interior.*

Corvette Coupe with optional leather-trimmed Sport seats.

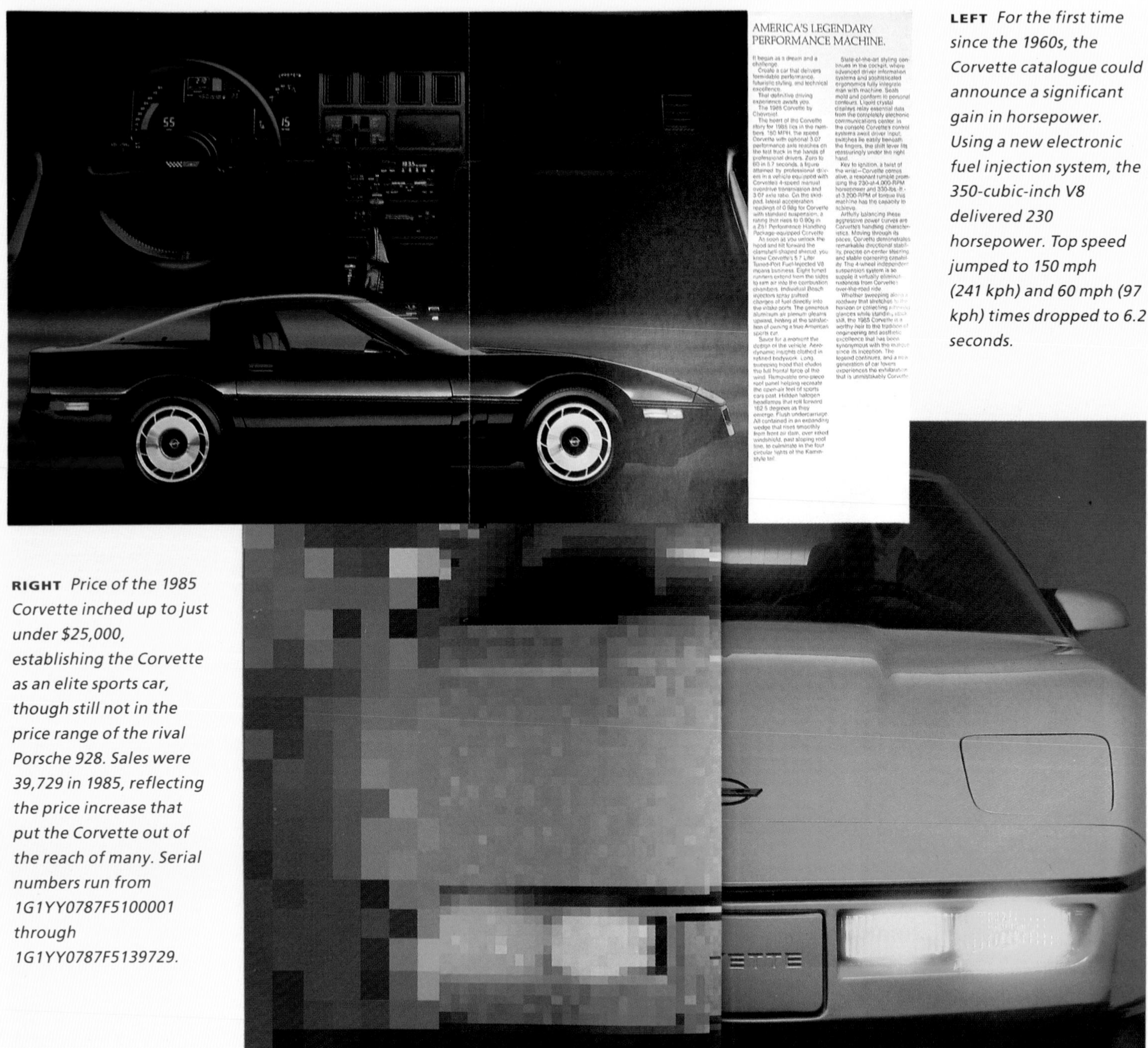

AMERICA'S LEGENDARY PERFORMANCE MACHINE.

It began as a dream and a challenge.

Create a car that delivers formidable performance, futuristic styling, and technical excellence.

That definitive driving experience awaits you.

The 1985 Corvette by Chevrolet.

The heart of the Corvette story for 1985 lies in the numbers. 150 MPH, the speed Corvette with optional 3.07 performance axle reaches on the test track in the hands of professional drivers. Zero to 60 in 5.7 seconds, a figure attained by professional drivers in a vehicle equipped with Corvette's 4-speed manual overdrive transmission and 3.07 axle ratio. On the skid-pad, lateral acceleration readings of 0.88g for Corvette with standard suspension, a rating that rises to 0.90g in a Z51 Performance Handling Package-equipped Corvette.

As soon as you unlock the hood and tilt forward the clamshell-shaped shroud, you know Corvette's 5.7 Liter Tuned-Port Fuel-Injected V8 means business. Eight tuned runners extend from the sides to ram air into the combustion chambers. Individual Bosch injectors spray pulsed charges of fuel directly into the intake ports. The generous aluminum air plenum gleams upward, hinting at the satisfaction of owning a true American sports car.

Savor for a moment the design of the vehicle. Aerodynamic insights clothed in refined bodywork. Long, sweeping hood that eludes the full frontal force of the wind. Removable one-piece roof panel helping recreate the open-air feel of sports cars past. Hidden halogen headlamps that roll forward 162.5 degrees as they emerge. Flush undercarriage. All contained in an expanding wedge that rises smoothly from front air dam, over raked windshield, past sloping roof line, to culminate in the four circular lights of the Kamm-style tail.

State-of-the-art styling continues in the cockpit, where advanced driver information systems and sophisticated ergonomics fully integrate man with machine. Seats mold and conform to personal contours. Liquid crystal displays relay essential data from the completely electronic communications center. In the console Corvette's control systems await driver input; switches lie easily beneath the fingers, the shift lever fits reassuringly under the right hand.

Key to ignition, a twist of the wrist—Corvette comes alive, a resonant rumble promising the 230-at-4,000-RPM horsepower and 330-lbs.-ft.-at-3,200-RPM of torque this machine has the capacity to achieve.

Artfully balancing these aggressive power curves are Corvette's handling characteristics. Moving through its paces, Corvette demonstrates remarkable directional stability, precise on-center steering and stable cornering capability. The 4-wheel independent suspension system is so supple it virtually eliminates rudeness from Corvette's over-the-road ride.

Whether sweeping along a roadway that stretches to the horizon or collecting admiring glances while standing stock still, the 1985 Corvette is a worthy heir to the tradition of engineering and aesthetic excellence that has been synonymous with the marque since its inception. The legend continues, and a new generation of car lovers experiences the exhilaration that is unmistakably Corvette.

LEFT *For the first time since the 1960s, the Corvette catalogue could announce a significant gain in horsepower. Using a new electronic fuel injection system, the 350-cubic-inch V8 delivered 230 horsepower. Top speed jumped to 150 mph (241 kph) and 60 mph (97 kph) times dropped to 6.2 seconds.*

RIGHT *Price of the 1985 Corvette inched up to just under $25,000, establishing the Corvette as an elite sports car, though still not in the price range of the rival Porsche 928. Sales were 39,729 in 1985, reflecting the price increase that put the Corvette out of the reach of many. Serial numbers run from 1G1YY0787F5100001 through 1G1YY0787F5139729.*

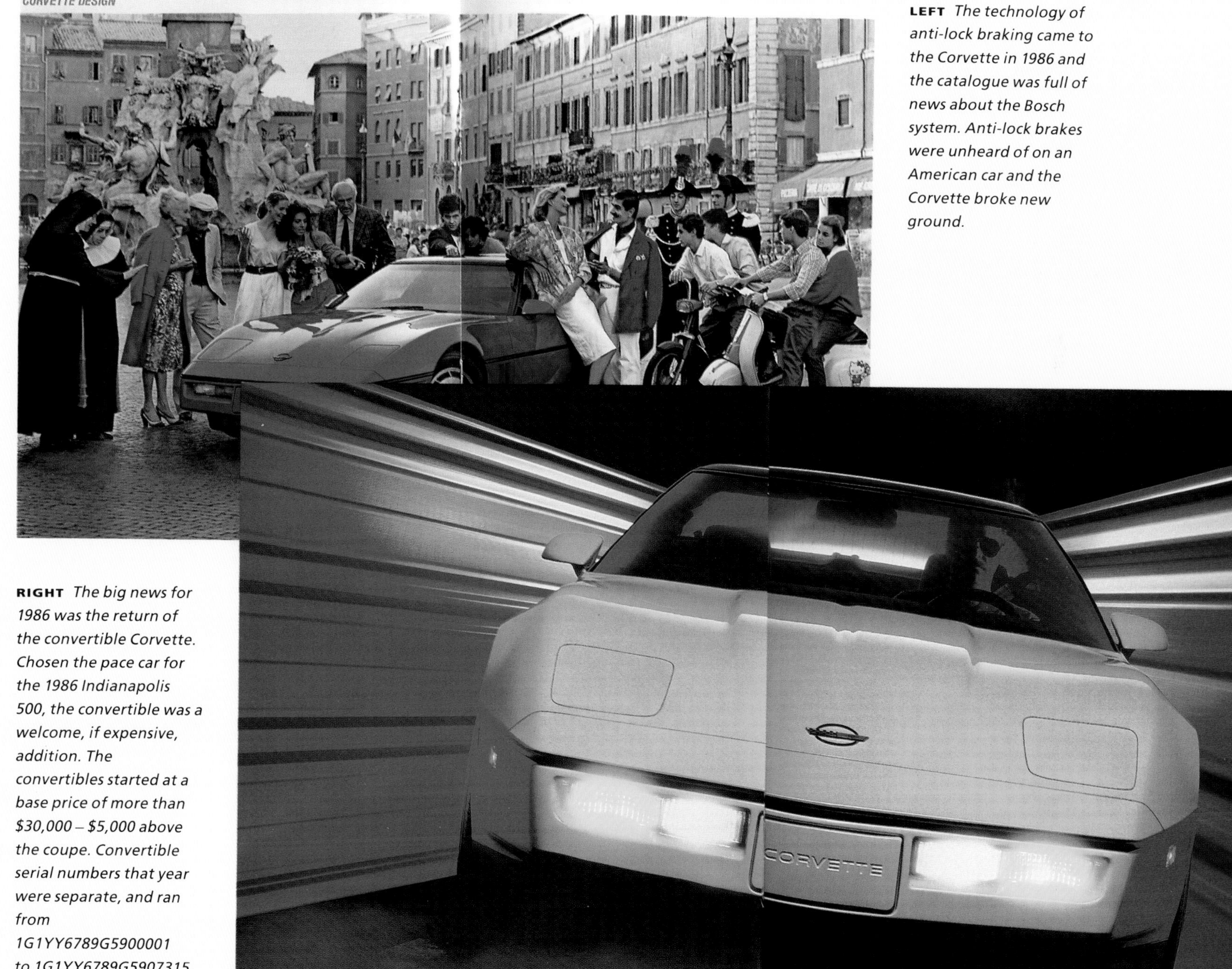

LEFT *The technology of anti-lock braking came to the Corvette in 1986 and the catalogue was full of news about the Bosch system. Anti-lock brakes were unheard of on an American car and the Corvette broke new ground.*

RIGHT *The big news for 1986 was the return of the convertible Corvette. Chosen the pace car for the 1986 Indianapolis 500, the convertible was a welcome, if expensive, addition. The convertibles started at a base price of more than $30,000 – $5,000 above the coupe. Convertible serial numbers that year were separate, and ran from 1G1YY6789G5900001 to 1G1YY6789G5907315.*

RIGHT *Squeaks and rattles still plagued the Corvette, and in 1986 the engineers started to do something about it. The convertible benefitted from a plethora of chassis stiffening measures that made it more solid than the coupe. Sales were a brisk 35,109. Coupe serial numbers run from 1G1YY0789G5100001 through 1G1YY0789G5127794.*

LEFT *The graphics on the Corvette dashboard were still of the pinball variety but they were cleaned up considerably from when the car first appeared. Although there were many calls for analog gauges, Chevrolet has stuck by the electronic dashboard.*

LEFT *By 1987, the Corvette was again dominating amateur racing in the United States, as this catalogue photo illustrates. Corvettes not only had their own race series – the Corvette Challenge – they were also frequent winners in the Showroom Stock category. Using the option list, a customer could specify a Corvette with the Z-51 suspension that was showroom stock ready.*

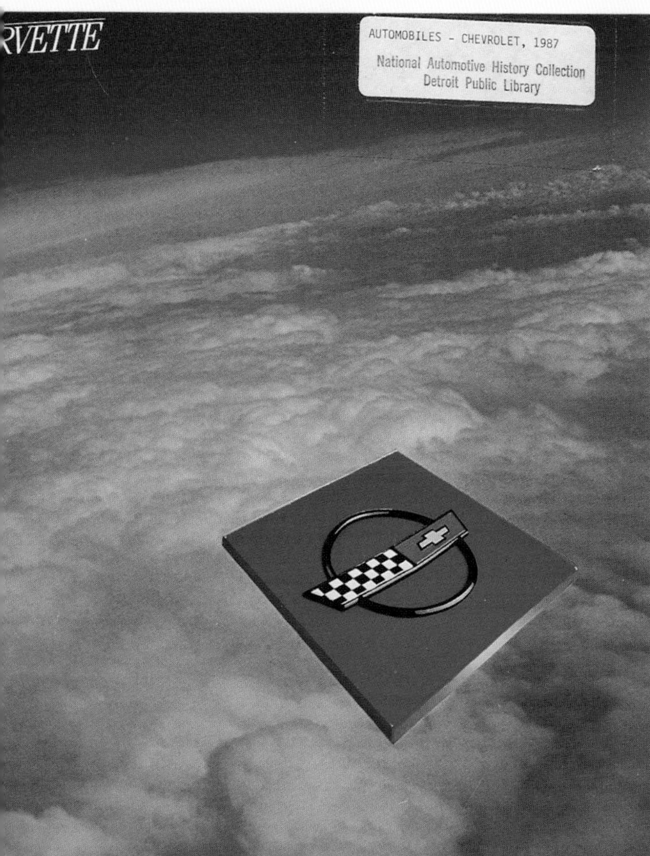

LEFT *By the 1987 model year, the Corvette was flying high. More power was on tap in 1987, thanks to some refinements to the 350-cubic-inch V8. Horsepower climbed to 240, pushing zero-to-60 mph (97 kph) times below six seconds.*

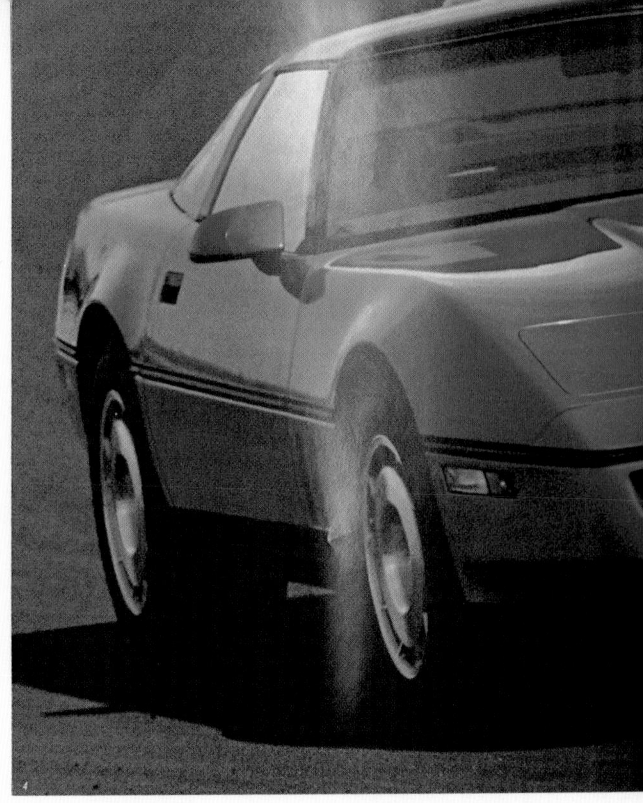

BELOW *While there was a lot of refinement going on in the engineering labs, the Corvette programme was being furthered by all-out racers and experimental cars, such as the Corvette Indy.*

SHOWN PRECEDING PAGE:

CORVETTE IS THE CAR TO BEAT IN SCCA-SANCTIONED SHOWROOM STOCK COMPETITION. THESE 6-, 12- AND 24-HOUR ENDURANCE RACES OFFER PROOF OF CORVETTE'S WORLD-CLASS CREDENTIALS.

THE EXOTIC GTP-SERIES CORVETTE PUTS TECHNOLOGY TO THE TEST ON THE WORLD'S RACETRACKS. POWER IS SUPPLIED BY A TURBOCHARGED V6.

Capturing the checkered flag is a long-running Corvette tradition. It is a tradition upheld in spectacular fashion in a variety of racing events by the current-generation Corvette.

CORVETTE DOMINATES SCCA SHOWROOM STOCK RACING

Showroom-stock road racing, sanctioned by the Sports Car Club of America, has become one of the most popular forms of motorsport competition in the U.S.A. And it is everything the name implies. The cars are production vehicles, modified only with SCCA-mandated safety equipment. This kind of racing, in 6-, 12-, and 24-hour endurance events, puts stock automobiles to a true test of their performance capabilities on the racetrack. The specially modified Corvette finished 1-2-3 in all six SCCA races in 1985.

Last year SCCA officials decided Corvette had just too much of a performance advantage over its nearest competitor, the Porsche 944 Turbo. After all, Corvette specifications include the legendary 5.7 Liter V8 with Tuned-Port Fuel Injection, the confidence of a Bosch ABS II anti-lock braking system and the tenacious road-holding capability of four-wheel independent suspension mated to Goodyear Eagle VR50 16" tires.

Modified SCCA rules placed the 1986 Corvette in an unlimited production class. New competition included Ferrari 308 Quattrovalvole, Lotus Esprit Turbo and a reworked 944 Turbo that the Porsche folks built specifically to loosen Corvette's stranglehold on America's most prestigious meaningful racing series.

The rules-shuffling hasn't been enough to overcome the proven performance thunder of a world-class champion. Corvette topped its competition again in 1986 and for 1987 it remains the car to beat.

THE PRODUCTION-BASED GTO-SERIES CORVETTE

GTO-series racing, sponsored by the International Motor Sports Association, is limited to production-based cars with engines displacing more than 3.0 liters. Except some cars are closer to production specifications than others.

While every other competitor in this fast-paced series, including Porsche and Toyota, discards its standard chassis in favor of a tube-type racing frame, Corvette doesn't have to. Corvette's stock uniframe (modified for racing) offers the lightweight strength required to compete successfully against some of the world's finest racing machines.

Under the hood of every GTO-series Corvette, a race-prepared version of the small-block V8 proves yet again that Corvette has what it takes to go the distance.

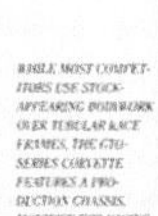

WHILE MOST COMPETITORS USE STOCK-APPEARING BODYWORK OVER TUBULAR RACE FRAMES, THE GTO-SERIES CORVETTE FEATURES A PRODUCTION CHASSIS MODIFIED FOR RACING.

THE EXOTIC GTP-SERIES CORVETTE

The International Motor Sports Association's (IMSA) GTP series features all-out race cars. Once again, Corvette is participating with a specially prepared aerodynamic mid-engined car.

In its first 1986 outings, the GTP Corvette has earned pole positions and two overall victories, establishing itself as a formidable competitor. But that's not the real reason this racing Corvette exists.

Herb Fishel, Director, Chevrolet's Special Products Group, describes the role of the GTP this way:

> There are many similarities between production and pure-performance machinery, particularly in the areas of design, construction and the application of high technology. Our intent is to turn the knowledge gained through on-track experience into viable applications for our production vehicles. Thus the rationale for the GTP Corvette.

In addition to a turbocharged V6 developing over 770 HP, the GTP features an aluminum honeycomb-type frame for high strength and light weight. Body panels are constructed of high-strength carbon fiber fabric bonded with epoxy resin, one of the strongest, lightest combinations of materials known.

This incorporation of advanced materials, engine technology and aerodynamics not only makes the GTP Corvette a contender on the world's racing circuits, it puts technology to the test so that it may be applied to future production Corvettes.

CORVETTE INDY

THE SHAPE OF TECHNOLOGY TO COME

The critics agree: The shape of Corvette Indy introduces a new milestone in automotive design. Yet this prototype Corvette Indy is far more than a "dream car" created simply to impress crowds at auto shows.

Don Runkle, Chevrolet Chief Engineer, explains:

> Corvette Indy is Chevrolet's latest innovation vehicle for studying new engineering and design concepts. We do these cars as much for inspiration as experiment, because it gives our people a chance to turn their dreams into reality.

CORVETTE INDY POWER

As its name implies, Corvette Indy is powered by a version of the Indy engine: a 2650-cc dual overhead cam V8 designed for Indianapolis 500 competition.

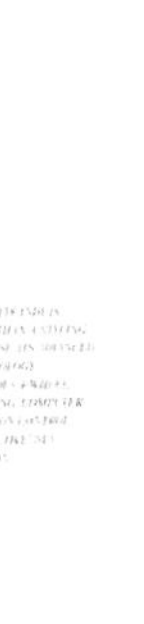

LEFT *Little items distinguish the 1987 Corvette. The chassis stiffening that went into the 1986 version convertible now applies to all Corvettes. And there's a nifty option of a tyre-pressure sensor system. The two-pound package monitors the air pressure of each tyre and switches on a warning light when a tyre is low.*

BELOW CENTRE *The Corvette catalogue has become not only a sales tool but a piece of literature detailing the ongoing Corvette saga from development through racing. One option not mentioned is the Callaway Twin-Turbo Corvette, a 175 mph (282 kph) version of the car that can be ordered through Chevy dealers. Price is a stiff $57,000.*

BELOW *Coupe and convertible styling carries over almost unchanged from 1986. The only addition is a federally mandated centre brake light, which supposedly cuts down on rear-end collisions. Chevrolet sells 30,632 Covettes that year, with serial numbers running from 1G1YY2182H5100001 to 1G1YY2182H5130632.*

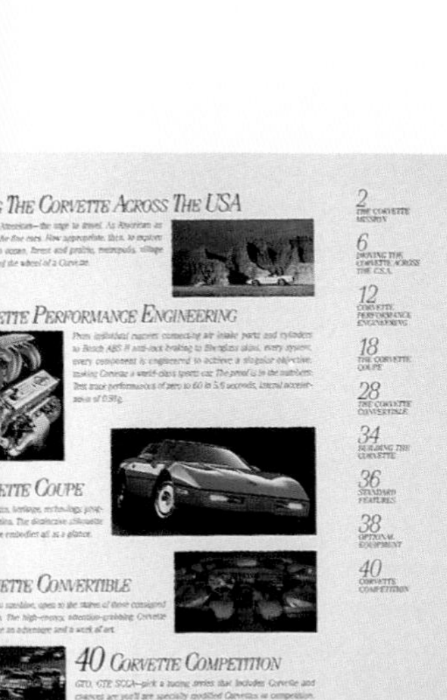

RIGHT AND LEFT *The Corvette had become a fashion statement by 1988, with the car appearing in all manner of magazine ads for other products. Though the body style has remained unchanged for more than four years – unusual in an American car – the Corvette style is still appealing, and is perceived by buyers and critics alike as being timeless.*

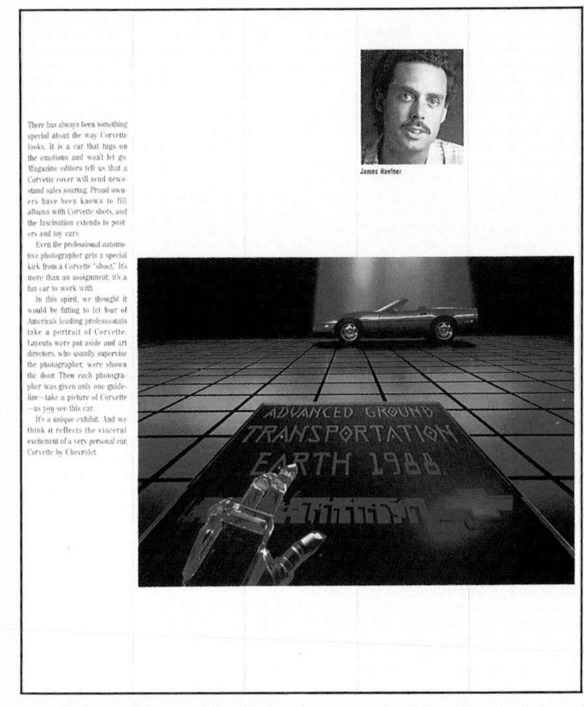

There has always been something special about the way Corvette looks. It is a car that tugs on the emotions and won't let go. Magazine editors tell us that a Corvette cover will send newsstand sales soaring. Proud owners have been known to fill albums with Corvette shots, and the fascination extends to posters and toy cars.

Even the professional automotive photographer gets a special kick from a Corvette "shoot." It's more than an assignment; it's a fun car to work with.

In this spirit, we thought it would be fitting to let four of America's leading professionals take a portrait of Corvette. Layouts were put aside and art directors, who usually supervise the photographer, were shown the door. Then each photographer was given only one guideline—take a picture of Corvette —as you see this car.

It's a unique exhibit. And we think it reflects the visceral excitement of a very personal car. Corvette by Chevrolet.

James Haefner

BELOW *New to the catalogue in 1988 are 17-inch (432 mm) aluminium wheels, which are an option and also are included in the Z51 handling package. The new wheels also allow larger brake rotors and the suspension geometry has been changed to make the car more stable under braking.*

In addition to the artwork displayed on various pages throughout this brochure, Chevrolet commissioned three artists of national stature to share their personal impressions of Corvette. The exhibit, shown on these and following pages, reflects the highly individual approaches of serious artists, portraying serious (and not-so-serious) Corvette moods.

Robert Cunningham

"I've always admired the Corvette but this new one really appeals to my eye. It has a simplicity of line, with the excitement of a shark."

Robert Cunningham appreciates "fine designs, those with substance." His illustrations demonstrate a fondness for vibrant colors and clean shapes. With an economy of brushstrokes, he conveys impressive detail.

"The scene I chose for my portrait of Corvette is Route 45 in Connecticut. It's a fine touring highway for a car like Corvette," says Cunningham. Robert Cunningham's illustrations have appeared in many of America's leading magazines. He studied art at the University of Kansas, Kansas City Art Institute and Art Students League and taught at the Pratt Institute in Brooklyn. Philatelists know Cunningham as the designer of the U.S.A.'s 1980 Olympic stamp.

BELOW *By the 1989 model year, the Corvette had firmly established itself as a glamour vehicle with the guts to match. Selling the car became an art form unto itself. In that vein, Chevrolet produced a brochure that asked several prominent modern artists to put their visions of the car on to canvas.*

ABOVE *While the outside of the Corvette was becoming a classic, there were still changes aplenty under the skin. A premature announcement by Chevrolet held out the possibility that the Corvette ZR-1, a 180 mph (290 kph) supercar, would debut in 1989. It was held up until 1990 by last-minute design work.*

RIGHT *Minarets and a desert landscape are in sharp contrast to the totally modern nature of the Corvette. New to the Corvette in 1989 is a sophisticated computer-controlled suspension system that allows varied setting to match road and driving conditions. Called FX-3, it can be manually selected or allowed to function automatically.*

Artists' Impressions

Robert Giusti

The paintings of Fra Angelico, a pre-Renaissance Italian master from the 1400s, were inspiration for Giusti's "red Corvette." Giusti explains, "The artists of the 1400s were precision-oriented craftsmen. The frescoes, murals and other paintings were all well-designed and exacting in detail. So it is certainly appropriate to portray Corvette, an example of the best in automotive art and engineering, in this way."

Bob Giusti has been drawing as long as he can remember. After attending the Tyler School of Art in Philadelphia, Giusti graduated from the Cranbrook Academy of Art in Bloomfield Hills, Michigan. He has worked as an advertising agency art director and artist at Random House. His free-lance assignments have included television animation, record album covers, magazine and book covers, calendars and posters.

Giusti loves to paint animals, and now Corvettes. "I appreciate the esthetics and lineage of the car. It represents good, classic design."

Artists' Impressions

Paul Coker Jr.

To some it was expressive. To others, outrageous. It was "pop art," and it was born in the Sixties.

Pop art took many forms, from Warhol's soup cans to Roy Lichtenstein's comic-strip-inspired paintings.

Paul Coker studied the pop art phenomenon and faithfully created this Corvette interpretation. "I used the simple dot pattern and red-blue-yellow colors of the comic strips. Then I put the dot pattern over a black-and-white pen and ink drawing. I wanted to express – in a fun way – the romance that is Corvette."

Coker has made fun a major ingredient in his work. An art graduate of the University of Kansas, he has illustrated for Mad Magazine, created artwork for "contemporary" greeting cards, and has drawn characters for animated television specials.

LEFT *The Corvette was no cartoon car by 1989. New in the catalogues was the six-speed transmission, replacing the 4+3 manual transmission. The new gearbox is smoother than the old model but still uses a computer override sytem to ensure shifts at certain speeds that will result in maximum fuel economy.*

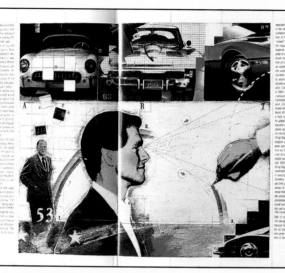

LEFT *Form and function were not always compatible in a Corvette, but by the 1989 model year, the two concepts worked hand-in-hand. In this artwork, the Corvette's original designer, Harley Earl, looks in the background as the evolution of the car is depicted.*

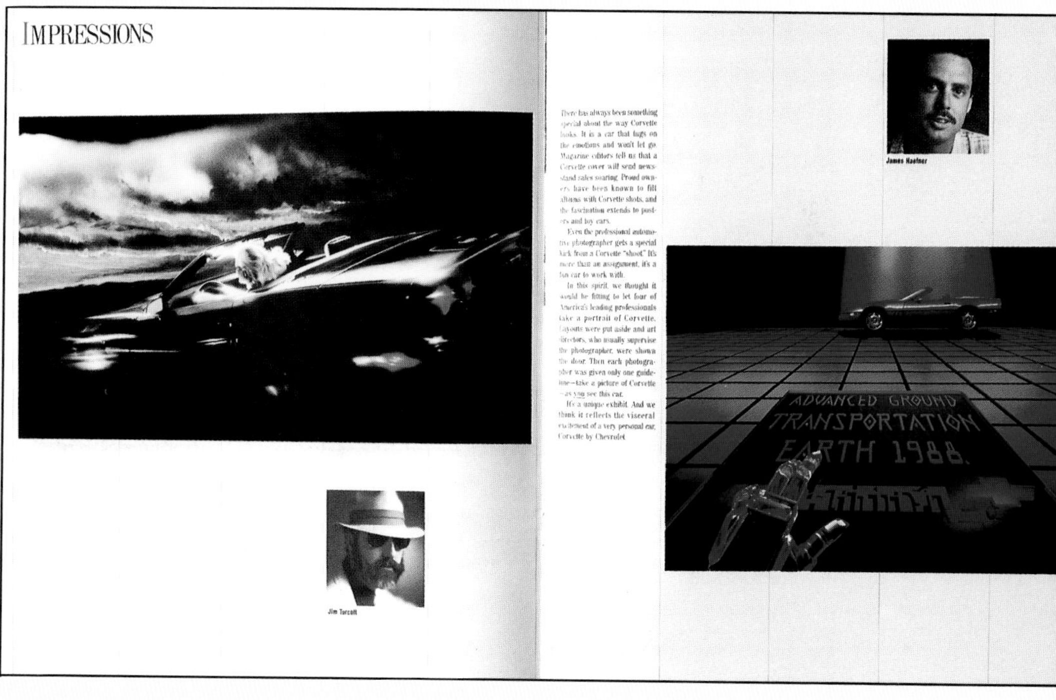

IMPRESSIONS

There has always been something special about the way Corvette looks. It is a car that tugs on the emotions and won't let go. Magazine editors tell us that a Corvette cover will send newsstand sales soaring. Proud owners have been known to fill albums with Corvette shots, and the fascination extends to posters and toy cars.

Even the professional automotive photographer gets a special kick from a Corvette "shoot." It's more than an assignment, it's a fun car to work with.

In this spirit, we thought it would be fitting to let four of America's leading professionals take a portrait of Corvette. Layouts were put aside and art directors, who usually supervise the photographer, were shown the door. Then each photographer was given only one guideline—take a picture of Corvette—as you see this car.

It's a unique exhibit. And we think it reflects the visceral excitement of a very personal car, Corvette by Chevrolet.

RIGHT *The impression a Corvette leaves on a driver is one of speed, as this catalogue shows. But the car stops and corners equally well, thanks to larger brake rotors and the addition of 17-inch wheels as standard equipment. Base price is now just above $30,000, with the convertible selling for about $38,000. Sales were 26,412, with serial numbers running from 1G1YY2186K5100001 through to 1G1YY2186K5126412.*

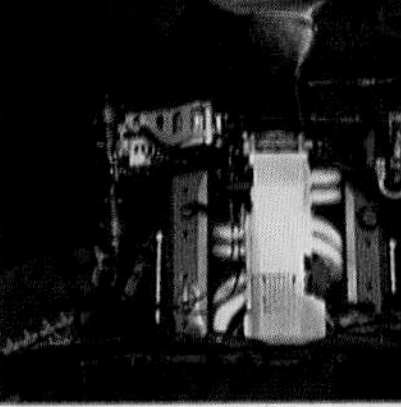

ABOVE *The long awaited ZR–1 makes its appearance in 1990, though it takes a ton of cash to own one. On top of the base price of $58,000, collectors and greedy dealers tack on premiums of as much as $30,000 to buy one of the first models. With the ZR–1, a buyer gets a 5.7 litre aluminium V–8 with 32 valves and a unique system of tuned fuel intake runners. Horsepower is 380, and top speed is 178 mph (284 kph), putting it in the range of the Ferrari Testarossa and the Lamborghini Countach. Outside, ZR–1s are distinguished by a wider, convex rear body assembly and huge 315/35ZR–17 Gatorback tyres, ZR–1 production numbers run from 1G1YZ23J6L5800001 through 1G1YZ23J6L5803049.*

RIGHT *Inside, all 1990 Corvettes receive a new dash layout that attempts to use electronic graphics to duplicate analog gauges. Overall the dash layout resembles a concentric pod that puts all controls within easy reach of the driver.*

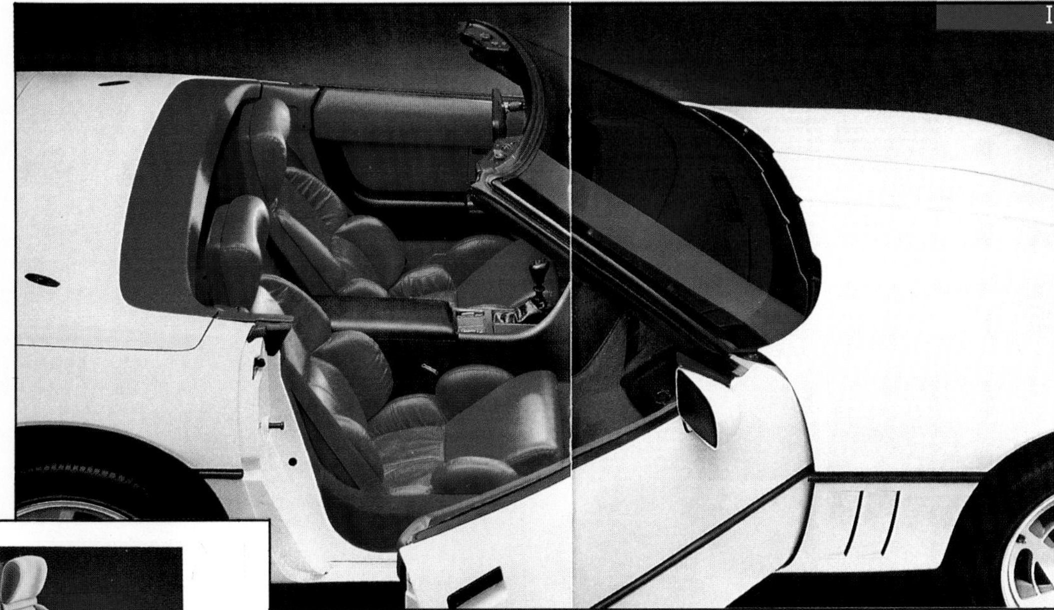

INTERIORS

The Corvette interior is designed to American tastes. With comfortable seating. Powerful air conditioning. Advanced sound systems. And power everything.

It is fair to say the 1990 Corvette is an extremely well-equipped, driver-oriented automobile. In fact, few cars in the world can match Corvette on the single criterion of creature comfort.

The following interior features are standard in every Corvette:

☐ Superbly luxurious and ergonomically correct seating for two, with a choice of standard sport cloth or optional leather buckets.
☐ Air conditioning, power windows, power door locks, leather-wrapped Comfortilt steering wheel and intermittent wipers.
☐ Delco AM/FM stereo radio with Seek and Scan, cassette tape player, digital clock and power antenna.
☐ Electronic Speed Control with Resume Speed feature.
☐ Dual electrically adjusted and heated mirrors.

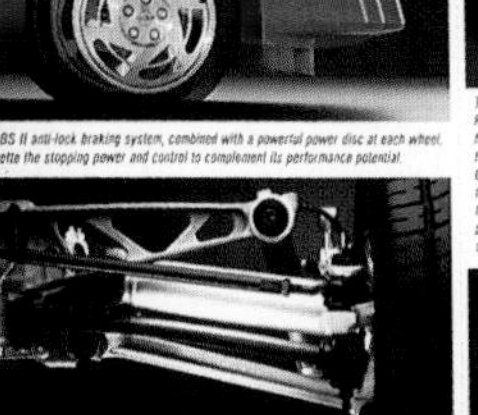

ABS II anti-lock braking system, combined with a powerful power disc at each wheel, ...rvette the stopping power and control to complement its performance potential.

The new-for-1990 Supplemental Inflatable Restraint system (air bag) is located in the hub of the steering wheel. The S.I.R. is designed to provide added protection in the event your Corvette is involved in a moderate to severe frontal collision. For maximum protection in frontal and all other collisions, both driver and passenger should be properly restrained with safety belts.

Standard fully reclining cloth bucket seats are available in Black or Saddle.

...'s sophisticated fully independent sus... is an important reason why this car ...uch fun to drive. Components include aluminum control arms, transverse and stabilizer bars and a 5-link inde... rear design that helps maximize tire contact with the road surface.

Comfortilt steering wheel adjusts to your personal driving style.

Corvette Coupe features a standard removable roof panel (one piece with no center T-bar).

The Convertible's soft top disappears below a fiberglass panel when lowered.

ABOVE LEFT *The base Corvette, no slouch on its own, continued unchanged under the hood for 1990. The 245-horsepower engine still provided more than enough punch for most Corvette buyers. Standard production numbers run from 1G1YY2386L5100001 through 1G1YY2386L5120597.*

ABOVE *Overall, the seats and door panels on the 1990 car are freshened. Most significant addition is an air-bag safety system on the driver's side. Sales dropped to about 20,000, a reflection of a slumping market overall.*

RIGHT *First planned for the 1990 ZR-1 but put off due to development deadlines, the new nose does a better job of integrating the directional and driving lights. All Corvettes get redesigned 17-in (432 mm) wheels as well.*

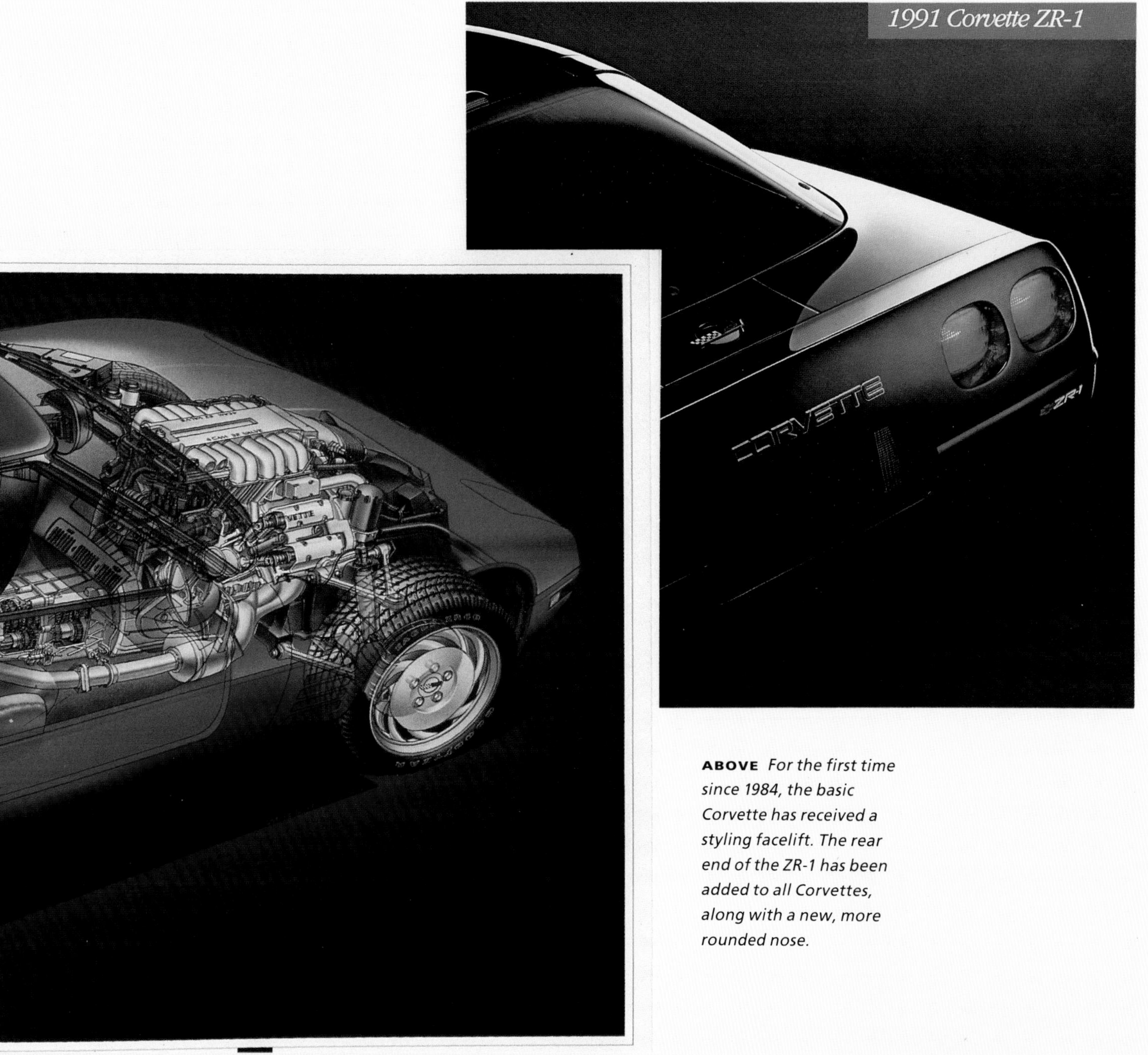

ABOVE *For the first time since 1984, the basic Corvette has received a styling facelift. The rear end of the ZR-1 has been added to all Corvettes, along with a new, more rounded nose.*

Features & Options
One Corvette ... with
everything ... to go.
18
19

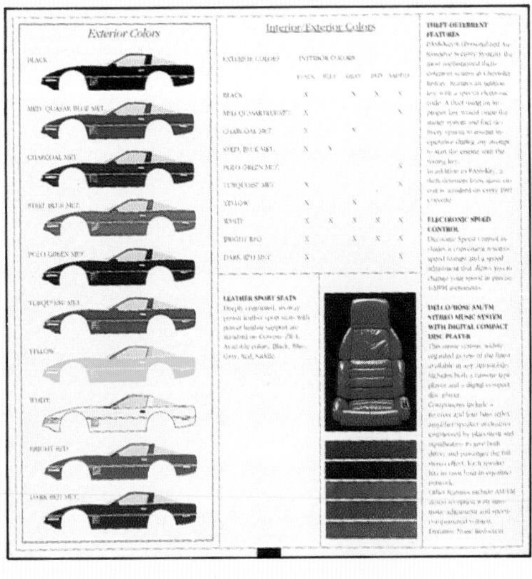

LEFT *Corvette buyers in 1991 get a rainbow of colours to choose from, including six metallic finishes. The Polo Green is particularly popular, but red remains the No. 1 colour chosen by Corvette owners.*

ABOVE *Underneath, there's little new for 1991. The new exterior styling will make it difficult to distinguish basic Corvettes from ZR-1s. The only tip-off is that the basic car now has the centre-mounted tail stoplight integrated into the rear assembly. On the ZR-1, the light still rides on top of the rear hatch.*

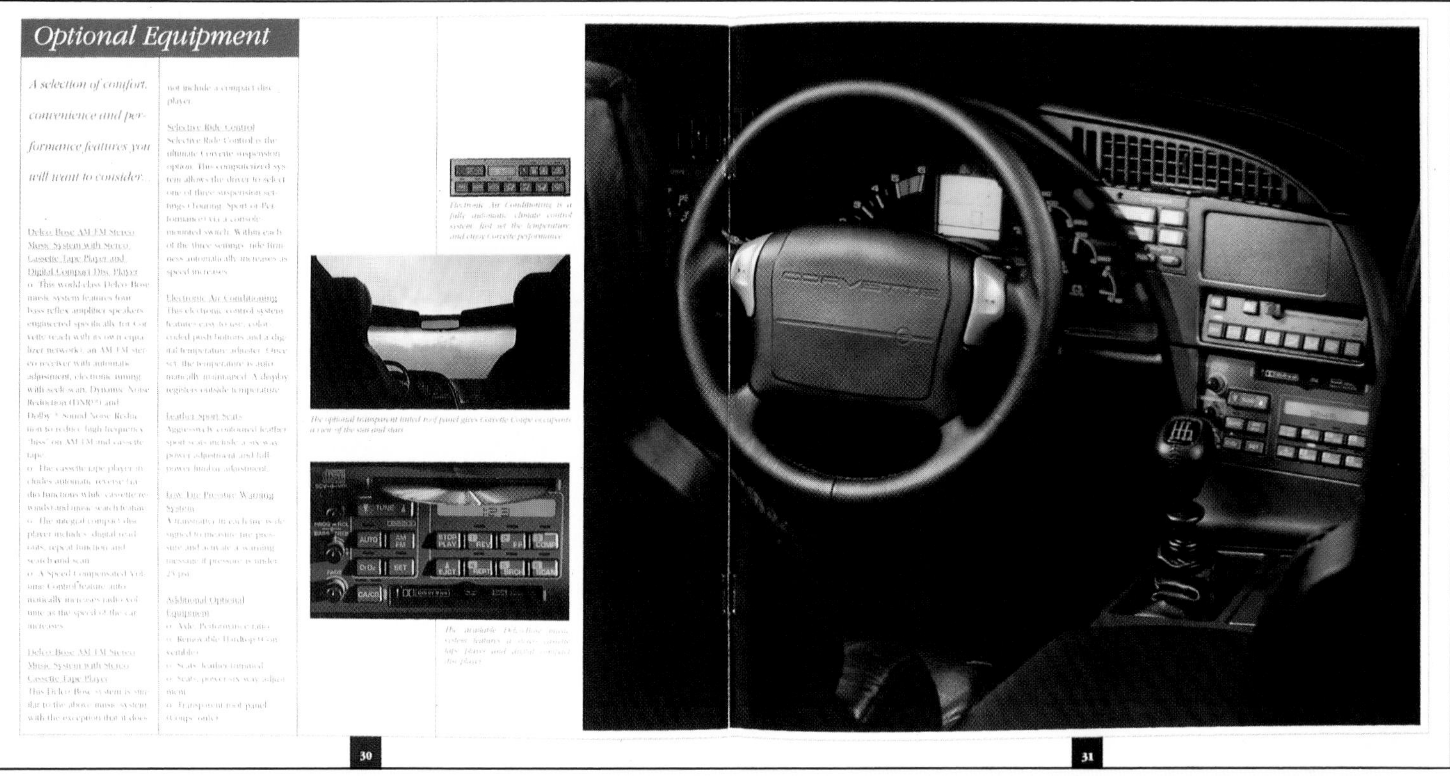
Optional Equipment

A selection of comfort, convenience and performance features you will want to consider.

30

31

ABOVE *Among options available in 1991 are a compact disc player addition to the stereo system, a computerized ride control system, electronically controlled air conditioning and a system to monitor tire pressure at each wheel.*

RIGHT *It's tough to tell the difference between a run-of-the-mill 155 mph (248 kph) Corvette from a 178 mph (284 kph) ZR–1. Both get the same rounded tail, but the tipoff is that the standard Corvette has slightly narrower tires and an integrated center tail light.*

INDEX

ACKNOWLEDGEMENTS:

The author and publishers would like to thank the following for providing catalgoues: Pete Atkins; National Automotive Archives, Detroit Public Library, Michigan; Pooks Motorbooks.

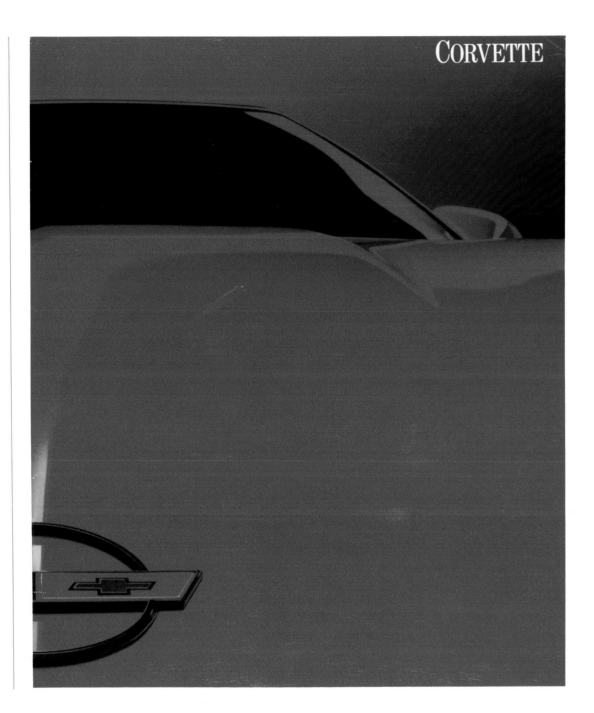